Dostoevsky and the
of Religious Experience

To George and Judith
with affectionate
regards

Malcolm
2.11.10

Anthem Russian and Slavonic Studies

Other titles in the series:

Dostoevsky and the Dynamics of Religious Experience

MALCOLM JONES

Anthem Press

Anthem Press
An imprint of Wimbledon Publishing Company
75-76 Blackfriars Road, London SE1 8HA
or
PO Box 9779, London SW19 7ZG
www.anthempress.com

This edition first published by Anthem Press 2005

British Library Cataloguing in Publication Data
A catalogue record for this book is available from the British Library.

Library of Congress Cataloging in Publication Data
A catalog record for this book has been requested.

1 3 5 7 9 10 8 6 4 2

ISBN 1 84331 205 0 (HB)
ISBN 1 84331 202 6 (PB)

Cover illustration: Footprint Labs

Typeset by Footprint Labs Ltd, London
www.footprintlabs.com

Printed in the United Kingdom

Dedicated to the memory of two good friends and outstanding scholars, Roger Poole and Sergei Hackel, who died while this book was being written, and who contributed more than they ever realised to its conception and realisation.

Contents

Author's Preface

In 1990, CUP published my book *Dostoevsky after Bakhtin*. When the reviews began to appear, I was not surprised to find that what most troubled some otherwise sympathetic Western readers was that I had tried in my final chapter to relate Dostoevsky's religious insights to a narrative structure that in many ways anticipated a post-modernist sensibility. In particular, it was my reintroduction of the notion of an originary truth ('The Whisper of God') into critical discourse that gave offence. Clearly, I was thought to have failed to grasp something essential (if that is not a contradiction in terms) about the post-modernist enterprise. The fault may well have been mine, but I suspect that some readers still secretly prefer a Dostoevsky whose religious insights, as in Soviet days though for quite different reasons, have been suppressed, or translated into the sort of discourse that is politically acceptable to them.

I am afraid that I remained incorrigible, and in my introduction to the Russian edition (1998), I went further, stating that if I were to rewrite the book now I should expand rather than delete that section. I was also aware by that time that some of my Russian readers, themselves adherents of a resurgent Orthodoxy that regards Dostoevsky as a great Christian prophet with a unique word for the twenty-first century, might take the opposite view, and consider me culpably neglectful of the religious dimension of his work. With the end of the Soviet Union, the study of literature from a religious point of view has become a serious growth area in Russia, where long-standing Western essays in this genre were, until recently, hardly known.

So there were two quite different contemporary critical movements vying for Dostoevsky's soul. In my presidential address to the Tenth International Dostoevsky Symposium in New York in 1998, I intimated that this presented problems for the contemporary reader that demanded urgent attention. Not only did I believe that both these approaches were valid for different reading communities, but also that each reflects deep structures of Dostoevsky's text that must be incorporated in any adequate modern reading.

A wealth of new writing on the religious dimension of Dostoevsky's novels has been appearing in both Russia and the West in recent years, some of it of very high quality. In many cases, an attempt is being made to show

how his fiction expresses his developing understanding of the way in which the truths of Russian Orthodox Christianity, with its emphasis on *sobornost'* (togetherness or conciliarity) and the image of Christ, offered the only possible salvation to a Russia, and indeed to a world, riven by what he called *obosoblenie* or fragmentation. His novels, according to such readings, depict this fragmented world, but also hold out the promise, especially in *The Brothers Karamazov*, of rebirth and renewal through the Christian faith.

It seems to me that there are two problems with this kind of reading. The first is that it follows too slavishly the agenda that underlies most critical endeavour, to find order where there appears to be chaos, clarity where there appears to be confusion, coherence where there appears to be conflict, precision where there appears to be indeterminacy; to reconcile all apparent contradictions, and to smooth over all apparent inconsistencies. Suddenly, as even at the hands of the great Bakhtin, we find that the turbulence of Dostoevsky's fictional text is stilled, and it takes on a reassuring and seductive coherence and tranquillity, which Dostoevsky may very well have liked, but which hardly reflects the actual texture of his fictional world, the character of his own inner turmoil, or the unsettling narrative techniques that he unleashes upon his reader. In response, I would paraphrase Dmitry Karamazov and reply, no. Dostoevsky's novels are too broad for such treatment. The world they depict is both mysterious and fearful. The devil is struggling with God. The battle is not yet won and the battlefield is Dostoevsky's text.

The reader will correctly infer from this that my interest in the present book will be in the religious dimension of Dostoevsky's fictional world rather than in any coherent philosophy of religion that may be distilled from it in the light of his extra-fictional statements or his preferred reading matter.

This brings me to the second problem. It must be granted that Dostoevsky's soul was sometimes suffused in a spiritual tranquillity that brought him peace from its accustomed turbulence, and to which he attached supreme importance. But it must also be granted that its most characteristic state, throughout his life, was one of unrest, and that it is this state, not one of serenity, that his novels principally reflect. As he says himself, he reached his hosanna through a crucible of doubt, and the spiritual map of human experience that he offers us includes only the occasional small island of serenity in vast, turbulent oceans of doubt, rebellion, rejection, indifference and unbelief. All belong to the human condition and, so far as Dostoevsky's world is concerned, in roughly these proportions. Moreover, it was necessary for Dostoevsky himself as creator, as well as for us as his conscientious readers, to navigate the stormy oceans to find the islands of peace: it is not simply a question of choosing a calm route rather than a stormy one.

It is for this reason, it seems to me — the arguments will come later — that Dostoevsky consciously and repeatedly chose to reveal his glimpses of salvation by means of a narrative structure that might almost have been designed — and was perhaps unconsciously conceived — to destabilize and to subvert them, and through characters that, in almost every case, experience this destabilization to the full. He could, after all, have restored the semblance of control by choosing omniscient narrators, as his great contemporary Tolstoi did in his major novels. But he did not do so. Or he could have given his 'saintly' characters an aura of imperturbability and spiritual peace that protected them from worldly shocks and human cynicism. But he did not do this either; quite the reverse. In the one case where we might be tempted to believe that such a saintly character has indeed reached an accommodation with the creation of which he is a part — that of Zosima in *The Brothers Karamazov* — nature itself seems to rise up and deny it, as his corpse decomposes, denying his admirers the satisfaction of a miracle and playing into the hands of his detractors. To say this is not to deny that, as Frank Seeley would have put it, they are closer to the pole of wholeness on the continuum of personality. It is to say that not even they can escape the slings and arrows of outrageous fortune and their destabilizing effect on the personality.

Why, if Dostoevsky was, at least towards the end of his life, a committed Orthodox Christian, did he give in his final novel a portrait of metaphysical rebellion that has seemed unanswerable to many a modern mind? One answer is that he wanted to juxtapose the suffering that goes with such rebellion to the spiritual tranquillity that accompanies faith, and to leave the reader to choose. Such a reading often assumes that the Holy Scriptures and other great works of religious literature and art are part of the intertext, and that the text of the novel itself, where it does not make them explicit, repeatedly gestures in their direction as a reminder to the reader that they form its true foundation. According to this view, any lapses or gaps in, say, Zosima's religious testament, should be filled by the reader from his or her knowledge of the Orthodox intertext. This is what, it is implied, Dostoevsky would have wished, and what he undoubtedly hoped and intended. It seems to me that this leaves out of account not only Dostoevsky's own confession that he experienced the turmoil of unbelief and doubt to the last months of his life, but also that there can be two kinds of answer to the question, 'what are an individual's religious beliefs?' One kind of answer reels off uncritically the words of a creed or statement of belief authorized by the Church, or other responsible institution, or invites the questioner to immerse him or herself in that tradition by way or response. This is the kind of discourse that Bakhtin calls 'Holy Writ'. The other brings to the surface only those beliefs that the honest believer actually knows, understands and treasures from his or her own personal experience, and acknowledges or omits those areas of traditional doctrine that have no personal meaning. This is what Bakhtin calls 'inwardly persuasive discourse'. It leads to a kind of 'minimal religion', which may lack the power and authority of the interpretative tradition, but has the direct impact of lived, personal testimony and it is this kind of religious belief, I shall argue, that Dostoevsky embodies in his last novel and which had been evolving, via many diversions and cul-de-sacs, throughout his life. If I am right, then this has serious implications for the debates, past and current, about the way in which we read the religious dimension of Dostoevsky's work in the twenty-first century.

When I go on to write about Dostoevsky's deconstructive anxiety, it is in order to see more clearly what problems he was addressing, not in order to claim him for a later phase in the history of human thought. I shall not attempt to 'deconstruct' Dostoevsky. Interesting though such a task might be, I am content to leave it to others, or indeed to him, for as often as not the Dostoevskian text deconstructs itself before our eyes. I shall also not foreground the claim that Dostoevsky is a post-modernist writer *avant la lettre*. Such a view is by no means absurd. Dostoevsky had a notable talent, which leaves a clear trace on both his journalism and his fictional writing, for discerning processes by which weaknesses in a particular system of thought may lead to the development of unplanned and unforeseen consequences, and indeed culminate in their opposite. To take a case that he states unambiguously, the Great Schism in the Christian Church led in the West to Catholicism, whose illegitimate offspring were the Protestant sects, which in turn gave birth to Christian socialism and subsequently to atheistic socialism (XXV, 7). Here is the 'logic of the supplement', as Derrida would put it, at work in history. If Dostoevsky was able to state as much explicitly, it is not too fanciful to imagine that he might have intuited further stages, which he was not able to conceptualize because they had not yet actually occurred, and this is exactly what we witness, I shall argue, in his treatment of religious experience in his major novels.

It is not then difficult to conceive of Dostoevsky as a precursor of modernism and post-modernism, and it is perhaps surprising that so little recent Dostoevsky criticism has taken up the challenge, when so many modernist and post-modernist writers, both in Russia and abroad, are so clearly and avowedly in his debt. To focus on such a reading, however, would inevitably neglect the degree to which his text conforms to the canons of nineteenth-century psychological and social realism, his yearning for a stable centre for human experience and the primacy of the epistemological dominant in his work.[1] What I am suggesting does not neglect this yearning or this heritage, but acknowledges that Dostoevsky, throughout his best known and most characteristic work, displays a dread that reality, whatever that might be, forever eludes our grasp and that the world of our experience is devoid of all meaning apart from that with which we may choose to endow it; in the compulsive decentralization of the subject; in a fascination with ontological pluralism; in the prominence given to the theme of writing itself. Why do I call this a deconstructive *anxiety*? Since the fascination with an infinitely multi-layered reality is balanced by a yearning for solidity, truth, a lost 'binding idea', born out of a deep sense of disorientation and uncertainty. It is against this anxiety that we must measure the strength of Dostoevsky's commitment to Orthodoxy. This pervasive anxiety, I shall argue, does not make Dostoevsky a post-modernist, for he does not celebrate the post-modernist vision. However, it does make him into an anticipator and precursor of much that is characteristic of post-modernism.

In evolving a model for the dynamics of religious experience in Dostoevsky's fiction, I have found several recent essays by Mikhail Epstein particularly useful, though he may never have envisaged that they would be put to such use. Since my argument does not depend on this connection, and since some reviewers — I can almost predict which ones — may too readily infer that it does, I had thought of airbrushing it out. But that would be both ungrateful and self-defeating, because what I have called the Epstein model does in fact map so well onto the religious dynamics of Dostoevsky's text that one is tempted to believe that it was unconsciously inspired by it: it certainly throws into relief exactly those features of Dostoevsky's text that I wish to emphasize and will therefore help the reader to follow my argument. So I must begin by acknowledging this particular debt. I must also acknowledge a profound debt to several Dostoevsky specialists whom I know personally, whose interests overlap with my own and the theme of this book, and who have influenced my thinking down the years. We do not always agree, it is true, but that does not lessen my respect for their work or my gratitude to them for sharing with me the fruit of many years' research and personal reflection. Although my interest in the subject goes back many years, it was W J Leatherbarrow who first encouraged me to write explicitly on the subject; before him Jostein Børtnes invited me to contribute to a conference whose theme allowed me to develop some of the ideas that underlie this book; long ago I drew inspiration from the work of Stewart Sutherland on Dostoevsky's contribution to the philosophy of religion. I have benefited enormously over the course of time from conversations and discussions on my topic with him and with Sergei Hackel, Irina Kirillova, Robin Feuer Miller, Diane Thompson, Valentina Vetlovskaia, Sarah Young and Vladimir Zakharov, as well as from their publications, and I am extremely grateful to my Nottingham colleague Lesley Milne for reading an earlier version of the typescript of this book. Finally, I must acknowledge with profound gratitude the many stimulating conversations I had over the years with my late colleague Roger Poole on questions of religion and philosophy, the sort of questions that would have interested Dostoevsky himself.

In the essays that follow, I have frequently drawn on material that has already been published under my name elsewhere in academic publications, and I should therefore also like to express my gratitude to those publishers who own the copyright, namely the Cambridge University Press, the Dresden University Press, the *New Zealand Slavonic Journal* and Solum Forlag. Full references are given in my Bibliography.

Finally, references to Dostoevsky's fiction in the body of my text are to the Soviet Academy Edition, *Polnoe sobranie sochinenii v tridtsati tomakh*, Nauka, Leningrad, 1972–1990. I am aware that this will not help non-Russian speaking readers, but they may perhaps be less interested in following up references than their Russianist colleagues and it seemed cumbersome to overload the text or footnotes with two or more sets of references. This leads me to conclude my preface by expressing the hope that my book may be of interest not only to Dostoevsky specialists but also to those who teach and study courses in comparative literature and in literature and religion.

Malcolm V. Jones
Nottingham 2005

ESSAY I

Dostoevsky's Journey of Religious Discovery: A Biographical Introduction

I

If Christianity often went by default in educated Russian families in Dostoevsky's day (as it did, for example, in the Herzen, Tolstoi and Turgenev families), this was certainly not the case with the Dostoevskys.[2] In 1873, now aged 52, Dostoevsky recalled that he had been brought up in a pious Russian family and had been familiar with the Gospels from an early age (XXI, 134). Both factors — the early memories and the pious family environment — were vitally important to his development. As a child, he would sometimes be called on to recite prayers in the presence of guests. His brother Andrei remembered that they would attend mass every Sunday, preceded by vespers the previous night, in the Church attached to the Moscow hospital where their father worked as a doctor. They would do the same thing on Saints' days as well.[3] Their parents were evidently not just conventional observers of religious practice. Both, especially their mother, said Andrei, were deeply religious: every significant event in the life of the family would be marked by the appropriate religious observance. Dostoevsky himself received religious instruction from the deacon at the hospital. Before he even learned to read, his imagination had been fired by events from the ancient lives of saints (XXV, 215), who provided models of asceticism, compassion, suffering, humility and self-sacrifice, based on the example of Christ. Such impressions were reinforced by the family's annual pilgrimage to the St Sergius Trinity Monastery, about 60 miles outside Moscow. These major family events continued until Dostoevsky was ten. In fact, in a letter written in A N Maikov in 1870, he would claim to be an expert on monasteries, on the grounds that he had been acquainted with them since childhood (XXIX, i, 118). As Dostoevsky's biographers never fail to mention, his mother taught him to read from a Russian translation of a well-known German eighteenth-century religious primer by Johannes Hübner, entitled *One Hundred and Four Sacred Stories from the Old and*

New Testaments Selected for Children,[4] which was also the childhood reading of the Elder Zosima in Dostoevsky's last novel (XIV, 264). This book, which was supposed to be learned by heart, contained many of the Bible stories that were later to play a key role in Dostoevsky's major novels, including the stories of the Fall in the Garden of Eden, of the trials of Job and of the raising of Lazarus. It was probably the story of Job's unmerited sufferings and his rebellion against God (which he also associates with Zosima and which is the implied response to Ivan Karamazov's rebellion) that made the deepest impression on Dostoevsky. He had read it for himself by the age of eight and we know that he read it again in his mid-fifties, when he was working on *A Raw Youth* and *The Brothers Karamazov* (XXIX, i, 43).

It was also in childhood that he discovered the deep spirituality of the Russian people. The story of the peasant Marei, who rescued the young Fedor when he thought that he was being pursued by a wolf, is well known to all Dostoevsky enthusiasts. The memory of the peasant's surprising tenderness as he made the sign of the cross over the comforted child remained with Dostoevsky all his life. He told the story in his *Diary of a Writer* in February 1876 (XXII, 46–50). One recent Dostoevsky scholar, Sarah Hudspith, even sees the story as having iconic significance in his work.[5]

Childhood memories were of great importance for Dostoevsky, a fact stressed in the *Diary of a Writer* and emphasized in some of his character portrayals. At the end of *The Brothers Karamazov*, Alesha says that people talk a lot about education, but a beautiful, sacred memory, preserved from childhood, is perhaps the best education of all (XV, 195).[6]

At the Military Engineering Academy in St Petersburg, where Dostoevsky studied from 1838 to 1841, he was known to his fellow-pupils for his hermit-like habits, and for spending all his free time reading. Some of this reading served to reinforce his religious upbringing.

A I Savelev, who was an officer at the Academy at the time, noted that Dostoevsky was very religious and scrupulously observed all his obligations to the Orthodox Church. He possessed copies of the Gospels and of Heinrich Zschokke's *Die Stunden der Andacht* (*Hours of Devotion*). After Father Poluektov's lectures on religion, Dostoevsky would stay behind and engage in long conversations with him. The other students called him 'the monk Fotii'.[7] An interesting feature of Zschokke's book, in the words of Dostoevsky's biographer Joseph Frank, is that it 'preached a sentimental version of Christianity entirely free from dogmatic content and with a strong emphasis on giving Christian love a social application',[8] a creed which Dostoevsky tried actively to put into practice in the Academy and which apparently won him the respect of his fellow-students. Perhaps we see here the origins of his later interest in a Christian socialism with Western European sources. While it did not apparently involve any lessening of his Orthodox observance, it was nevertheless in harmony with his romantic enthusiasm for those Western novelists, poets and playwrights, whose work he began to devour with such enthusiasm at about this time. Some of them, for example Schiller, Hugo and George Sand, he saw as great Christian writers (XXVIII, i, 69–70; XXIII, 37) and this was not for reasons which were unique to the Orthodox faith. On the occasion of George Sand's death in 1876, Dostoevsky wrote that, while she was never able to bring herself to subscribe consciously to the central idea of Orthodoxy (that 'in the whole universe there is no name but His by which one may be saved'), she nevertheless, in acknowledging both intellectually and emotionally the freedom and moral responsibility of the human personality, accepted one of the basic ideas of Christianity. Dying a deist, with a firm faith in God and immortality, she was possibly, Dostoevsky thought, the most Christian woman of her age (XXIII, 37).

There is little doubt that these words reflect the views of both the young and the mature Dostoevsky. It was a Dostoevsky capable of seeing Western European Christian socialism not simply as a step on the baleful, downward path from Catholicism to atheistic socialism, as he was later to insist (XXV, 7), but also as a bright reflection of the central idea of Orthodoxy. For Dostoevsky was able to appreciate the central ideas of Christianity wherever he found them, even in Western Europe, even when entirely shorn of their Orthodox context and colouring.

At the Engineering Academy, his infatuation with the works of Schiller, Sand and the cohorts of romantic writers whose work enshrined all that was pure and noble in the human spirit, was stimulated and reinforced by his intense friendships with his two young friends, Berezhetsky and Shidlovsky. At the same time, he was reading those other romantic writers who celebrated the supernatural, the dark side of the human soul, the individual's Faustian pact with the devil and the sacrilegious attempt to usurp God's place in the universe; works by such writers as Hoffmann, Balzac, Sue and Goethe himself, which were to merge in his creative imagination with the traditions of Russian sectarianism and Old Belief.[9]

In 1844, Dostoevsky resigned from the army for the precarious life of a professional writer and not long afterwards the manuscript of his first novel, *Poor Folk*, received a rapturous welcome from the doyen of the Natural School, the critic Vissarion Belinsky. It was inevitable that the young Dostoevsky, like everyone who met him, should fall under Belinsky's spell, and this encounter was to mark a new phase in the evolution of his religious thought. For a while he was fêted in the literary circles of St Petersburg. Many years later he recalled Belinsky's passionate socialism, which in many ways accorded with values to which he was already attracted. For example, Belinsky acknowledged the moral basis of true socialism and appreciated the dangers of the 'anthill society', as Dostoevsky called the socialist ideal. Yet unlike the utopian socialists, Dostoevsky recalls, Belinsky's socialism was of the atheistic variety, and he therefore felt impelled to attack Christianity. Writing in 1873, Dostoevsky remembered an occasion when in the middle of a tirade against Christ, Belinsky pointed straight at him and turned to a friend with the words, 'Every time I mention Christ the expression on his face changes and he looks as though he's going to burst into tears.' Belinsky, says Dostoevsky, went even further than Renan, who saw Christ as the ideal of human beauty, seeing him as the most ordinary man, and even as a possible recruit to socialism. Dostoevsky remembers George Sand, Cabet, Pierre Leroux, Proudhon and Feuerbach as Belinsky's particular heroes at the time; Fourier had already fallen out of fashion (XXI, 8–12). Quite likely, Belinsky also introduced him to the works of Strauss and Stirner. In the same article of 1873, Dostoevsky gives the impression that he had been completely won over to Belinsky's position, which presumably included his atheism, and later in that year he even reflects that he might have been capable of becoming a follower of the unprincipled nihilist Nechaev (XXI, 129). If so, then his youthful enthusiasm for socialism had certainly taken a dramatic turn. But there is other evidence, of that of Dr S D Ianovsky,[10] who saw him frequently in the mid to late 1840s, which contradicts this, and most scholars nowadays believe that in this respect Dostoevsky retrospectively exaggerated his youthful capitulation to Belinsky. Joseph Frank has argued persuasively that he found better support for his own progressive, moral-religious views in the Beketov Circle, and in his friendship with Valerian Maikov.[11] It may well be that Belinsky's charismatic personality exercised an influence over Dostoevsky that faded when he was in the more relaxed company of other friends.

Dostoevsky was now in his mid-twenties, at an age when intellectual views often take shape. It seems very likely that he wavered in his religious views and observance at this time, finding himself caught between two irresistible forces, his emotional attachment to Orthodoxy and the image of Christ on one hand, and his rage at the Church's apparent indifference to the oppression of the lower social classes on the other. Both sometimes led him to excess, and the resulting pressures must have caused him considerable anguish. When he was eventually arrested for his part in the Petrashevsky Conspiracy in 1849, the principal charge against him was that he had read Belinsky's letter to Gogol in public. In this letter, Belinsky had taken Gogol to task for confusing the Christ who brought freedom, equality and brotherhood to humanity, with the Orthodox Church, the servant of despotism, superstition and the knout.[12] No doubt, Dostoevsky agreed with Belinsky's view of Gogol; but however far he strayed into the utopian socialist camp under Belinsky's influence, and later, in his fateful association with the Petrashevsky Circle, he always drew the line when it came to attacks on the image of Christ, which never ceased to move him deeply. Much later, in 1876, he was to reflect in *The Diary of a Writer*, 'In Russian (that is, genuine) Christianity, there is no mysticism at all; there is only love for mankind and the image of Christ — at least, these are its main points' (XXIII, 130).

Notwithstanding his commitment to the image of Christ, Dostoevsky continued to expose himself to philosophies that incorporated and gave expression to radical atheistic ideas, and to be drawn into their orbit. His regular visits to meetings of the Petrashevsky Circle began in the autumn of 1848 and the details are too well known, and too easily accessible, to require rehearsal here. But A B Gibson is right in reminding us that Feuerbach's *Essence of Christianity* is a work always to be reckoned with in the study of Dostoevsky, and whether he read it or not is beside the point, because all around him were talking about it. According to Feuerbach, religious experience is not to be discounted, but is to be seen as a projection of the human mind.[13] Whatever Dostoevsky's intention was, there was to be no depiction of religious experience in his novels that could not be satisfactorily interpreted in this way; and the degree to which the most radical questioning of religious claims becomes the ideological cornerstone of his major novels likewise testifies to the deep and permanent impression that thinkers like Belinsky, Petrashevsky and the even more extreme Speshnev made on his creative consciousness during this formative period in his life, when he was still in his 20s and finding his feet as a writer.

While there is plenty of evidence that, during the period of his association with the Petrashevsky Circle and its offshoots, Dostoevsky was moved to indignation by violence against the oppressed and the underprivileged, and that he had a wide intellectual curiosity, there is none that, like Petrashevsky and Speshnev, he looked to revolution from below as a solution. Nevertheless, he was arrested on 23 April 1849. There followed incarceration in the Peter-Paul Fortress, and the gruelling investigation that followed. When conditions were alleviated, he managed to read and even to write a bit. Though he read anything available, he seems to have been particularly interested in two accounts of pilgrimages to the Holy Places, and the works of St Dmitry of Rostov (XXVIII, i, 157), which included plays on religious themes in the medieval tradition. He asked his brother for the Bible (both Testaments), in both the French and Slavonic versions (XXVIII, i, 158–59).[14] However, there is no suggestion that under the pressure of events he entirely abandoned worldly thoughts in order to immerse himself in religion, for he also urgently requested copies of the journal *Notes of the Fatherland* and Shakespeare. It was here too that he wrote *A Little Hero*, which had no more religious significance than the rest of his early work. Nevertheless, as Frank speculates,[15] this period may well mark the beginning of that process of close reading of the Scriptures which reached its zenith during the four years in the Fortress at Omsk, with the New Testament as his only reading matter.

First, however, came the death sentence and the last-minute reprieve at the site of execution. In spite of Dostoevsky's words to Speshnev at the scaffold ('Nous serons avec le Christ'),[16] his spirit was understandably far from tranquil at that moment. The unexpected sentence, followed by the unexpected reprieve, would have put the faith of the most devout saint to test. Even Christ seems to have suffered desolation on the Cross (Matthew, 27: 46; Mark, 15: 34). Dostoevsky seems to have continued to hope for something after his physical death and to be terrified more by confrontation with the unknown than by the imminent prospect of total extinction. It would be inappropriate to draw any general conclusions about his religious views from his feelings at such a moment, yet they are likely to have left a deep imprint on his imagination. Some years later, he was to put the experiences of a condemned man on the way to execution into fictional form, notably in *The Idiot* (VIII, 51–52) and also, more briefly, in *The Brothers Karamazov* (XV, 146). Whether or not they faithfully reflect his own experience in every detail, he was undoubtedly able to write from first hand experience. From that moment on, he knew that matters of faith were not peripheral to living and dying, but vitally relevant to every minute of his experience. His unexpected, last minute reprieve must have seemed like a veritable resurrection.

II

The years in the Fortress at Omsk also made an indelible impression. At Tobolsk, each of the Petrashevsky convicts was given a copy of the New Testament in modern Russian. This was the only book that was allowed in prison and therefore the only book Dostoevsky read for the next four years. Miraculously, his copy has survived, complete with markings made with his fingernail at the time, and later underlinings and annotations in his own hand. It has been carefully scrutinized by scholars, especially by the Norwegian scholar Geir Kjetsaa, for clues as to what was most important to Dostoevsky,[17] and some of these findings are reflected in what follows.

His outlook on life, and with it his spiritual life, could not fail to undergo lasting change as a result of the eight years of exile, especially the four years in the fortress. He encountered concentrated evil at first hand and the Schillerian utopianism of his youth suffered a fatal blow. He got to know the Russian people in their deepest degradation and yet, at the same time, came to believe in their underlying spiritual worth. In 1880, in response to Gradovsky's objections to his Pushkin speech, he recalled his experiences at Omsk, defying his critic to say that he does not know the Russian people, and adding that it was from them that he again received into his soul the Christ whom he first knew in his parents' home as a child, and whom he nearly lost when he reinvented himself as a European liberal (XXVI, 152).

For all the alleged shortcomings of the Orthodox Church, he insisted, it had kept the Russian people faithful to the truth of Christ through their long centuries of suffering, by its hymns and its prayers, and in particular by the prayer of Saint Ephraim the Syrian, beginning 'God and Lord of my life', which contained 'the whole essence of Christianity' (XXVI, 151). The devout prayers of the prisoners, in whom the spark of the divine had never been extinguished, had deeply impressed Dostoevsky.

It was on his release from the fortress in January 1854 that he wrote his now-famous and much-quoted letter to Natalia Fonvizina, from whose hands he had originally received his copy of the New Testament at Tobolsk:

> I have heard from many sources that you are very religious, Natalia Dmitrievna. However, it is as a result of my own experience and not because you are religious that I am telling you that there are moments when one thirsts for faith like 'parched grass'; and one finds it, for the very reason that truth shines more brightly in affliction. As for myself, I confess that I am a child of my age, a child of unbelief and doubt up to this very moment, and I am certain that I shall remain so to the grave. What terrible torments this thirst to believe has cost me and continues to cost me, burning ever more strongly in my soul the more contrary arguments there are. Nevertheless, God sometimes sends me moments of complete tranquillity. In such moments I love and find that I am loved by others, and in such moments I have nurtured in myself a symbol of truth, in which everything is clear and holy for me. This symbol is very simple: it is the belief that there is nothing finer, profounder, more attractive, more reasonable, more courageous and more perfect than Christ, and not only is there not, but I tell myself with jealous love that there cannot be. Even if someone were to prove to me that the truth lay outside Christ, I should choose to remain with Christ rather than with the truth (XXVIII, i, 176).

The significance of this passage for the later Dostoevsky has been much debated, especially his prediction that he would remain a child of doubt and unbelief to the grave. But the ability to identify imaginatively with the extremes of doubt and unbelief never left him, and this is something which those who wish to stress the depth of his faith in his later years sometimes gloss over.[18] Dostoevsky himself never glossed it over. At the same time, the letter testifies to three important, positive facts; the first is that Dostoevsky sometimes experienced moments of great spiritual tranquillity associated with human love. The second is that atheistic arguments, far from undermining his faith, seemed to provoke an intense thirst for it, and adversity seemed to make it shine more brightly. The third is the immense power over him of the image of Christ as ideal, a power that would withstand, as one of his characters later puts it, even mathematical refutation (X, 198).

On his release and transfer to Semipalatinsk, Dostoevsky certainly did not become a wholly conventional Orthodox believer. Wrangel recalls how in Semipalatinsk their favourite occupation would be to lie on the grass on a warm evening gazing at the millions of stars twinkling in the deep blue sky. These moments calmed him and an awareness of the greatness of the Creator, of an omniscient, omnipotent divine power, softened their hearts, while the consciousness of their own insignificance quietened their spirits. Wrangel observes that in Semipalatinsk Dostoevsky 'was rather pious, but did not often go to Church, and disliked priests, especially Siberian ones. But he spoke about Christ ecstatically'.[19] There is some evidence too that he was keen to explore the philosophical and psychological aspects of spiritual life, including Islam. Writing to his brother in February 1854, he entreats him to send copies of the Koran, Kant's *Critique of Pure Reason* and Hegel's *Philosophy of History* (XXVIII, i, 173).

At about the same time Wrangel reports that they were planning to translate together Hegel's philosophy and Carus's *Psyche*.[20] Such evidence, combined with what we know of Dostoevsky's intellectual interests after his return to metropolitan Russia, suggests that he was keen to place Christianity in a wider context and to explore ways in which modern idealist philosophy had enabled his contemporaries to re-evaluate the religious tradition without entirely abandoning it. A further dimension of his religious experience at this time is provided in an anecdote told by S V Kovalevskaia, according to which Dostoevsky related to her the experience of an epileptic fit one Easter in Siberia, during which he was convinced that, like Mohammed, he had really visited Paradise and apprehended God.[21] Such experiences are reflected in those of Prince Myshkin in *The Idiot* (VIII, 188). 'For several moments,' Dostoevsky told Strakhov, 'I experience a happiness that is impossible under ordinary circumstances, and of which most people have no comprehension. I feel a complete harmony within myself and in the whole world, and this feeling is so strong, and affords so much pleasure, that one could give up ten years of one's life for several seconds of that ecstasy, perhaps one's whole life.'[22]

In spite of the occasional moments of tranquillity, the epileptic aura, and the ecstatic commitment to the image of Christ, the picture we have of Dostoevsky as he returns to Russia at the close of the 1850s is that of a troubled, questing spirit, open to intense momentary mystical experiences, who becomes progressively convinced of the spiritual treasures in the soul of the ordinary Russian people and of the damage done to the Russian spirit by Westernization and the divorce of Russian youth (including, for a time, himself) from its native traditions.

On his return to European Russia such views were reinforced in Dostoevsky's mind in a variety of ways. His travels in Europe, his experience of the revolutionary movement after the Emancipation, his discussions with the exiled Russian socialist Herzen in London and Italy, and with Grigorev and Strakhov on the two journals *Time* (*Vremia*) and *The Epoch* (*Epokha*) which he edited in St Petersburg with his brother Mikhail, until Mikhail's death in 1864, led him to formulate, with his colleagues, a doctrine which they called *pochvennichestvo*,[23] a term which is easy to understand, but difficult to translate. Some call it 'native soil conservatism'; its object was to bridge the gulf between Westerners and Slavophiles in post-Reform Russia. In later years Dostoevsky moved further into the orbit of the Slavophiles. While accepting the need to take the best of Western civilization on board, he called for a return to Russian values, which he increasingly saw as the key to universal salvation, and not only to the salvation of Russia. Like the Slavophiles, he preached that Europe had long ago sold its soul to the principles of abstract rationalism, legalism, materialism and individualism, which the Catholic Church had inherited from Rome and passed on to Protestantism and thence to socialism, which had inevitably become atheistic. Russia, on the other hand, with its ideals of universality and reconciliation, and its ability to understand other people and unite them in a grand synthesis, had preserved its sense of organic community in the Orthodox conception of *sobornost'* (the Church as fellowship under God). These values are reflected in his *Winter Notes on Summer Impressions* (an account of his visits to Europe in 1862 and 1863), in the editorial policies of the two journals, in the articles published in his *Diary of a Writer* (from 1873 to 1880), and from time to time through the mouths of characters in his novels. Such ideas underlay his sensationally successful Pushkin Speech in 1880. It is this outlook to which Dostoevsky was referring when he wrote in 1873 of the 'regeneration of his convictions' (XXI, 134). The source of the values underlying it was to be found in the tradition of the Russian Orthodox Church as interpreted by the leading Slavophile thinkers, and there is no doubt that the development of a coherent world-view along these lines did much to stabilize Dostoevsky's intellectual and emotional life, and to restore his respectability in Russian high society. In later years, he even became close to Konstantin Pobedonostsev, the Procurator of the Holy Synod, and to the Imperial Family, but he continued to bring the radical ideas of his youth back to life through his fictional characters. Dostoevsky was never able, perhaps never tried, to put the radical ideas of his youth entirely out of his mind. Had he ceased to entertain these seriously to the end of his life, in favour of the religious beliefs of his maturity, he would have written none of his great novels.

It has to be admitted that most non-academic admirers of Dostoevsky have not found his '*pochvennik*'/Slavophile ideas very interesting, and there are good reasons why this is so. In the first place there is their strident, didactic, nationalistic tone, at times tinged by anti-Semitism; in the second, they display little intellectual originality and lack intellectual integrity. Not least, as Geir Kjetsaa, puts it, one is irritated by his tireless assertion of Russia's excellence, and by his bitter complaints that this excellence cannot be understood by West Europeans.[24]

But, most importantly, they seem to cast little light on what is original and insightful in Dostoevsky's major fiction and to have little in common with those qualities which have established him as a world-ranking author. Although it is arguable that Slavophile values inform the text of his novels at the level of implied author, not a single character in the great novels, and that includes the narrators, subscribes to Dostoevsky's personal 'Slavophile' philosophy as a whole. Even Shatov in *The Devils*, who shares his views about many things (Russia as a God-bearing people; the importance of the aesthetic principle; the prospect of the Second Coming of Christ taking place in Russia), cannot yet bring himself to confess belief in the existence of God.

In fact, we shall see that it is not the ideology of the later Dostoevsky but the spiritual struggles of the earlier Dostoevsky that give us the most valuable clues to the reading of his mature novels. And this should not surprise us. As we have noted, Dostoevsky reminds his readers more than once that it is the voyage that matters, not the arrival at one's destination. In the words of Ippolit in *The Idiot*:

> 'You can be certain that Columbus was really happy not when he actually discovered America, but during the process of discovering it. You can be certain that he was perhaps happiest of all exactly three days before he discovered the New World, when his mutinous crew almost turned the ship back to Europe in despair [...] It is life that matters, life alone — the continuous and everlasting process of discovery, and not the discovery itself' (VIII, 327).

Similar sentiments are expressed in Dostoevsky's article of 1861 'Mr –bov and the Question of Art' (XVIII, 97) and by the hero of *Notes from Underground* (V, 118). What one observes in his novels is a reflection of the process of discovery — or rediscovery — of the Christian tradition, in the face of its most deadly (one might say 'mutinous') opponents, some of which were, it seems, permanently lodged in his own mind. It is a process of rethinking Christianity in dialogue and, whatever may have been the case with his own spiritual pilgrimage, it is a process that reached no final conclusion in his works of fiction.

When Dostoevsky committed his thoughts to paper in 1864 on the occasion of the death of his first wife, Mariia Dmitrievna, he made this very argument the cornerstone of his belief in immortality.[25] Reflecting that to love another person as oneself according to Christ's commandment is impossible, because a man's ego holds him back, Dostoevsky affirms that Christ alone was able to do this; and he is the perpetual ideal towards which the individual vainly strives, and must strive in accordance with a law of nature. Since the appearance of Christ in the flesh, it has become evident that he represents the ultimate development of the human personality.[26] To put it in modern terms, human beings have a genetic disposition to seek to emulate the ideal of Christ. The highest use the individual can make of his ego is therefore to annihilate that ego, to give it totally and unselfishly to everyone. At this point, the law of the ego and the law of humanism annihilate themselves and fuse. But if this were the final goal of humanity, there would be no more point in living once it had been achieved. Therefore, on earth the individual is in a state of development, unfinished, transitional. 'It is completely senseless to attain such a great goal, in my view, if on attaining it everything is snuffed out and disappears, that is, if there is no more life for the individual on the attainment of this goal. It follows that there is a future, heavenly life' (XX, 172–73). As we shall see, belief in immortality is one traditional Christian doctrine that Dostoevsky consistently affirms and it is predicated on the belief that here on earth the individual's spiritual business is necessarily unfinished.

By the mid-1860s, Dostoevsky's religious consciousness had many strands. Publicly, he had succeeded in knitting them together in the ideology of *pochvennichestvo*, but the uncritical passion with which he sometimes preached its precepts, especially in later years, is perhaps a measure of the fragility of the edifice that he had created. At all events, when it came to writing novels, he adopted quite a different mind-set, a mind-set which has still perhaps not been satisfactorily described and modelled in the voluminous critical literature, but which has something in common with his metaphor of Columbus and his mutinous crew on the verge of discovering America.

III

We thus come to the major works, beginning with *Notes from Underground* in 1864. Although religious motifs are difficult to find in *Notes from Underground*, it is typical in taking as its central character an intellectual obsessed — as Dostoevsky was — with ultimate philosophical questions. Ostensibly the hero is in rebellion against the dominant progressive ideas of the 1860s, above all the idea that human beings are rational creatures, who have only to be shown their true rational interests to follow them, and the idea that human beings are part of a natural world which has been shown by science to be subject to iron laws of cause and effect, with the result that belief in freedom of the will is deluded, and all notion of moral responsibility illusory. Liza Knapp has shown that the terminology of Newtonian physics and mechanistic models of the universe is repeatedly used by Dostoevsky in characterising the concept of a materialist world without a spiritual dimension.[27] Against these ideas, the hero protests that reason accounts for only a fraction of human faculties and rarely if ever determines actions; moreover, whatever science may say about freedom being illusory, people will simply refuse to accept it. In fact, if ever a perfectly rational society were created, people would willingly conspire to bring it tumbling down. The hero also has deeper philosophical problems, which are more rarely commented on, such as the impossibility of finding any stable basis at all for philosophical certainty. Ostensibly, again, the hero's answer is frantically to assert the claims of the individual will, a stance that has caused Dostoevsky to be seen as a proto-existentialist. However, there are both textual and extra-textual reasons for rejecting this protest as the hero's final word. The appalling consequences of the unfettered play of the individual will are depicted in Raskolnikov's Siberian dream in *Crime and Punishment* (VI, 419–20) and again in 'The Grand Inquisitor' in *The Brothers Karamazov*; and we know that Dostoevsky had originally intended to provide a Christian solution to the Underground Man's problems (XXVIII, ii, 73). He wrote the words on the death of his wife, about seeking to emulate the ideal of Christ and a future heavenly life, just as he had completed Part I of his story, so perhaps they give a clue to what this might have been. We are left however only with hints in the text, the most important of which is the hero's intuition that there is a better solution than the one that he has inscribed in his notes, and that this perhaps has something to do with 'living life' (*zhivaia zhizn'*) (V, 121, 178). This is a vitally important point to note in respect of Dostoevsky's treatment of religion. It recalls Christ's words 'I am the way, the truth and the life' (John, 14: 6)[28] and reminds us that, for Dostoevsky, Christianity was to be less a set of prescribed doctrines and more what Stewart Sutherland, taking his cue from Wittgenstein, has called a 'form of life',[29] a form of life which takes all human faculties, including the thirst for the holy, fully into account. As Dostoevsky said in one of his notebooks: 'The Gospels foresee that the laws of self-preservation and scientific experiment will discover nothing and will never satisfy people, that people are satisfied not by progress and necessity, but by a moral acceptance of a higher beauty.'[30] *Notes from Underground* seems to pose the question 'What happens to an intellectual of our time who has lost his sense of the holy and his grasp of living life, and finds himself in the thrall of fashionable progressive ideas?' The Man from Underground is Dostoevsky's answer. In this way he sets out to counter some strong and insistent challenges to religion: rationalism; deterministic physics; historical optimism; utilitarian ethics; nihilistic amoralism. But he does so here by a negative route, by displaying the inadequacy of human language to reach certain truth, and the dreadful consequences for the individual, and for society, of such ideas taken to their logical conclusion, hinting that there is another, infinitely better way on offer.

In *Crime and Punishment* the main challenge to religion once again comes from an intellectual of the 60s, who hubristically takes on himself the role of God (the Man-God as Dostoevsky was to call him later), believing that he has the right to determine the life or death of others, to sit in judgement on other people and even to divert the course of history if he is in truth a great man with a new word for humanity. Raskolnikov fitfully persuades himself that he is such a person (though this is a gross oversimplification of his psychology) and he commits two murders on the strength of this belief. The rest of the novel is taken up with the events that accompany a process of self-questioning and eventual voluntary surrender to the authorities. Dostoevsky saw this intellectual hubris exemplified in the young nihilists of the 1860s, inspired not just by a utilitarianism debased by a form of social Darwinism, but also by the cult of the great man, typified by the achievements of Napoleon I and the aspirations of Napoleon III. Together with an emphasis on the individual will, the novel shows that Raskolnikov feels that destiny is playing a hand in his life.

It is in planning his murder that Raskolnikov accidentally hears of the young prostitute Sonia Marmeladova, and resolves eventually to make his confession to her. Sonia is the first of Dostoevsky's major saintly characters, characters who accept life, rather than take up arms against it, characters who echo the tradition of the *iurodivyi* or 'holy fool'[31] and whose personalities express a simple faith, characterized by humility (*smirenie*), compassion (*sostradanie*), insight (*prozorlivost'*) and spiritual tenderness (*umilenie*). Perhaps it is this last characteristic which is the least accessible to the Western mind. V N Zakharov has shown how the idea plays a key role in Dostoevsky's poetics, from his very first novel, the sentimental *Poor Folk*, onwards. A Western reader may mistake *umilenie* for sentimentality. But there are further dimensions to the Russian idea; it is a softening of the heart, an arousal of tender emotions that combines the richness of Christian love with a veneration and piety, expressive of the grace of God.[32] Sonia is by no means a tranquil person. Her faith is easily disturbed. But she is the agent of Raskolnikov's spiritual rebirth, which she sets in motion when she reads him the story of the raising of Lazarus from St John's Gospel (VI, 250; John, 11: 1–46). The story expresses the idea of death and resurrection, the Easter motif,[33] and looked at from the Christian point of view it is this myth that structures Raskolnikov's destiny in the novel, from his spiritual suicide when he commits murder to the beginnings of his spiritual renewal in Siberia. It can be argued, as Roger Cox does, that in fact it structures the whole novel,[34] cutting across the counter-structure of pride and retribution, into which the reader is lured by the novel's title, with the result that most secular readers seem to find the religious alternative implausible. Cox also argued, long before the fact was rediscovered by specialists working in Russia, for the special importance of the Johannine scriptures for Dostoevsky (that is, John's Gospel, the first Letter of John and the Book of Revelation), in particular John's insistence on the priority of Grace over Law, an emphasis which, of course, he shares with Paul. It is an idea associated with the Russian acceptance of the criminal as an 'unfortunate' rather than as an outcast, an idea that pervades the whole of *Crime and Punishment*. Geir Kjetsaa has noted that a study of the underlinings in Dostoyevsky's copy of the New Testament confirms the significance of the Johannine scriptures for him, with its emphasis on the commandment to love and its definition of sin as a rejection of Jesus.[35] There is much in this argument, though we shall see later that it is not the whole truth about Dostoevsky's relationship to the New Testament.

However, neither traditional Orthodox theology nor the Church plays a significant role in the novel and, for that matter, nor does the notion of *sobornost'*,[36] which was later to be so important to Dostoevsky. Raskolnikov's 'resurrection' is made possible by Sonia's evocation of his Christian upbringing for, like Dostoevsky, he has warm childhood memories which seem to have been revived by the arrival of his mother and sister in St Petersburg.[37] Neither Sonia, nor any other character, seeks to mount counter-arguments against Raskolnikov's atheism. She is no intellectual, nor is she a traditional Orthodox saint. And if she echoes the type of the Holy Fool, it is only distantly. She has not chosen a life of renunciation, feigning foolishness in order to vanquish her spiritual pride; she has been forced into prostitution to support her family. Her literary ancestry includes representatives of the 'pure prostitute' of the European romantic tradition of which the prototype is Eugène Sue's Fleur de Marie in his famous novel *Les Mystères de Paris*. She presents an alternative form of life, but Dostoevsky does not simply juxtapose the alternatives. He causes his characters, with their philosophies, to interact. And as we shall see, there is no certainty as to which will emerge victorious within the framework of any given fiction.[38]

The figure of Prince Myshkin in *The Idiot* has produced much heated discussion. If we did not know that Dostoevsky had conceived him (very late in the day, within two months of completing Part 1) as a 'positively beautiful man', had referred to literary models such as Dickens' Mr Pickwick, Cervantes' Don Quixote and Hugo's Jean Valjean (XXVIII, ii, 251), and left notes in which 'The Prince' is juxtaposed with the name of Christ (IX, 246, 249, 253), there might be less to dispute. But it is certainly true that, especially in the first part of the novel, Myshkin is associated with many Christian motifs, deriving from both the New Testament and the Russian religious tradition. In his long stories to the Epanchin women, Myshkin evokes the Gospels, not least in his own childlikeness and in his liking for children, his fondness for the donkey he talks about, the story of Marie, and the very fact that he is prone to contribute to conversation by means of parables.[39] L Miuller stresses that Myshkin displays all the qualities emphasized in the beatitudes in the Sermon on the Mount: he is 'poor of spirit', meek, merciful, pure of heart and a peacemaker. Likewise he displays the virtues commended by St Paul in 1 Corinthians 13, verses 4–7: he is patient, kind, envies no one, is never boastful, nor conceited, nor rude, never selfish or quick to take offence, keeps no score of wrongs, does not gloat over other men's sins, delights in the truth, believes that there is nothing that love cannot face, and that there is no limit to faith, hope and endurance based on love.[40] Above all, Myshkin's religious experience incorporates a spiritual dimension unique in Dostoevsky's fiction, based on his own epileptic aura, a blinding inner light which momentarily floods his soul and conveys a deep calm, full of serene and harmonious joy and hope, full of understanding of the ultimate cause, the very synthesis of beauty and prayer, the highest synthesis of life (VIII, 194).

At first sight, *The Idiot* seems an exception to the rule that Dostoevsky's novels focus on the mutinous crew rather than on the captain inspired by faith in what lies over the horizon. Yet, although it begins by introducing a saintly hero in the person of Prince Myshkin, it is evident, both on textual grounds and from what we know of its complex creative history, that the author/narrator becomes increasingly uncomfortable with this arrangement. Something odd happens at the end of Part 1. It is as if some magnetic force draws Dostoevsky, and his fiction, back into their usual configuration. By the time he is writing the third part of the novel, his notes contain a marginal reminder to write concisely and powerfully about Ippolit, and to focus the whole plot on him (IX, 280). Shortly before, he had noted, 'Ippolit is the main axis of the whole novel. He even has a hold on the Prince, though in essence he realises that he can never possess him' (IX, 277).

This is an extraordinary move with respect to a character who in other respects seems minor and peripheral, and who is essentially an afterthought in the author's scheme of things.[41] Yet it is foreshadowed as early as Part 2, where a quite different and devastatingly negative image of Christ is introduced, by means of Rogozhin's copy of Holbein's picture of Christ taken from the Cross. Rogozhin likes looking at the picture. Myshkin is horrified, remarking that it could cause a person to lose his faith (VIII, 182). Much later in the novel, as he confronts his own imminent death, Ippolit gives an extended comment on it:

'Here one cannot help being struck by a question: if death is so horrible and the laws of nature so powerful then how can they be overcome? How can they be overcome when they were not even conquered by the one who during his lifetime conquered nature and whom nature obeyed...? When one looks at that picture, nature appears in the form of some huge, implacable and dumb beast, or to be more exact (much more exact, however strange it may seem) in the form of some huge machine of the latest design which has senselessly seized, cut to pieces and swallowed up, impassively and unfeelingly, that great and priceless being, a being alone worth the whole of nature and all its laws, the whole earth, which was possibly created solely for the appearance of that being' (VIII, 339).

There is no doubt that the mutinous crew comes into its own as the novel progresses — embodying cupidity, pride, humiliation and the demand for individual rights — and if Myshkin for a time learns to cope with it, it is at the expense of his tranquillity, his innocence and his saintliness. The transition is marked by a shift from motifs reminiscent of the Gospels to apocalyptic motifs recalling The Book of Revelation.[42] One of the characters, Lebedev, even sets up as an interpreter of the Apocalypse, and the narrative soon takes on a dizzy momentum which Myshkin is powerless to stop. The key to life now remains for him beyond the horizon, as it does for the novel's neurotic and tragic heroine Nastasia Filippovna, who also presents an image of Christ, this time accompanied by a child, his gaze fixed on a distant point on the horizon, a great thought, as great as the universe, in his eyes (VIII, 380). It is worth noting that the one positive image of Christ contained in the novel is presented not by Myshkin but by the deeply neurotic, melodramatic and suicidal Nastasia Filippovna. At the end of the day Myshkin is not the Russian Christ, as some readers have wished to see him — he succeeds in 'resurrecting' no one — and he is scarcely a traditional saint. Although he embodies to an unusual degree those features which Dostoevsky associates with the Christian personality (compassion, insight, humility, sensitivity to beauty, tenderness of heart, forgiveness) and shares Dostoevsky's own glimpse of paradise through the aura of an epileptic fit, this glimpse is followed by a sense of utter desolation, and is associated more with the Prophet Mohammed than with Christ. Moreover, he is unable to remember his Russian roots, bringing with him into the novel only mixed memories of Protestant Switzerland. Nor does he seem to be a practising Christian in the conventional sense; he does not attend Church services or observe the Church calendar, and General Ivolgin's seems to be the first Orthodox funeral he has ever attended. The other characters perceive him in a wide variety of ways, ranging from idiot, holy fool, democrat and manipulative rogue to Pushkin's 'poor knight' and Cervantes' Don Quixote, but not as an Orthodox saint. Those readers who persist in seeing in him the image of an Orthodox saint should ask themselves whether he is really the sort of person the Russian Orthodox Church would be likely to canonize. Yet he succeeds in holding up to the other characters an image of the best in them and a hint of a higher reality in which time shall be no more (VIII, 189). Although the conception and characterization of Myshkin is an artistic triumph, and almost certainly the most memorable portrait of the Christian personality in a realistic novel, his performance as an embodiment of Christian virtues, a 'positively beautiful man', to use Dostoevsky's own phrase, remains controversial.[43] Among those who lament his failure, there are some, like G M Fridlender,[44] who ascribe it to his Christianity, and others, like A B Gibson, for whom he is not Christian enough.[45] Both positions are defensible. Dostoevsky himself felt that he had not achieved his aim, that the novel did not express a tenth of what he had intended (XXIX, i, 10), yet he had poured his most intense spiritual experiences into it, raising the discussion from the level of historical processes in his previous novel to that of the nature of the universe.

IV

Dostoevsky spent the years 1867–1871 in Europe with his second wife, Anna Grigorevna, whom he had married in 1867. As Gibson remarks,[46] so far as we can tell Dostoevsky was, in 1869, full of religious sentiment and less suspicious of the Church than previously; but still in trouble on the intellectual front. He did not seem to have advanced much beyond the Myshkin who, convinced that 'compassion is the chief law of human existence' (VIII, 192), tried to persuade himself that 'the atheist is always talking about something else' (VIII, 184).[47]

Yet by the time he returned to Russia, his friend Nikolai Strakhov could testify (and Anna Grigorevna confirms what he says) that it was while abroad that the revelation of the Christian spirit, which had always dwelt in him, came to fruition. He continually steered conversation onto religious themes. Moreover, his personal conduct changed, and took on a great gentleness, expressive of the highest Christian feelings.[48]

Of course, Dostoevsky was certainly not always like this, as other witnesses testify,[49] but his years of exile in Europe do seem to have strengthened the Slavophile Christianity of his last decade, at least so far as his personal life is concerned. There is another significant change. Christ appears in his thoughts not as an ideal of perfection, unattainable here on earth, but as the Word incarnate of St John's Gospel:

> Many think that it is enough to believe in the moral teaching of Christ to be a Christian. It is not Christ's moral teaching, not Christ's doctrine, that will save the world, but faith that the Word has become flesh […] Only in this faith can we achieve divinisation, that ecstasy which binds us most closely to him and has the power of preventing us from straying from the true path (XI, 187–88).[50]

Though there is a clear development here in what has come down to us of Dostoevsky's private thinking, it remains to be seen what significance this would have for his fiction. *The Devils*, Dostoevsky's next major novel, based in part upon his unrealized plan for *The Life of a Great Sinner*, contains many religious motifs, some notable dialogues on religious topics, hallucinations in which the devil appears, a holy fool and a 'Bible woman', even, for the first time, an epigraph from the Gospels; but it does not make a major contribution to his religious evolution. There is no doubt that the mutinous crew is in command here and it is therefore not surprising that many of the religious motifs are apocalyptic, as they were in the later parts of *The Idiot*. Dostoevsky reverts to his preferred structure, in which the central character expresses, or provokes others to express, forms of desolate atheism and amoralism. Although the novel was inspired by the Nechaev episode, and Nechaev is represented in the novel by Petr Verkhovensky, the central character is Nikolai Stavrogin. In a note reminiscent of the one on Ippolit, Dostoevsky wrote in his notebooks: 'Everything is contained in the character of Stavrogin. Stavrogin is ALL' (XI, 207).

Indeed, as the novel shows, Stavrogin has inspired the ideas not only of Verkhovensky, but also of Shatov and Kirillov. As for himself, he has never found a task worthy of his strength, or even capable of commanding his attention for any length of time. In the censored chapter, 'At Tikhon's', where he presents his confession to the Bishop Tikhon in a local monastery, he asks Tikhon to recite a passage from the Book of Revelation in which the 'lukewarm' are condemned (Rev. 3: 14–16). That is Stavrogin himself. Tikhon declares that a complete atheist stands on the next to top rung of the ladder of perfect faith (XI, 10), but Stavrogin cannot manage even that. His short-lived intellectual enthusiasms have produced passionate disciples, however. From the point of view of Dostoevsky's presentation of religion, Shatov and Kirillov are the most important. Shatov, who displays some of the personal characteristics of Dostoevsky's saintly types, also, as we have already noted, subscribes to some of the main points of his Slavophile creed; in particular he proclaims his belief that the aesthetic principle in human affairs is much more important than science and reason, that Russia is a God-bearing people, that the Second Coming of Christ will take place in Russia, and, significantly, he expresses in his own words Dostoevsky's idea that humanity is driven by a force which is the source of 'an unquenchable desire to continue to the end and at the same time to deny an end' (X, 198). But although Shatov believes in these things, he can affirm only that he *will* believe in God. As a representative of Dostoevsky's Slavophile creed, Shatov seems to fall at the vital hurdle. Gibson is surely right in saying that the Shatov–Stavrogin dialogue shows us Dostoevsky ruthlessly probing his own religious advances, and finding them hollow.[51] Kirillov, confused though he seems to be, does, however, fatally assert his atheism. His picture of a universe without God is as bleak as Ippolit's, and seems to echo Dostoevsky's own exchange with Speshnev at the scaffold. In it, Christ, without whom the whole planet is utter madness, founded on lies, 'a vaudeville of the devil', is himself the victim of an illusion, for there is no paradise or resurrection (X, 471).

Kirillov shares Myshkin's epileptic aura. He too momentarily feels eternal harmony in all its fullness, and has a joyful sensation of the whole of nature and truth for which he would give his whole life, but it is an experience alien to a physical life in which people are tormented by pain and fear, and Kirillov sees it as his quasi-messianic mission to sacrifice himself in order to demonstrate that if God does not exist then everything is a matter of the self-will of the individual who can now conquer pain and fear in the most significant way possible, by taking his own life (X, 470).

If Shatov's and Kirillov's religious views have fatal flaws, the same may be said for that of Stepan Verkhovensky, father of the young nihilist and mentor of Stavrogin. At the close of his life, he too stumbles upon the key passage from Revelation (3: 14–16) and is enthused by it, together with the passage from Luke about the Gadarene swine (Luke, 8: 32–37), which Dostoevsky's narrator uses as his epigraph to the novel. But, unlike Stavrogin, of whom it is said that 'when he believes he does not believe that he believes and, when he does not believe, he does not believe that he does not believe' (X, 469), Verkhovensky senior discovers that his main trouble is that he believes himself even when he is lying (X, 497). It hardly needs to be said that such thoughts put huge question marks against the reliability of all belief systems. It may be asked why Dostoevsky should have devoted so much space to various forms of eccentric religious beliefs in a novel that was ostensibly based on political events with no evident religious content.

The answer is not only that Dostoevsky hypothesized that the political events and the accompanying moral and spiritual confusion were the inevitable by-product of a society which had lost its 'binding idea' and faith in the image of Christ. It is probably even more because he was still wrestling with the 'accursed questions' himself and his novels inescapably reflect that process. This is true even of *A Raw Youth*, his penultimate major novel. Although space precludes its detailed treatment here, this novel, as Gibson reminds us, not only contains interesting religious discussions, but the characters quote scripture as they never did, for example, in *The Idiot*.[52] Moreover the narrator's stepfather (Makar) and his natural mother (Sofia) embody a positive conception of peasant religion unparalleled elsewhere in Dostoevsky's fiction, in which *umilenie* has a prominent place. The novel also takes up a curious theme which found its first expression in Stavrogin's Confession (XI, 21–22), subsequently in *A Raw Youth*, (XIII, 290; 374–79), in the story 'The Dream of a Ridiculous Man' (XXV, 104–119) and finally in Ivan Karamazov's poem on 'The geological upheaval' (XV, 83). This theme is that of the 'Golden Age' on earth. In three of its manifestations, it is based on Dostoevsky's interpretation of Claude Lorrain's painting 'Acis and Galatea', which he saw in the Dresden Art Gallery. What they have in common is a depiction of an idyllic, pastoral life in the distant past in a mythical Greece, a paradise on earth in which human beings lived in joy, peace, harmony and plenty. Gibson compares and contrasts all these passages.[53] In 'The Dream of a Ridiculous Man', paradise is destroyed by the introduction of the lie. It is a reworking, using classical rather than Hebrew motifs, of the myth of The Fall as told in book of Genesis. And the consequences of the Fall from innocence, as retold here, are that human language ceases to be a reliable vehicle of truth. Makar Dologoruky, in extolling God's creation in the present, represents an advance on Myshkin in this respect. The latter typically feels alienated from Nature, while the former believes that everything is a mystery, the greatest mystery of all being what awaits us after death (XIII, 290). The word most often associated with Makar is *blagoobrazie* (beautiful form); what he has to offer is not an abstract philosophy of life, nor reflections on the atheistic desolation of an Ippolit or a Kirillov, but an alternative 'form of life' in which a foretaste of eternal life is to be experienced here and now.

Dostoevsky's last novel is unique in many important ways. But we have it on his own repeated authority that he wished *The Brothers Karamazov* to serve as a vehicle for the vindication of the Orthodox faith. There is no doubt that he went to great lengths, both in his reading and his field research, to give an authentic rendering of the life of the Orthodox monastery. His visit with the young philosopher Vladimir Solovev to the monastery at Optina Pustyn in the summer of 1877 played a part and was supplemented by his extensive reading of relevant religious texts.[54] It is impossible to do full justice to the richness of the religious texture of this novel in this chapter. This will be attempted later. Here, we may note that it contains many of the features that we have observed in the earlier novels, including the apocalyptic motifs. The association of the Christian life with tender spiritual feelings, compassion, humility, beauty, childlikeness, non-judgementalism, love for one's neighbour, are all present, together with allusions to transfiguration and *sobornost'*. Zosima's address to the company as he brings his duel to an end (XIV, 272) seems to echo Makar in its paean to God's creation. It is arguable that the Easter motif, echoed in the epigraph taken from John, 12: 24, structures the whole novel. The powerful antireligious polemic contained in the chapters entitled 'Rebellion' and 'The Grand Inquisitor' has alone inspired a multitude of articles and even books; it has attracted the attention of leading Catholic, Protestant and Orthodox theologians and philosophers of religion. To a lesser extent, the same is true of the figure of Zosima and his 'Testament', designed, according to Dostoevsky's plan, to refute the views of the Grand Inquisitor. Nor, of course, is the religious significance of the novel limited to these chapters. All three brothers, Ivan, Alesha and Dmitry make their own contributions to the dialogue, as, in semi-caricature, do Fedor Karamazov, Miusov, Smerdiakov, Rakitin and the monks in the local monastery.

In brief, the heart of the religious polemic is again the mutinous crew, whose chief representative is the young intellectual Ivan Karamazov. Echoing Belinsky's famous rejection of Hegel in his letter to Botkin,[55] he tells his brother, the novice Alesha, a whole series of heart-rending anecdotes about inhuman atrocities committed against children, which he has collected from the newspapers, and concludes that he reserves judgement about the existence of God, but if He exists, and this suffering is the price we are required to pay for future entry into paradise, then the cost is too high and he 'respectfully returns the ticket' (XIV, 223). He continues by recounting a narrative poem of his own composition, full of allusions to religious texts, set in Seville in the sixteenth century, where an aged Grand Inquisitor is supervising the burning of heretics. Into this scene steps the figure of Christ who, having performed a number of acts which echo the Gospel narrative, makes his way to the Inquisitor's cell where the latter, far from acknowledging the incongruity of burning one's fellow humans in the name of a doctrine of love, proceeds to justify his procedure, and that of the Catholic Church, at very great length. This he does by allusion to the Gospel story of Christ's temptation by the Devil in the wilderness (Luke 4: 1–13), concluding that the Devil was right and that Christ was mistaken. Christ offered people freedom, but the burden of freedom, and knowledge of the truth that there is no God, is too much for all but a small élite to bear. What people really crave are the three principles (which the Inquisitor derives from the Devil's temptations) of 'mystery', 'miracle' and 'authority', or in more concrete terms, something to worship, the political and moral authority of the Church, and the satisfaction of their daily material needs. This is what the Church offers, having corrected Christ's teaching. Christ has no right to come back and interfere. In Ivan's poem, Christ makes no answer, but kisses the old man and is allowed to leave. The significance of that act has been much debated by readers of Dostoevsky's novel, as indeed has the significance of the poem as a whole, some seeing it as a brilliant anticipation of the totalitarian orders of the twentieth century, not least in Dostoevsky's homeland. One of the best discussions of 'The Grand Inquisitor' is by Roger Cox, who acutely points out that what the Inquisitor is really offering is not 'mystery, miracle and authority' but 'magic, mystification and tyranny'.[56] These two chapters have been widely seen as containing powerful and irrefutable arguments against the Christian faith, the first being that a God who permits such suffering is unworthy of worship; the second being that Christ fundamentally overestimated the spiritual resources of the human race and their ability to act as morally free agents. Dostoevsky was aware of the strength of these arguments and anxious lest he fail to refute them effectively in the rest of the novel. Refutation was to be achieved not by logical argument, however, but indirectly by the juxtaposition and interaction of alternative forms of life. The chief exponents of the Christian form of life were Ivan's brother Alesha and his Elder in the local monastery, Zosima.

To Ivan's hatred of the order of creation and his assertion that if there is no immortality and God does not exist, then everything is permitted, Zosima juxtaposes a belief in the efficacy of a life of active love and the conviction that each is responsible for everything and for all (XIV, 270), a view which the whole novel demonstrates in relation to the murder of Fedor Karamazov and the conviction of his son Dmitry.

Zosima believes that the source of such a life of active love lies beyond the natural world. It certainly has nothing to do with the atheist's abstract love for humanity. If you actively love everything, you will perceive the divine mystery in things and you will begin to comprehend it more every day (XIV, 289):

> For on earth we seem in truth to be wanderers, and, without the precious image of Christ before us, we should have perished and lost our way altogether, like the human race before the flood. Many things on earth are hidden from us, but in exchange for that we have been given a mysterious, precious sense of our living bond with another world, with a higher, heavenly world, and the roots of our thoughts and feelings are not here but in other worlds. That is why philosophers say that it is impossible to fathom the essential nature of things on earth (XIV, 290–91).

The precious image of Christ, preserved in the Russian monasteries, is our sole reliable compass. Without it, humanity would have destroyed itself (XIV, 288). To Ivan's complaint about innocent suffering, Zosima juxtaposes the magnificence of the Book of Job, whose hero praises God in spite of his undeserved suffering (XIV, 264–65), a suffering which may be necessary as a condition of happiness.

The young Alesha has a mystical experience himself after falling asleep at the reading of the story of the Wedding at Cana in Galilee (John 2: 1–11) over Zosima's coffin, where he has experienced something glowing in his heart, something that filled it until it ached with tears of ecstasy welling up from his soul. Outside he throws himself on the ground and kisses the earth, drenching it with his tears. In this mystical experience Alesha senses the threads of all God's innumerable worlds meeting in his soul; *something* as firm as the firmament itself enters it. He has the sensation of *someone* visiting his soul, of *an idea* gaining ascendancy over his mind that would last for the rest of his life (my italics). The silence of the earth seems to merge with the silence of heaven; the mystery of the earth with the mystery of the stars (XIV, 328). In three days time, following his Elder's command, Alesha leaves the monastery to live in the world. This emphasis on the silence of heaven evokes the apophatic strain in Orthodox theology, according to which the essence of God is unknowable and a sense of the presence of God is to be attained only through spiritual tranquillity and inner silence, for which all mental images are obstacles. At all events, it harmonizes with Dostoevsky's view that human language is incompetent to express the deepest truths (XXIII, i, 326; XXIX, ii, 102).

In letters to his editor N A Liubimov (XXX, i, 63–65) and to the Procurator of the Holy Synod, Konstantin Podedonostsev (XXX, i, 120–22), Dostoevsky affirms both his intention of vindicating Christianity and his anxiety lest he should fail. But to read the novel exclusively from this point of view is highly problematic, for both structural and biographical reasons. In the first place many readers find such a reading counter-intuitive. They sense correctly that Dostoevsky's point of departure is not 'A Saint's Life' but 'The Life of a Great Sinner'; they are also aware that Dostoevsky's novels are so constructed that they do not privilege one point of view over another. The novel can equally well be read from Ivan's point of view, and more profitably still, as what Bakhtin has called a 'polyphonic novel', in which all voices carry equal weight, including that of the author/narrator. Whatever the 'real author' may have protested, the 'implied author' of the text confronts us with a world in which such questions are ultimately unresolved and unresolvable, in which we are travelling, but, like Moses, never quite reach the promised land.

While the religion of *The Brothers Karamazov* bears a strong family resemblance to Orthodoxy in its general ethos, there are also significant departures that have been widely discussed. It is often justly remarked that Zosima's doctrine that each is responsible for everything and for all is an expression of the Orthodox notion of *sobornost'*, but in this case it is extremely odd that the traditional corporate life of the Church, with its liturgy, its dogma, its regular observance of its rituals and sacraments, plays such a slight role. As Gibson says, Dostoevsky revered Christ but sat loose to all theology.[57] Moreover, as Hackel, Linnér and others have shown, the images of Zosima and Alesha owe at least as much to European fictional models (for example, Victor Hugo and George Sand) as to those of Orthodox sainthood. Gibson has pointed out, and Hackel agrees, that in the last analysis the novel seems evasive even about God, preferring to describe the profoundest religious ecstasies in terms which at best seem cosmetic from a Christian point of view. This is not to say, of course, that the religious text of the novel may not be illuminated and energized by reference to the Orthodox intertext. It is to say simply that Dostoevsky's text as we have it presents us with something significantly different. It is this 'something different', the shoots of a new religious perception growing in an Orthodox soil and fertilized by an admixture of European images, which has sometimes caught the imagination of thinkers wrestling with the problems of religious faith in the twentieth century.

And what of Dostoevsky's biography? Whatever other sources may be available, his fiction is itself the best testimony to what was actually going on in Dostoevsky's mind. While we may indeed hope that he ended his troubled life in a haven of spiritual serenity, Dostoevsky himself always insisted that the important thing was not the achievement of the goal but the process of striving to reach it. And, in his case, this process was very far from tranquil or complete. His declaration that he achieved faith through a furnace of doubt is usually seen as an affirmation of triumphant faith. It is no less a statement about the intensity of the experience of doubt. Perhaps doubt is actually too weak a word. Unbelief, a word that he used in his letter to Fonvizina, might be nearer the mark. Right up to the end, in the person of Ivan Karamazov, we hear the authentic voice of a soul in torment. No one could write like this unless his own soul partook of that torment, at least during the process of literary creation. No one could bring himself to write like this, unless these issues were intellectually and emotionally compelling for him at that very moment. Yet, as he said in his letter to Fonvizina so many years before, it was in such moments of affliction that the image of Christ burned strongest. And perhaps, after all, this is the true measure of Dostoevsky's legacy. What we cannot doubt, in reading his work, is that we are in the presence of a genius wrestling with the problems of rethinking Christianity in the modern age. It does him less than justice to represent him as a devotee of unreflective theological conservatism.

ESSAY II

An Introduction to Current Debate

I

Some readers will regard the statement that Dostoevsky was a Christian novelist, as a simple statement of an obvious truth, while others may regard it as a denial of all that is modern and of enduring importance in his work. It is easy to see why. However, both camps will agree on one thing. Dostoevsky and his novels take the claims of religion seriously on its own terms. Religion does not occupy the peripheral place that it does in most notable English novels of the period: it is not just depicted from the outside as a social phenomenon nor, with some minor exceptions, is it the subject of caricature. In both Dostoevsky's life and work, Christianity was engaged in pitched battle with the most desolate atheism, and neither is of that untroubled, optimistic variety often held to be characteristic of the Victorian age. When, awaiting his own execution on the Semenovskii Square in 1849, he had murmured the words 'Nous serons avec le Christ', his companion, the atheist Speshnev, had rejoined dryly, 'un peu de poussière.'[58] Whatever thoughts on life and death had passed through Dostoevsky's mind before this moment, the burden of Speshnev's words, in one form or another, refused thereafter to go away. In a letter to A N Maikov of 25 March/6 April 1870 about his plan for *The Life of a Great Sinner* he wrote, 'The main question, which runs through all the parts, is the one that has tormented me consciously and unconsciously all my life, the existence of God' (XXIX, I, 117). The plan as such remained unrealized, but it fed into all his subsequent major works. Only towards the end of his life, while writing *The Brothers Karamazov*, was he able to note with some semblance of tranquillity that he had reached faith ('my hosanna') through a furnace of doubt (XXVII, 86). Yet this was at a time when that furnace of doubt was itself receiving its most memorable fictional expression in the person of Ivan Karamazov. Even his note about his hosanna follows remarks (also penned in 1880–1881) to the effect that 'all Christ's ideas can be disputed by the human mind and seem incapable of realisation', 'Christ was mistaken — that has been proved, but some burning feeling tells me that I should remain with error and with Christ' (XXVII, 56, 57). It seems that Dostoevsky's prediction to Fonvizina that he would remain a child of his age to the end of his life turned out to be accurate. These glimpses into the complexity of Dostoevsky's thinking about religion are sufficient to warn us that any reading of his religious thought that focuses primarily on his 'hosanna' will detach it from the spiritual and intellectual travail that gave it birth, and therefore from its most characteristic and most modern features.

Most disagreements about the nature of Dostoevsky's presentation of religion consequently pivot on the ratio of faith to unbelief in his fiction. Some readers do see his life and writing as a triumphant affirmation of the Christian spirit (a *podvig*), in which an ultimately unshakeable faith in the image of Christ sustained him from the cradle to the grave and preserved him from succumbing to the many radical challenges which he encountered in his own tormented life and in the intellectual climate of his time, all graphically and passionately reflected in his fiction. According to such a view, his ambition, in the years of his maturity after his return from Siberia, to use his novels as vehicles for a religious debate in which the Christian world-view would ultimately prevail, is reflected in the structure and content of his major literary works, which in turn cannot be fully appreciated unless they are read against this background. Such, in summary, is the view propounded in a recent book by Donald Nicholl,[59] which in this respect reflects a traditional Orthodox reading. It is the view that underlies readings of his mature works as expressions of the Easter motif of death and resurrection.

Other readers, while granting that in times of desolation he found personal comfort in a traditional religious piety, particularly on the scaffold, in his travails in Siberia and again towards the end of his life, see his greatness in his ability to transcend such comforting illusions and to present, through his characters and narrators, those unresolved and unresolvable conflicts of the human spirit which he called the 'accursed questions' (*prokliatye voprosy*). Such readers may doubt whether his restless mind ever reached any final solution, or, if it did, whether this is in the least bit relevant to our reading of his novels, which are essentially about conflict and unresolvability. Indeed, it has been observed, Dostoevsky presents the case for atheism so persuasively, and so variously, that many readers, among them such eminent literary figures as Albert Camus, D H Lawrence and V Rozanov, have been forced to conclude that this is what, in his heart, he really believed. Such readers stress the strength and persistence of his religious doubts, amounting nearly to atheistic convictions, and his undiminished ability, one might almost say compulsion, to express them in their most ardent and compelling form to the very end of his life. By contrast, many such modern readers find his depiction of saintly characters and arguments far from compelling. He was, as he says in that letter to Fonvizina, a child of his age (XXVIII, i, 176), and this was an age in which a radical intelligentsia, which had finally rejected religion, was energetically propounding various forms of scientific atheism, an age, like our own, in which Christianity, at least among the educated classes, was liable to go by default, to be seen as a curious survival of pre-scientific folk lore, or as evidence of feeble-mindedness, of the denial of reality or of mental derangement.

A less fundamental, but no less passionate debate hinges on the character of Dostoevsky's Christianity. Is it to be read in the spirit of that Slavophilism which he professed with increasing urgency towards the end of his life, an Orthodoxy deprived of its dogmatic aspects and infused with Russian nationalism? This is a view which has won favour among some Orthodox readers and which is currently being rediscovered by Dostoevsky scholars in post-Soviet Russia and abroad.[60] Or is the Christianity of his novels essentially of a non-sectarian and even heretical brand, still bearing traces of the Christian socialism of his youth, a religion in which there is so little sign of God, of theology, of dogma, of the Orthodox liturgy, or indeed of church-going, that it has even prompted comparisons with Buddhism?[61] Does it even prefigure, as some have argued, radical developments in Christian spirituality and theology in the latter part of the twentieth century?

A final approach, which may commend itself to practitioners of Cultural Studies, is simply to note and appreciate the Orthodox colouring of Dostoevsky's literary texts, without drawing any conclusions about his own beliefs or intentions, or getting caught up in the soul-searing (and some would say, outdated) religious and philosophical issues raised in his novels. There is much to be said for this relaxed point of view, for those who read novels and biographies for passive enjoyment, or for whom the issues have no actuality. But Dostoevsky's novels, more than most, invite intellectual engagement, and this is what they have generally provoked.

It was the appearance of George Pattison and Diane Thompson's book *Dostoevsky and the Christian Tradition* in 2001[62] that prompted me to take up these issues once more. Full of fine examples of individual scholarship, and with excellent contributions from the editors themselves, the book nevertheless left me feeling that fundamental questions remained un-addressed and that (to borrow from Dostoevsky himself with respect to atheist discourse on God) many of the contributors had missed the main point. Before proceeding with my own analysis I wish therefore to pause to consider some recent contributions from other scholars.

From my own point of view, the main point is not whether Dostoevsky's imaginative fiction can fruitfully be read from a religious viewpoint, or viewpoints — even Buddhist or Muslim — nor is it whether the mature Dostoevsky saw himself as an Orthodox Christian with a mission to convey the truth of Orthodoxy to his readers, nor is it whether the traditions of Orthodoxy, or Christianity more generally, are inscribed in his text at many levels. All these claims, though they may give rise to various sorts of controversy, are demonstrable. The main point is the degree to which his novels may legitimately be read, without distortion, as *expressions* or *vehicles* of Orthodox Christianity, or of Christianity more generally. And it is remarkable how often the weight of evidence in favour of the former kind of reading slips over into implicit or explicit claims and assumptions of the latter kind, and even of theories designed to sustain them. It may be a matter, ultimately, of what we think the 'ideal author' of his text is saying. What I shall try to show in the pages that follow is that there is another way of reading Dostoevsky religiously (to use the expression coined by Pattison and Thompson) which is more in keeping with the complexity and the emphases of Dostoevsky's text and with the evolving religious experience of the nineteenth and twentieth centuries, which is wholly in keeping with his own outlook, and which neither neglects the Orthodox dimension of his work nor makes implausible claims for it.

Pattison and Thompson's book serves as a microcosm of recent critical literature on the subject. It proffers, and here and there attempts to theorize, a wide variety of perspectives from which Dostoevsky can be 'read religiously'. It did not, of course, set out to provide a summation of all the extensive work on Dostoevsky and religion that had preceded it down the years. It does, however, present such a wealth of issues of interest to the Dostoevsky scholar that I have not hesitated to draw on it for examples to illustrate my own argument. I hope that readers will regard this as a compliment to its power to stimulate debate, not to a desire to single it out for special criticism.

The three main sections of its 'Introduction', jointly authored by its two editors, give a helpful background to the subject. The first surveys the historical context, illustrating the way in which, during the eighteenth and nineteenth centuries, the Russian intelligentsia became progressively polarized between those who sought a solution to Russia's problems in the adoption of Western ideas with an increasingly atheistic tendency, and those who, albeit under the influence of European Romanticism, identified with the people's religious faith and native traditions, a split reflected in Dostoevsky's depictions of contemporary society, and still evident today.[63] In fact, Dostoevsky did not only *depict* this split; much more importantly he *experienced its full force* in his own intellectual and emotional life, and to this we shall frequently return.

The second section reviews the vicissitudes of Dostoevsky criticism from his day to ours, with particular reference to religious questions. While (Marxist–Leninist) antireligious responses are now primarily of historical interest, critics well-disposed to the religious dimension of his works range from those who have seen him as a great preacher and prophet of our time, to those who see him as a heretic; from those who stress his adherence to Russian Orthodoxy, to those who see in him significant traces of Protestantism. Some seek spiritual illumination in his work, or recruit him for their own religious (and sometimes Russian nationalist) cause, while others 'scrupulously disclose, analyse and interpret the Christian basis of Dostoevsky's art'.[64]

The third section discusses Dostoevsky's place in the debates surrounding the religious crisis of the West. To all appearances his impact here has been even more diverse, ranging, as the editors remind us, from those who see in it a thinly veiled atheism to those who see him as one of the great prophets of Christian faith for a post-Nietzschean world, this latter view often being connected with his recruitment to existentialism. Among the Orthodox, Berdiaev based his own philosophy of religion, with its emphasis on the freedom of the human spirit, on his reading of Ivan Karamazov's poem about the Grand Inquisitor. There were also important Catholic and Protestant studies of his work. Foremost among Catholic readings (though not mentioned by the editors) is that of Romano Guardini.[65] Among the Protestant theologians who acknowledged Dostoevsky's religious significance were the gigantic figure of Karl Barth[66] and his friend and colleague Edward Thurneysen,[67] whose book typifies the view of Dostoevsky as the prophet of religious horror of a life without God. Among more recent approaches listed by the editors are Henri de Lubac's assessment of Dostoevsky as the prophet of a Christian faith which has taken the measure of modern atheism 'and lived to tell the tale',[68] William Hamilton's assimilation of Dostoevsky to the cause of 'death of God' theology, René Girard's debt to Dostoevsky for the basis of his theory of the role of violence in the origin of religion and culture, the 'polyphonic' approach of A B Gibson[69] and last, but certainly not least, the refreshingly dispassionate work of Stewart Sutherland,[70] a Scottish philosopher of religion steeped in the tradition of Anglo–Saxon philosophy.

The intention of the volume, it would seem, is to give free rein to the variety of responses that the religious dimension of Dostoevsky's life and work stimulates among contemporary scholars, including literary critics, theologians and those who seek to bridge these disciplines. Its programme is therefore expressed in catholic terms: Dostoevsky had a gift, virtually unique among modern writers, for making Christianity dynamic, for subtly forcing the ideological challenges of the modern age to interact dialogically with his Christian vision and for embodying this vision in psychologically compelling characters. To 'read Dostoevsky religiously', then, would mean to engage with this dialogue which runs through his entire post-Siberian oeuvre. This makes those who would rather bypass the religious issues uneasy; they are more comfortable discussing the psychology of his characters and the ideas debated in his fiction. But given the prominence in Dostoevsky's work of biblical motifs and of references to doctrinal, liturgical and devotional elements in the Christian tradition, it is almost impossible *not* to read Dostoevsky religiously.[71]

As a programmatic statement, this is attractive and plausible. Of course, the last claim is hyperbolic: virtually all the voluminous, critical and scholarly literature published in the Soviet Union managed *not* to read Dostoevsky religiously, and the same is true of much Western writing on the subject too. Yet, while one may readily accept its general thrust, the statement contains a number of ambiguities and begged questions. The first is the reference to Dostoevsky's Christian vision, which itself is a highly disputed concept.

Is there one Christian vision only in Dostoevsky? How far is it Orthodox and how far eclectic, how far is it traditional and how far heretical? Does it, as some have argued, derive from primitive pre-schism Christianity? Is it seriously indebted to European Christian socialism? Is it essentially a vision of the image of Christ, and if so, which image, or does it extend to a fully developed theology? Is the vision constant throughout his work, or does it evolve? Does it bathe his works in its glow or does it flicker fitfully? Do we see the same vision in his novels that we see in his non-fictional work and, if not, how are they related? Is there a single religious vision embodied in his characters, and how far is this vision primarily or exclusively Christian? Is there a Christian vision at all in the novels outside the visions of his characters, or are there contending visions of equal moment within a world that is capable of sustaining them all?

The claim that religious values and beliefs are embodied in psychologically compelling characters may seem less contentious, though some critics will insist that psychological plausibility is in inverse proportion to religious vision, that is, that Sonia Marmeladova, Myshkin and Alesha Karamazov are a good deal less convincing psychologically than their irreligious antagonists. Albert Camus thought that Dostoevsky's heart was with his atheistic heroes rather than with his religious ones.[72] Nor does it follow — and here further questions are begged — that discussion of the psychology of his characters, or the ideas debated in his fiction, is an irrelevant or unconnected exercise, or that to focus on them is necessarily to 'bypass religion'. Perhaps there is confusion here between religion and theology. After all, few would claim that the psychologist William James 'bypasses religion', though he certainly bypasses theology, in his famous book *Varieties of Religious Experience*.[73] And what of the work of Karl Jung? Or perhaps the confusion is between religion and individual religious experience. Any comprehensive study of Dostoevsky's presentation of religion will need to ask in what ways and how far religious experience in his work is adequately grounded in (or even explicable in terms of) psychology. As we shall see, the narrator of *The Brothers Karamazov* is himself attracted by psychological explanations of religious phenomena. A reading that takes this as the basis for a discussion of the religious dimension of Dostoevsky's work is clearly a legitimate option. A single book cannot cover everything — the present one is no exception — and it is helpful to know its self-defined limits, yet the implication that such preoccupations are beyond the natural limits of the subject inevitably causes uneasiness. All these are questions that have often been explicitly discussed in critical literature and remain open.

Finally, the proposition that to 'read Dostoevsky religiously' is to engage with the dialogue between religious vision and the ideological challenges of the modern age embodied in his novels is both a statement of intent and a matter of definition. Paradoxically, the articles that follow very rarely address what might seem to be the most topical questions for readers in the latter half of the twentieth and the beginning of the twenty-first centuries, namely those raised in the work of latter-day theologians and philosophers of religion who have themselves grappled with the challenges of a 'post-Christian' culture, challenges whose origins pre-date Dostoevsky and which he in turn influenced. Almost all the contributors read Dostoevsky religiously by seeking out traditional Christian motifs in his work, often those with a distinctively Orthodox pedigree; they very rarely, if at all, venture to discuss the dialogue with the ideological challenges of the modern age, which, outside the introduction, get barely a mention.[74] To view Dostoevsky's texts from a religious point of view, rather than from the point of view of the dialogue with these secular challenges, may justifiably make some readers uneasy and I shall later suggest why this is so.

The introduction to a book of this kind, in which contributors are given much leeway in their choice of material and approach, can be only of a general kind, so we are entitled to look to individual contributions for further enlightenment.

The essay that makes the strongest claims for the role of Orthodoxy in Dostoevsky's major work is that of Diane Thompson herself. She maintains that 'the Christian world-view *permeates* and *shapes* all Dostoevsky's post-Siberian works, from the large narrative structures of his redemptive plots, whether failed, realized or suspended, to single words charged with Christian significance' (my italics).[75] The implication is that 'the Christian world-view' is in these respects uniquely dominant in Dostoevsky's work.

But this appears to beg the same questions. Avril Pyman, in the article that immediately follows, reminds us that every artist works within a cultural context (what she, following Lotman, calls the semiosphere[76] and another contributor, David S Cunningham, following Calvin Shrag, calls its 'space of subjectivity'[77]). The artistic vision emerges within and in response to this complex contextual material, which in its turn permeates and shapes it. In Dostoevsky's case, Christian traditions undeniably form an important part of this contextual material. But Pyman goes on to remind us that there were many other cultural factors shaping and permeating Dostoevsky's semiosphere, including the space occupied by his own inextinguishable furnace of doubt. Among these were his knowledge of the Russian classics (Karamzin, Zhukovsky, Pushkin, Griboedov, Lermontov, Gogol, all of them examples of Westernized, post-Petrine, post-Enlightenment culture), None of the Westernizers such as Belinsky and Herzen, and European writers such as Fourier, Schiller, Shakespeare, Molière, Cervantes, Balzac, Dickens, Schiller, Eugène Sue and George Sand were Orthodox Christians. These were all part of Dostoevsky's cultural environment from childhood and youth and remained so throughout his life, leaving their mark on his fiction and nowhere more than on *The Brothers Karamazov*, his last novel. So, while many of the essays in the book usefully explore the ways in which Orthodoxy left an imprint on Dostoevsky's fiction, we are left without clear answers to the questions 'how' and 'to what extent' Dostoevsky's 'Christian vision' may be said to permeate and shape his world and what exactly this Christian vision is.

Thompson's approach deserves further consideration, however, for she attempts to ground her reading theoretically. She tells us that, although Dostoevsky was a master of irony, of the word spoken with reservations, his works are hardly 'completely secularized'. They are permeated and shaped by 'the biblical word' which, she tells us, means 'any saying, image, symbol or thought whose source can be traced to the Bible.' For Thompson, this is evidently not the same thing as saying that the 'Pushkinian word' is any saying, image, symbol or thought that can be traced to Pushkin, for the Biblical word, she goes on to say, is a direct proclamation of the Word of God. Proclamation is a mode of speech characteristic of Biblical style used to transmit sacral messages and divine commands, either directly (God speaks) or by witnesses to divine acts and words. The requisite style was no longer available to Dostoevsky as a nineteenth-century novelist: his discourse is double-voiced, which means that Biblical words inserted into his text undergo refraction and testing by the pervasive medium of double-voiced discourse. However, double-voiced words in Dostoevsky still manifest the impress of the Biblical word, and 'it is on this turbulent boundary, where the biblical word interacts with double-voiced words, that Dostoevsky's dynamic art lives'.[78] For her, therefore, the issue is not simply one of Biblical motifs or themes, or characters motivated by religious visions, or even of the religious dimension of Dostoevsky's work being one among many factors inhabiting the semiosphere that gave birth to the novels and permeates and shapes them. The Biblical word as divine proclamation, though refracted through double-voiced discourse, remains the fundamental structuring principle in his mature fiction, and gives his novels their unique vitality. This is a bold and attractive hypothesis, which draws on Bakhtin and develops his work in ways that might well have appealed to him. Yet she does not tell us how we might in practice distinguish the kind of intertextuality that relates to Pushkin from that which relates to the Biblical word as direct proclamation of the Word of God. She does tell us that it is not a question of stylistic markers. Though she does not say so explicitly, her solution seems to make a distinction between 'the *living word*', which evokes a religious awe in characters and is capable of changing their lives, and other neutral instances of Biblical quotation and allusion. On this basis she comes to the following conclusion:

> Dostoevsky's feeling for the dynamic aspect of the Logos was exceptionally strong, as was his gift for making it a living rejoinder in the great dialogue of his works. He never seals off the Biblical word from other words, from the life depicted in his works, but makes everyone, from deniers to affirmers, respond to that word, thus maximising its sphere of contacts and opening it up to further development, and further revelations. Dostoevsky disseminates his characters' and his own deeply subjective responses to Christianity through every word he writes.[79]

Against this background, instances of the 'living word' radically affecting the lives of characters turn out to be disappointingly few and peripheral. It comes as a surprise to discover that in *Crime and Punishment*, Thompson's evidence relates principally to a minor character (Marmeladov), and that *The Idiot* is dismissed as 'Dostoevsky's bleakest work'[80] in which 'there are no readings or faithful interpreters of the biblical word, no prayers, no heavenly visions, no biblical epigraphs, no references to the Kingdom, and no one moves towards redemption or renewal through the Word'.[81] As with *Crime and Punishment*, the Biblical word in *The Devils* is represented by a secondary character (Stepan Trofimovich Verkhovensky), who experiences its impact only towards the very end of the action (and his life) when it is too late to influence anyone else. *A Raw Youth* is omitted from consideration, while lesser works (*Bobok*, *The Meek One* and *The Dream of a Ridiculous Man*) are made to carry the burden of the argument forward to *The Brothers Karamazov*, which, we are told, is saturated with the Biblical word.[82] Presumably Thompson must mean this differently from the sense in which *The Idiot* might be so described, and is referring to the effect of what elsewhere she calls the 'living word'. Or perhaps she would wish to maintain that where there is evidence of the 'living word' in action (as in *The Brothers Karamazov*) this lights up and brings to life all the other Biblical motifs in a way that does not happen when, as in *The Idiot*, it is absent. Here again there are problems, and perhaps symptomatic of the difficulty is the fact that Smerdiakov, of all characters, is drafted in to clinch the case. To my mind, the question is not whether the novel contains quotations from the Bible to which characters respond, or even whether they respond to such quotations differently from the way in which they respond to quotations from secular literature (of which, as Nina Perlina has shown,[83] there are very, very many), or even whether in some cases (notably Alesha Karamazov's) a reading from the Bible arouses religious emotions, which by various stages (of which the latter and the most affecting are in fact not Biblical at all), they have a life-changing effect on him. All this is beyond dispute. The question is whether the extent of Thompson's claims is thereby justified and how she would reconcile her patchy findings (for example, that 'the Word never enters Raskol'nikov's consciousness' and 'In *The Idiot* the *living* Word is absent')[84] with her own sweeping conclusion that Dostoevsky makes everyone, from deniers to affirmers, respond to that Word. For all the article's stimulating and provocative insights, it is therefore clear that there are problems still to be addressed.

II

If the editors do not themselves suggest a basis for resolving these problems, one of the contributors does. Avril Pyman makes a number of important points that, with some possible minor amendments, any researcher in the field would do well to keep in mind.

The first is that though his vision and 'metaphysical experience' may be Christian, and in many ways specifically Orthodox Christian, Dostoevsky is a nineteenth- century writer whose dreams are influenced not by Christian theology but by secular European Utopianism and Romanticism.

Perhaps even Pyman, who is generally so meticulous, is using evidence selectively here, in claiming that Dostoevsky's 'metaphysical experience' is always Christian (whether by 'his' one is referring to the historical author or to the ideal author of the novels). Serious doubts must remain about two of the most vivid and most often cited examples in his major novels: Prince Myshkin's intense epileptic experience in *The Idiot* and Alesha Karamazov's life-changing mystical experience after his Elder's death. Moreover, Western models undoubtedly influenced Dostoevsky's image of Christ. As Pyman herself notes elsewhere: a young man who compares Jesus Christ to Homer, as Dostoevsky did in a letter to his brother Mikhail of 1 January 1840, can hardly then have been thinking of the Russian people and the Russian Christ (XXVIII, i, 69).[85] Nor can the same young man, in referring to Hugo and Schiller as 'Christian poets' (XXVIII, i, 70). But let us accept that Christianity, and specifically Orthodox Christianity, is the cultural background against which Dostoevsky received his religious vision, and that its mark is frequentlydiscerned in his imaginative fiction: the second part of Pyman's proposition is undoubtedly true and, even more importantly, the interrelationship of 'secular dream' and 'religious vision' affects, and perhaps distorts, both. Pyman sagely advises: 'One can only accept these contradictions, and work from within this paradox'; 'it is not necessary to put everything in its place so that everything can be reconciled.'[86]

It is within a context of undecidability, she reminds us, that Dostoevsky speaks of his 'hosanna' having passed through a furnace of doubt (XXVII, 86), and adds, 'I think [...] that one has to accept that, throughout his life in literature, this furnace was kept well-stoked.' We must consider the possibility, which many of those critics who write on the subject seem reluctant to do, that Dostoevsky's furnace of doubt permeated and shaped his oeuvre at least as powerfully as his 'Christian vision'. With some notable exceptions, such as Stewart Sutherland, the majority of Dostoevsky critics seem incapable of entertaining such a notion, perhaps because they themselves tend to be either indifferent to religious questions or to hold so strongly to a particular position, for or against Christianity, that they are unable to escape its thrall. Another possible explanation may be the Russo-centrism of much Dostoevsky criticism. When Erich Heller writes 'Thus he knows two things at once, and both with equal assurance: that there is no God, and that there must be a God,' he is speaking not of Dostoevsky, nor of any of his characters, but of Kafka.[87] Whatever may be true of the maximalist traditions of Russian nineteenth-century thought, the modern European mind, of which Dostoevsky was also a part, knows many similar cases. This particular blindness is all the more remarkable because critics who seem reluctant to acknowledge this duality in Dostoevsky himself, or at least to apply it to their analysis of his work as a whole, often emphasize its presence in his fictional characters. Pyman herself concludes that in reading Dostoevsky it is necessary to accept both the hosanna and the furnace, or seek the hosanna beyond literature.[88] Stewart Sutherland puts it even more starkly: Dostoevsky is pre-eminently a man divided, inhabiting simultaneously the worlds of belief and unbelief. It is vain to seek a 'final word' from Dostoevsky on the subject of religious belief — the dialectic defined in Ivan and Zosima remained Dostoevsky's final word to the grave.[89]

Pyman notes a growing tendency in Dostoevsky criticism to attempt a 'theological', semiotic approach to Dostoevsky by stressing such features of Eastern Orthodox worship as the veneration of icons, the emphasis that the Orthodox tend to place on Incarnation, Transfiguration and Resurrection (that is, on contemplating the cosmic majesty and kenosis of Christ rather than on expounding his moral teaching), and the tendency to make more of 'image' than of 'likeness'. She confronts this tendency with a number of pertinent questions, asking 'How Orthodox was Dostoevsky, the writer?' 'Was it natural for the young author to regard men and women as icons or, for that matter, to regard icons as works of art which might inspire even the secular artist to catch at some refraction of the divine?' She reaches the conclusion that the answer to these important questions would appear to be 'no', or at least 'not entirely'. For most of his life, notwithstanding his Orthodox upbringing, 'the great novelist seems to have been a man of the Book rather than the Church.'[90] This observation raises further important issues. Although it is possible to find numerous significant instances of icons, parables of divine grace and many other echoes and refractions of Orthodoxy in Dostoevsky's novels, his work is notably free of both Orthodox ritual and dogma. This is the more significant because the Orthodox tradition, as Dostoevsky and his original readers knew perfectly well, sets very great store by both. It also means that, as a compulsive and conscientious reader of the Bible, particularly of the Russian New Testament, Dostoevsky was free to develop his own personal readings of the Scriptures, which of course was precisely why the Russian Orthodox Church, like the medieval Catholic Church, had resisted their circulation in the modern idiom for so long.

III

These reflections prompt me to suggest an experiment and examine Dostoevsky's imaginative fiction in the light of the seven different aspects or dimensions of religion identified by the eminent specialist in Comparative Religion, Ninian Smart.[91] The first is the *practical and ritual dimension*, which, as Smart points out, is especially important with faiths of a strongly sacramental kind, such as Eastern Orthodox Christianity. Orlando Figes has even observed recently that the Russian Church is contained entirely in its liturgy, and that there is no point in reading books to understand it: one has to go and see the Church at prayer. The Russian Orthodox service is an emotional experience. The whole of Russian life during the nineteenth century was permeated with religious rituals: baptism, the celebration of a person's saint's day, weddings and funerals, the priestly blessing required and expected for every important event in a person's life, religious holidays, fasts, especially Shrovetide, Lent and Easter.[92] It is therefore of some significance that in Dostoevsky's major novels, although Easter plays a recurrent symbolic role in characters' memories, Church attendance, and therefore active participation in the Orthodox liturgy and sacraments by any of his characters, including those who are most commonly seen as exemplifying Christian virtues, is extremely rare. The one major exception is Alesha Karamazov's participation in the ritual following Zosima's death. Indeed the Russian Orthodox liturgy and priesthood receive a more sympathetically consistent treatment in the work of Leskov, and even, arguably, of Chekhov, than they do in that of the self-proclaimed prophet of Orthodoxy, Fedor Dostoevsky; and this has been a constant source of disquiet among those assessing the claim that his novels express the essence of the Orthodox faith.

Smart's second category is *the experiential and emotional* dimension, and he points to the importance of the feelings that religion generates, for example, the sacred awe, the calm peace, the rousing inner dynamism, the perception of a brilliant emptiness within, the outpouring of love, the sensations of hope, the gratitude for favours that have been received. We have noted the religious experiences of Prince Myshkin and Alesha Karamazov. Such experiences are the exception rather than the rule and they are not necessarily characteristic of Orthodox, or even Christian traditions. We might include under this rubric, however, those peculiar features of Orthodox spirituality that draw on the kenotic tradition or the folk traditions of the Holy Fool that have attracted so much critical attention among Dostoevsky scholars. Some of these are discussed by Margaret Ziolkowski in her chapter on 'Dostoevsky and the kenotic tradition',[93] where she draws special attention to the emphasis he places on humility and self-humiliation. In his chapter, Henry M W Russell even argues that the insistence that humiliation is the necessary precondition for Christian life is the 'most disturbing message of Dostoevsky's *Crime and Punishment*'.[94] Here we are on surer ground, for some of Dostoevsky's characters do indeed have intense religious experiences, often with an Orthodox and Russian colouring, as he evidently did himself.

The third dimension is the *narrative or mythic dimension*. By this, Smart alludes to the way in which experience is channelled and expressed not only by ritual but also by sacred narrative or myth. Both the Biblical allusions and quotations in Dostoevsky's novels, and the markings in his own copy of the New Testament, have been extensively studied, and there is no doubt that the Biblical text constitutes an important element (though by no means the only one) in the semiosphere within which they acquire meaning.

It is also arguable that Dostoevsky's novels are themselves, in some measure, attempts to express religious experiences in narrative form, which is very different from that of Holy Scripture and, as Thompson avers, certainly not best suited to the direct proclamation of the divine word in traditional terms. There are many significant references in Dostoevsky's imaginative fiction to Biblical texts, some of which function as myth within the Christian tradition, and this is in part what Pyman means when she writes of Dostoevsky as a man of the Book. As she says, the religious subtexts on which Dostoevsky drew unconsciously all his life were largely pre-Schism, the common Greco–Judaic heritage, the Book of Job, the Gospels, the Fathers, liturgical texts. In Dostoevsky, such powerful mythical *topoi* sometimes spread out into the surrounding text and colour our reading of it. For example, the story of the raising of Lazarus read by Sonia to Raskolnikov at a critical juncture in *Crime and Punishment* (VI, 250) encourages and permits an analysis of the whole structure of the novel in terms of the myth of death and resurrection, a myth that V Zakharov has recently canvassed as one of the dominant structural features of Dostoevsky's mature work. The image of a serene Christ with a child, described by Nastasia Filippovna in *The Idiot* (VIII, 379–380), seems to hover behind all those scenes, projected and realized, in which Dostoevsky envisaged his saintly heroes with children, from Myshkin's prehistory in Switzerland to Alesha in the final scenes of *The Brothers Karamazov*. In both cases, however, the mythical image is powerfully challenged by images in which resurrection is seen as an illusion and children are seen as vicious or the victims of vice. Although the image of the crucified Christ appears in Dostoevsky (in *The Idiot*), that of the symbolic image of Christ (in Nastasia Filippovna's picture in *The Idiot* and Versilov's dream in *A Raw Youth*) and that of the living Christ (in *The Brothers Karamazov*), nowhere did Dostoevsky attempt to depict the events surrounding the central image of Christ's own resurrection, as distinct from his raising of Lazarus and Jairus's daughter, or to present his reader with the other-worldly Christ, coeval with God, of Johannine theology. Dostoevsky's image of Christ no doubt took on different emphases at different times but, as we have seen, there is strong evidence to support the view that the statement in his letter of February 1854 to Fonvizina remained valid for the greater part of his life. This was where he famously declared that there is nothing more beautiful, more profound, more arousing of sympathy, more reasonable, more courageous and perfect than Christ, and there cannot be; and that if it were proved that the truth is outside Christ then his choice would lie with Christ rather than with the truth (XXVIII, i, 176). It is this haunting image that stands both as a model and indictment of Myshkin in *The Idiot* and of Alesha Karamazov in *The Brothers Karamazov*, and even perhaps of the Jesus who appears in person in 'The Grand Inquisitor'. Finally, a Biblical myth is sometimes embodied in an epigraph. The epigraphs to *The Devils* (the Gadarene swine, Luke, 8: 32–35) and *The Brothers Karamazov* (the seed which falls to the ground and dies, to burst forth in new life, John, 12: 24) may stimulate us to read the whole novel in the light of them. Not surprisingly, it is on this level that the connections between the religious tradition and Dostoevsky's realist novel are most easily and effectively made.

The fourth dimension is the *doctrinal and philosophical dimension*. Dialogue in Dostoevsky's novels is notably light on the enunciation of traditional Christian doctrine, though it has frequently been argued that they exemplify it in subtler ways. Such an argument is advanced in David S Cunningham's article on 'The Brothers Karamazov as Trinitarian theology'[95] or Henry M W Russell's on 'Humiliation as Christian necessity in *Crime and Punishment*'.[96] The second of these articles emphasizes the importance of apophatic theology in Dostoevsky's religious vision, as does Margaret Ziolkowski's article on 'Dostoevsky and the kenotic tradition'.[97] This is an important recent emphasis in Dostoevsky studies and more will be said about the apophatic tradition below. However, as I have just mentioned, although metaphors of death and resurrection abound in Dostoevsky's work, even in the epigraphs to *The Devils* and *The Brothers Karamazov*, the doctrine of Christ's resurrection as a historical event confirming his unity with God, the Father, at the very centre of Orthodox Christian doctrine from the early Church onwards, is notably absent, even from *The Brothers Karamazov*.[98] Since the image of the resurrected Christ, by contrast with that of the crucified Christ, is commonly held to be the distinguishing image of Orthodoxy as opposed to Catholicism, this omission must be regarded as significant. As for the philosophical or intellectual basis of Christianity, this is something that Dostoevsky consciously underplays in favour of confronting his atheistic ideologues with characters who embody Christian features, and in this too he is in harmony with Orthodox tradition, which has always eschewed rational discussion of religious faith. Where arguments in support of religious belief do surface, it is usually in a negative context, as when Ivan Karamazov protests that if there is no God and immortality, there is no morality.

Smart's fifth category is the *ethical and legal dimension*. Notwithstanding recent critical emphasis on the cosmic majesty and kenosis of Christ in Dostoevsky, there is no disputing the prominence of the ethical aspect of religion in his mature work, from *Notes from the House of the Dead* to *The Brothers Karamazov*. Moreover, among the recurring questions of his major novels, especially *Crime and Punishment*, *The Idiot* and *The Brothers Karamazov*, is that of the relationship of the legal structures of society to the inner sense of responsibility and guilt of the individual and, in his last novel, of the relative priority of secular and ecclesiastical structures themselves. Moreover, this is one of the areas in which the preoccupations of his novels reflect his markings in his copy of the New Testament, as is shown by a comparison of Irina Kirillova's article on 'Dostoevsky's markings in the Gospel according to St John'[99] with Ivan Esaulov's on 'The categories of Law and Grace in Dostoevsky's poetics'.[100] The ethic of active love (compassion), which plays such a vital role in the lives of the saintly characters in his novels and in those who come into contact with them, and which finds final expression in Zosima's proclamation of active love and the notion that everyone is guilty for everyone and everything in *The Brothers Karamazov*, undoubtedly derives from Dostoevsky's image of Christ and the Orthodox doctrine of *sobornost'*. In keeping with the Orthodox tradition, it is an ethic based upon spirituality rather than a legalistic code.

The *social and institutional dimension* is Smart's sixth category and refers to the external embodiment of religion, its institutions, its social arrangements and the role of outstanding individuals. There is again very little reference to the institutional dimension in Dostoevsky's work until we come to his final novel. Even here, we are introduced to a somewhat eccentric example of Orthodox institutions in the form of a monastery not noted for its pervasive spirituality, and a character (Zosima) who occupies the suspect role of Elder. There have been notable studies of Zosima's prototypes in the Russian Orthodox tradition.[101] A valuable addition to this literature is provided by Margaret Ziolkowski[102] who argues convincingly that a number of central characteristics of the spirituality of Zosima and his brother Markel, and to a lesser extent of Bishop Tikhon in *The Devils*, derive from this tradition and its historical representatives.

Finally, there is the *material* dimension, in which religion becomes incarnate in buildings, works of art, music and other creations. Smart asks, 'How could we understand Eastern Orthodox Christianity without seeing what ikons are like and knowing that they are regarded as windows onto heaven?'[103] When one considers the richness of the material aspect of Eastern Orthodoxy, especially of its Church buildings and its liturgy, one is again struck by its relative invisibility in Dostoevsky's work. Buildings occasionally play a role in the psychology of Dostoevsky's characters, as Antony Johae shows in his article 'Towards an iconography of *Crime and Punishment*',[104] but by and large neither they nor Orthodox music plays a significant role in Dostoevsky's fiction. Icons do of course feature from time to time, but the patchy and marginal incidence of the 'living Biblical word' in Dostoevsky's imaginative fiction finds a parallel in Sophie Ollivier's article on icons in Dostoevsky's works, for it transpires that, apart from Dostoevsky's early, and immature story 'The Landlady', written during a period when his personal devotion to Orthodoxy was probably at its weakest, icons usually feature in his imaginative fiction as objects of desecration. Examples of the traditional Orthodox view of icons as gateways to the divine realm, linking the believer to the saints and the Holy Trinity, are hard to find in Dostoevsky's writing, though such a role is lightly sketched in the story of Zosima's dying brother Markel (XIV, 260–63). Leonard Stanton has raised another interesting possibility. He points out how the icon painter deliberately inverts the normal rules of perspective in the foreground of his painting, so that the lines of iconic perspective come together not at a vanishing point in the distant background, but where the human observer stands. In this way the human viewer is represented as the focal point of God's knowledge, which, notwithstanding the unknowability of his essence, actively penetrates into created space and time through his energies, thus enabling human beings to gain a partial understanding of him. Stanton's book is subtitled *Iconic Vision in Works by Dostoevsky, Gogol, Tolstoy and Others*,[105] and this could suggest that the structure of their work mimics that of the icon and acts as a vehicle whereby the reader may come closer to God. Apart from pointing to the uplifting effect of Zosima on subsequent generations of believers, however, it is a possibility that he does not follow up, and though the critic could quite easily point to aspects of the structure of Dostoevsky's work that metaphorically invert the normal laws of perspective — we shall examine some in a later chapter — it would be difficult to demonstrate that they play the spiritual role of the Orthodox icon. Any such argument would run into the same sort of difficulties as attempts to demonstrate that Dostoevsky's novels are privileged sites of the Orthodox faith. There is simply too much else going on. Moreover, the spirituality of Orthodox icons does not derive exclusively from their formal characteristics, but also from the traditional way, accompanied by fervent prayer, in which they are painted.

I think that a number of preliminary conclusions can now be drawn. The first is that many of the most visible and distinctive features of the institutional and doctrinal life of Eastern Orthodoxy, the sacramental, the material, the ritual, the institutional, are either peripheral or occasional in Dostoevsky's mature art. We may be convinced for historical and cultural reasons, or for reasons of personal religious faith, that they are present somewhere in the novels' subtext, but it is nevertheless significant that they are not thrust upon the reader's attention, thereby permitting, even encouraging readings which do not require them. The second conclusion is that, provided we interpret the words 'experiential' and 'emotional' generously, to include experiences that may not be distinctively Christian and characters who embody Christian features and impart them to others in their interpersonal relationships, Dostoevsky's novels do contain many examples of religious experience, and these, while not exclusively Orthodox do, taken together, often, though not always, have a distinctively Orthodox colouring. Thirdly, although our reading may be influenced by the powerful mythological *topoi*, with Biblical origins, which characterize all the major novels, the appearance of any or all of these religious features not only acts as a positive structuring force, but also stimulates opposite, antireligious images, which may behave as rival structuring principles on virtually equal terms. For, when all is said and done, the world depicted in Dostoevsky's novels is not one in which *sobornost'* or Christian harmony predominates. Quite the contrary, it is primarily a world of violence, greed, conflict and inner division; of alienation from others, society, the cosmos and the spiritual depths. The remarkable thing is that in such a world some characters do transcend such feelings and values and that Orthodox Christianity and the ethic of active love can and do play a legitimate and psychologically plausible role. Referring to Bakhtin's concept of polyphony in Dostoevsky, Pyman concludes that Dostoevsky presents this polyphony, this dramatic, artistic, tragic form of *sobornost'* as *un*resolved. 'He never gave the last synthesis', Florovsky writes, 'the feeling remained clear and firm for him always. [...] truth was revealed in this life [...]Dostoevsky believed from love, not from fear.'[106]

We may conclude that it is not so much that Russian Orthodoxy bathes Dostoevsky's imaginative fiction in its light as that it flickers fitfully from time to time in varying guises and contexts. But to say that is not to minimize its importance, for these flickers, and occasional flares, are not merely cosmetic, not simply reflections of prevailing culture. They are an integral part of human experience for Dostoevsky's characters, as they were for the author himself, and hold out to the divided, crippled and alienated personalities that people his novels, the genuine possibility of a personal salvation and wholeness through a life of active love. The extent to which this promise is realized may vary from novel to novel and character to character, but is ultimately for each reader to decide.

IV

There is one final point to be made. It has often been said of Dostoevsky that he had crossed the bridge of Kant's philosophy. By this is principally meant that he understood what Kant's philosophy had revealed about the limits of human reason, and the importance of not confusing religious dogma with knowledge of the kind that can either be demonstrated empirically or whose opposite would involve one in logical contradiction. To summarize, Kant's philosophy, in arguing that we can have knowledge only to the extent that the world conforms to our conceptual apparatus (for example, in time and space, and in relationships of cause and effect), ruled out all traditional metaphysics of the kind that deals with such questions as the existence of God, the immortality of the soul and the freedom of the will. Russian Orthodox theology in Dostoevsky's day had not crossed the bridge of Kant's philosophy. So to say that Dostoevsky had done so, and at the same time to claim that he was a pious Orthodox Christian, is at first sight contradictory and at the very least requires some elucidation. In fact, as I shall try to show, it was one of Dostoevsky's great projects to try to rethink Christianity for a post-Kantian world. He had this, though little else, in common with the post-Kantian Idealists — notably Schelling and Hegel — who were so influential in Russia in his youth, though he preferred fictional to abstract philosophical means. Sometimes Ivan Karamazov's view that without God and immortality there is no morality is ascribed to Kant's influence.[107] And it may indeed be the case that Dostoevsky thought that this is what Kant had said in his *Critique of Practical Reason*, where he argues for the possibility of freedom in a world of things-in-themselves, otherwise inaccessible to human knowledge. The popular influence of many great minds has focussed on misunderstandings, simplifications or distortions of what they actually said. But Kant does not claim that he has thereby proved the existence of God, immortality and freedom. He rather argues that such concepts must be assumed to allow for the complete realization of moral perfection, which cannot be realized in this life. In other words, morality is primary for Kant and the concepts of God, immortality and freedom are secondary. Kant's emphasis on ethics is paralleled in Dostoevsky, as is his view that it is only possible to make sense of this life if we posit another. It is an emphasis which may gain importance when confidence in metaphysical and doctrinal matters is on the wane.

Yet, in one sense, the Orthodox tradition, with its roots in the writings of the Church Fathers, had anticipated Kant's philosophy, and Dostoevsky, in his insistence (or that of his characters) that science and reason have never solved humanity's religious or ethical problems, and that individuals and people are moved by a quite different force, an aesthetic, ethical or religious force (X, 198–99), draws on this tradition. For the Church fathers too insisted that God is in his essence beyond time and space and the reach of human reason. Unlike Kant, however, they affirmed that he can be known through his energies, in which the divine penetrates the created world, by the individual aspiring to spiritual knowledge through his or her own *theosis* (the fullest possible sharing of Christ's divinity), guided by the image of Christ in whom God emptied himself out of his divinity (*kenosis*) in order to share our physical life. According to this tradition, the divine reality beyond the physical world may be mediated to us in a number of ways, supremely by Christ, but also through the veneration of icons or through individuals of great spirituality.[108]

V

It is clear that any attempt to give a satisfactory account of the religious dimension of Dostoevsky's work is fraught with problems, some of them deriving principally from different interpretations of the biographical data, some from different assessments of the text (these two approaches laying claim to some degree of objectivity) and some from the varying points of view of different reading communities or individual readers. As we shall see, the very structure of Dostoevsky's fiction facilitates this wide range of diverse readings. Indeed, some would go further and say that not only does it invite the reader to interpret it in a wide variety of different ways but also deconstructs any single reading: there is always some aspect of the text that refuses to be assimilated to any single coherent interpretation, and which may be used as the basis of an alternative reading that is no less (and ultimately no more) persuasive. No book on Dostoevsky and religion satisfactorily address all these issues, and mine is no exception. Elsewhere I have discussed theoretical questions regarding the legitimacy of various religious readings and I shall not repeat them here.[109] Among the important areas to which I have drawn attention but to which I shall do no more than allude in the pages that follow are the psychological basis for religious experience in Dostoevsky and, just as important, his impact on the dialogue between Christian faith and secular philosophy in the twentieth century. However, the title of my book may suggest to the reader that it at least implicitly addresses these questions, and this is in fact the case.

ESSAY III

Remodelling Religious Consciousness in Dostoevsky's Fiction: The Death and Resurrection of Orthodoxy

I

The previous two essays should have made a number of things clear. The first is that religious experiences and images of very diverse kinds play a very important role in Dostoevsky's life and work. The second is that, to do full justice to Dostoevsky's vision, we must extend the meaning of 'religious experience' to cover the whole spectrum from the fullness of belief to the desolation of unbelief, which itself has a mystical quality, and we must accept that these two extremes, though at first sight they may seem to be located at opposite poles of a continuum, often exist on each other's doorstep. This at least was Dostoevsky's own experience and, in different degrees, it is frequently replicated in the experience of his fictional characters. A third conclusion is that whatever certainty Dostoevsky might have longed for, and at times thought he had found, in the bosom of the Russian Orthodox Church, to read his text exclusively through the lens of the Orthodox faith creates as many problems for the reader as it solves. Moreover, Dostoevsky actually banishes many central features of the Orthodox tradition to the very margins of his text. It is as if, at the level of ideal author, his text is telling us that a situation has arisen out of the conflict between belief and unbelief in the modern age in which the richness of that Tradition has to be put aside in order that personal faith may be allowed to blossom again. To put it more graphically, the richness of the Orthodox tradition has to die in order that the shoots of a new faith be born, at first in minimal forms, in a semiotic space that is quite different from that in which Orthodoxy itself originally developed and thrived, but which preserves the image of Christ to guide it. Whether Dostoevsky actually meant to say this or not is open to debate, but it seems to be very much what he ends up saying in his fiction.

We have several times noted the suggestion that the image of death and resurrection provides the underlying structuring principle for Dostoevsky's mature fiction. Sarah Hudspith has even suggested that the epigraph to his final novel, taken from the Gospel of John (John, 12: 24), might stand as an epigraph for his entire *oeuvre*.[110] Less ambitiously, it may serve us as a provisional model for understanding the religious dimension of his mature work, leaving for the time being unanswered the inevitable questions about what exactly dies and in what forms it is reborn.

Though central to Christianity, the image is, of course, not unique to it. It underlies all initiation rites and martyrologies and has parallels in other mythical systems. Its structuring role even in the Socialist Realist canon[111] should be sufficient to warn us that its presence in a modern literary text — even a Russian one — is not necessarily in itself a sign of Orthodoxy as an underlying belief system. The primary structuring role of Christian imagery in Dostoevsky's text has to be assumed, of course, unless there is strong evidence to the contrary; but just as importantly, the ubiquity of the image opens the door to a wide variety of other religious and philosophical readings.

We may remind ourselves here of the unique and unforgettable way in which Dostoevsky had himself experienced a sort of death and resurrection when, on 22 December 1849, he was taken from his cell in the Peter–Paul fortress to face the firing squad on Semenovsky Square. There he heard his death sentence announced. His whole life passed before him in his imagination in the half hour or so he stood there in the biting cold. As the first group of his fellows was lined up to be executed, an order commuting the sentences was publicly read. When able again to take pen in hand, Dostoevsky wrote to his brother, 'Now, with this change in my life, I am being born again in a new form... I shall be reborn in a better form' (XXVIII, i, 164).[112]

He was to see the long years in Siberia too, first in the fortress, then as a private soldier, as a process of gradual rebirth. Being released from the fortress of Omsk on 23 January 1854 was like a second resurrection from the dead (IV, 232). This was accompanied over the next few years by a rebirth of convictions, convictions, which in spite of his constant moods of doubt and unbelief, repeatedly brought Dostoevsky back to the ideal figure of Christ.[113]

Though recently promoted by both Russian and Western scholars, this is not a new idea. As long ago as 1891, Vasily Rozanov, in his famous book on Dostoevsky's *Legend of the Grand Inquisitor* wrote:

> We said that in *The Brothers Karamazov* a great analyst of the human soul depicted for us a new life emerging from an old one that is dying. According to certain inexplicable and mysterious laws, all nature is subject to such regeneration; and the main thing that we find in this is the inseparability of life from death, the impossibility that one can come about before the other has occurred. And here is the explanation of the epigraph that Dostoevsky took for his last work: 'Verily, verily, I say unto you, Except a corn of wheat fall into the ground and die, it abideth alone: but if it die, it bringeth forth much fruit' (John 12:24).

The fall, death, decay — this is merely a pledge of a new and better life. This is how we must look at history.

We must accustom ourselves to this point of view in watching the elements of decay in the life around us: it alone can save us from despair and fill us with the firmest of faith in moments when it seems that the end of all faith has come. It alone is in keeping with the real and powerful forces directing the flow of time, and not the weakly glimmering light of our mind, not our cares and fears with which we fill history and by which we do not in the least guide it.[114]

Zosima too quotes the verse from John 12 to his mysterious visitor when called upon to decide the latter's fate (XIV, 281). In one form or another, the metaphor had run right through Dostoevsky's major works. As we have seen, the story of the raising of Lazarus and associated metaphors had played a pivotal role in Raskolnikov's eventual change of heart in *Crime and Punishment*. Dostoevsky's notebooks to *The Idiot* indicate that he had envisaged Myshkin rehabilitating Nastas'ia Filippovna (IX, 252), as the Greek original of her first name, meaning 'resurrection', hints. In *The Devils*, Stepan Trofimovich Verkhovensky is inspired shortly before his death by the story of the miraculous recovery of the sick man when Jesus transfers the evil spirits that possess him into the Gadarene swine (Luke 8:32–37) who leap to their death. Dostoevsky's Biblical epigraph to this novel (the same passage) concludes with the words, 'Then they went out to see what was done; and came to Jesus, and found the man, out of whom the devils were departed, sitting at the feet of Jesus, clothed, and in his right mind: and they were afraid.' There is certainly no triumphant vindication of Orthodoxy, or any other form of Christianity, in either *The Idiot* or *The Devils*, but amidst scenes of almost universal spiritual desolation, the delicate shoots of new life are beginning to show through in the closing pages of both novels. Kolia, Radomsky and Vera Lebedeva seem to sense this, as does Stepan Trofimovich Verkhovensky.

If we follow Rozanov's approach, we should look not for a return to Orthodox theology in all its fullness, but for signs of the spirit working renewal in Dostoevsky's text. What we should expect to find are the shoots of a new faith, not a fully-grown harvest.

At first sight the metaphor of death and resurrection of Orthodoxy may seem a facile one, which tells us little, so I shall devote the greater part of this essay to explaining what it excludes and differs from, and this turns out to be a good deal of traditional Dostoevsky criticism.

II

Firstly, and most obviously, it excludes the view that Dostoevsky's world conclusively subverts Christianity (indeed monotheism) as a whole. There have been those, like Albert Camus, who have sensed that Dostoevsky had a deeper affinity with his atheist rebels than with his Christian apologists.[115]

Even Shestov, in acclaiming Dostoevsky as a rebel against reason and science, is dismissive of his positive religious views.[116] For such readers it is as if Dostoevsky acknowledges his true perceptions of the nature of the universe in the visions of Ippolit or Kirillov, or of Ivan Karamazov's Grand Inquisitor, and is being self-indulgent and inauthentic in expressing an allegiance to Orthodoxy, which he does under the pressures of nostalgia for childhood religious values, intense emotional turmoil and conformity to the values of the prevailing political and religious establishment. By his own admission, the argument continues, Dostoevsky was a 'child of his age' whose admiration for the ideal image of Christ could not allay those intellectual doubts which, as he had foreseen, persisted all his life (XXVIII, I, 176). This is why he struck such a responsive chord among agnostic and atheist readers of the twentieth century. According to such a reading, Dostoevsky's religious views, however expressed, are examples of what Sartre would call 'bad faith' and his authentic voice is heard in passages such as that which portrays Ippolit's reaction to Holbein's picture of Christ taken from the cross, quoted above. Kirillov, in *The Devils*, utters a similar despairing message. In both cases the protagonist is about to attempt suicide. In both cases the existential anguish is set against the ideal of Christ as the only possible source of meaning in an otherwise absurd world. The underlying idea is that Christ was deluded and his offer of salvation tragically null and void.

> 'Listen, I'll tell you something great. Once three crosses stood in the centre of the earth. One of the three on those crosses believed so completely that he said to another: "Today you will be with me in paradise." By the end of the day both of them had died. They went and they found nothing — no paradise, no resurrection — nothing. His words didn't come true. Listen now — that man was the best on earth — he represented all that makes life worth living. The whole planet with everything on it is sheer insanity without that man. There hasn't been anyone like him before or since — never; and therein lies the miracle — that there never has been and never will be such a man. Now, since the laws of Nature didn't spare even him, didn't spare even that miracle, and forced even him to live among lies and die for a lie, it proves that the whole planet is a lie and is based on a lie and an inane smirk. It proves too that the laws of Nature are a pack of lies and a diabolical farce. So, what's the point of living?' (X, 471)

Ivan Karamazov, in his rebellion, does not deny that God exists. He simply rejects his dispensation, particularly the implication that innocent suffering on earth can be compensated by future bliss in paradise (XIV, 223). His view, like that of Job's comforters, is that there should be some equivalence between the rewards of earthly life and human merit.[117]

In none of these key episodes, in Dostoevsky's last three great novels, are we confronted with a dispassionate affirmation, inspired by a scientific and secular world-view, that we live in a world without God. In different ways, each of these characters passionately proclaims the ideal of Christ and bitterly laments the unbridgeable chasm between that ideal and the natural world (whether or not it was created by some sort of God). The ideal of Christ has apparently been killed by the cross and by a massively hostile or indifferent nature. But it refuses to disappear from the human soul. Even Kirillov, who does commit suicide, rationalizes his death as a kind of messianic sacrifice for humanity on the model of Christ's death. Ippolit, in his confession, also talks of individual acts of charity sowing seeds of goodness (VIII, 336). Ivan Karamazov follows his conversation on rebellion against a world which permits innocent suffering with a 'poem' in which Jesus in person confronts an atheist Grand Inquisitor, engaged in burning heretics in the interests of creating a happier world.

As Dostoevsky's novels show, he fully understood the impact of the natural sciences on the claims of religion. Wherever in his mature novels the supernatural appears it is always possible to account for it in naturalistic terms; sometimes, as in *The Brothers Karamazov*, his narrator actually does so. In this sense too, Dostoevsky conforms to the spirit of modern times. Not only Ivan Karamazov, but also his saintly characters seem to have experienced the impact of Kant and Feuerbach, though, as we have seen, the idea that God in his essence is ultimately unknowable is also a tenet of Orthodox theology. Sonia, Myshkin, Shatov, Alesha all seem reticent about expressing their religious experiences in terms of belief in the existence of God in traditional terms. Perhaps the most menacing challenge to religion in Dostoevsky is not, however, science or rational argument (in whose ultimate authority in spiritual matters he did not believe), but his own psychological insight. He unremittingly explores those areas of human experience where the religious, the supernatural, the irrational (what he calls 'higher realism') break through into consciousness and he knew that they could be accounted for psychologically, without recourse to religious explanations. In our own day he doubtlessly would have explored the potential of evolutionary psychology for its insights into the source of religious experience. Yet he also believed that this did not itself invalidate them. As Svidrigailov affirms in *Crime and Punishment*, the fact that only sick people see ghosts does not prove that ghosts do not exist. It is another way of saying that the fact that some people are psychologically predisposed to have religious experiences does not necessarily mean that the experience of God has no objective correlative and that traditional ways of expressing it have no validity.

Dostoevsky also understood the sense of existential horror experienced in a world without the comforting presence of God, the experience that Tolstoi had at Arzamas. He understood, better than centuries of Western theologians, the powerlessness of reason to shore up a faltering religious faith. He explored, but was not ultimately convinced by the attempts of European Catholics and Protestants to meet these challenges.

But nowhere in Dostoevsky's text is the underlying Christian ideal finally erased. Even his great rebels (Raskolnikov, Ippolit Terent'ev, Kirillov, Ivan Karamazov) cannot banish it from their psyche. That ideal, for Myshkin, is the ideal of God as Father, the ideal of God rejoicing in humanity as a father rejoices in his own children and, vague as it may sound, Myshkin persists in affirming:

> The essence of religious feeling has no connection with reasoning, wrongdoing, crime or atheism; it is something entirely different and will always be so; it is something that atheists will always skate over; they will always skirt round the real issue. But the important thing is that you will notice it most clearly and quickly in a Russian heart. That's my conclusion (VIII, 184).

The idea that Orthodoxy is finally killed off in Dostoevsky's world arises because the radical challenges offered through such characters as Ippolit Terent'ev or Ivan Karamazov, although deriving from Western inspired polemics, seem equally applicable to Orthodoxy and indeed to all types of theism. Ippolit's terrifying vision of a world based on the principle of self-destruction, although inspired by Holbein's painting of the dead body of Jesus taken down from the cross, is no respecter of particular religious traditions. If this is how the universe is, then the truth claims of Orthodoxy as well as of those of Catholicism and Protestantism (and indeed of Judaism and Islam) seem to collapse. In more subtle ways the objections, which Ivan Karamazov raises against Christianity[118], if valid, are generally applicable. But Albert Camus's view that Dostoevsky's heart was with Ivan rather than with Alesha[119] is as one-sided as the opposite view. Dostoevsky's heart was clearly torn between the two extremes and, as in the case of his rebel heroes, even of Nastas'ia Filippovna, the image of Christ preserved by Russian Orthodoxy continued to glow defiantly.

I might add here as a postscript that a faithful reading of Dostoevsky's text will also dispose of the idea that it is essentially gnostic in orientation. Traces of gnostic influence are to be found in Orthodoxy itself, indeed, even in the New Testament, and certainly in Dostoevsky too, but the essential feature of the gnostic tradition, that the Godhead is to be distinguished from the principle that created the universe, is nowhere to be found in Dostoevsky. If the distinction between a higher spiritual world and the evil material world to which we belong, and from which we can be released only through privileged knowledge brought to us by a spiritual redeemer, is taken as the core of gnostic belief, then one can appreciate the temptation to read Dostoevsky's novels through the eyes of Ippolit or Kirillov. But, in fact, other characters, from Myshkin, through Makar Dolgoruky to Markel, even Ivan Karamazov, see the natural world in a much more positive light, with the result that a gnostic reading is no less reductivist than the others that I discuss in this essay.

The model which I propose here accepts the 'death' of the religious creed that Dostoevsky inherited from the religious tradition, while acknowledging the shoots of a new growth based on the image of Christ within the Orthodox tradition. If I am right, then Dostoevsky comes very close to fulfilling Simone Weil's requirement for integrity in religious thought:

> For religious feeling to emanate from the spirit of truth, one should be absolutely prepared to abandon one's religion, even if that should mean losing all motive for living, if it should turn out to be anything other than the truth. In this state of mind alone is it possible to discern whether there is truth in it.[120]

III

Secondly, the metaphor of the death and resurrection of Orthodoxy is different from that of the death and resurrection of Christianity in general. There is no doubt that the objections to Christianity expressed in Dostoevsky's novels are applicable to all its forms, and that his religious world draws on a wide variety of sources beyond the sphere of Orthodoxy, but Christian motifs in his work mostly adhere to clusters that have a distinctly Orthodox colouring deriving from his own religious and cultural background.

Konrad Onasch has recently returned to the question of Dostoevsky and the Orthodox Church. Onasch comes to the conclusion that in respect of his Christology, his ecclesiology and his understanding of the monastic life, Dostoevsky reflects the official teaching of the Orthodox Church only indirectly. He concludes, 'The less overtly such dogmatic principles make their presence felt in Dostoevsky's novels, the more convincing is their inner meaning. For the truth [*istina*] of poetry has a different structure from the truth of doctrine.' ('Je weniger sich in seinen Romanen dogmatische Determinanten bemerkbar machen, um so überzeugender sind ihre Inhalte. Denn die "istina" der Dichtung hat eine andere Struktur als die der Lehre.')[121]

Dostoevsky's hostility to the Catholic and Protestant traditions, expressed supremely in 'The Grand Inquisitor', is well known. Many Western critics nevertheless read his presentation of religion essentially through Western eyes, noting with wry interest his misreading of Western traditions, but finding in him nonetheless many true, common Christian insights. These readings are rarely anti-Orthodox. More usually they are ecumenical in orientation.

This situation has made it more than usually difficult to assess Dostoevsky's novels as expressive of both the 'hosanna' and the 'furnace of doubt' of which he speaks so eloquently, and of the 'regeneration of convictions' which forms the starting point for Shestov's famous and eccentric essay.[122] This is because if Dostoevsky's novels do indeed embody the shoots of new faith, these shoots are rooted not just in a Christian soil but in a specifically Russian Orthodox soil, which for better or for worse is in some respects inimical to the distinctive traditions of Western Christianity. In particular, as Dostoevsky himself repeatedly pointed out, it is inimical to the predilection of Western Christianity for rational argumentation and for its repeated attempts through the ages to accommodate theology to the prevailing secular culture.

In fact, as we have seen, there are common Christian seeds which take root in the soil of Dostoevsky's world (the ideals of humility, compassion, forgiveness, active Christian love, the idea of the accessibility of truth to the childlike mind, belief in a demonic principle which can take on a personalized form, belief that God is to be found in oneness with his creation, acceptance that God is not always just to the righteous on this earth, belief in spiritual rebirth and personal immortality, and the saving power of the suffering servant). But, by and large, those motifs which he discovered in the Western tradition wither in Russian soil, not least in the character of Myshkin who, in spite of the connections made with the Russian tradition, is in more ways than are usually acknowledged associated with Western Christianity. Myshkin appears on the scene fresh from education and convalescence in Switzerland. He is even dressed in Western clothes and looks like the Western (not the Orthodox) image of Christ. All his most obsessive memories, including religious ones, are associated with Western Europe. Dostoevsky's confessed models for Myshkin (Don Quixote, Mr Pickwick, Jean Valjean) derive from the Catholic or Protestant cultures of Western Europe (Cervantes, Dickens, Hugo). So, though he does not mention them, are such possible models as George Sand's Bishop Bienvenu (*Les Misérables*), Patience (*Mauprat*) or Alexis and Angel (*Spiridion*). So do the models which depict the historical Jesus (Strauss, Renan). The Orthodox tradition does not attempt a literal portrayal of the historical Jesus in its iconography. On the contrary, it avoids the representational. The Orthodox icon is seen not as an aid to understanding but as an aid to worship.

But although there are many motifs in Dostoevsky's novels common to all Christian traditions, the clusters in which they appear are usually peculiar to Orthodoxy. For example, Myshkin's humility, compassion and childlikeness have strong overtones of the Orthodox kenotic tradition, a fact that is pointed out by several contributors to Pattison and Thompson's book. Likewise, his image evokes the Russian tradition of the holy fool, deriving from the Russian folk tradition. His parables (which he uses to indirectly answer a direct question about belief in God) also call to mind Russian Orthodox folk spirituality (cf. VIII, 182ff.). Seen in this light, the Western associations of Myshkin's image fall away into irrelevance. Of course, Myshkin is not allowed so easy an escape. But the fact remains that his personal image, though incorporating many Western features, is inconceivable outside the Orthodox tradition.

V Zakharov, who reminds us of the significance of Easter and its symbolism in *Notes from the House of the Dead*, has suggested that Dostoevsky could well be regarded as author of the 'Easter Tale'. He has pointed to the particular prominence given to Easter in the Orthodox Calendar and also to the remarkable role of Easter motifs in both the narrative and thematic structure of Dostoevsky's works,

> The genre of the Easter tale first took shape in the story of Nelly in *The Insulted and the Injured*. In *Crime and Punishment*, it appears in Raskolnikov's first dream, about the beating and killing of the horse, and in Svidrigailov's dream, just before his own death, of the little girl who commits suicide. In *The Adolescent*, we find it in Makar's story of the merchant Skotoboinikov. In *The Brothers Karamazov* it is to be found in the stories from the life of the Elder Zosima. Dostoevsky's master-piece in this genre is the story of 'The peasant Marei' published in *The Diary of a Writer*. The Easter tale as a genre is linked to the events of the Passion cycle (in Dostoevsky this means Lent, Easter Week, Easter itself, St Thomas's week and Whitsun.) The Easter tale is a tale of edification. Its themes are 'spiritual awakening' and 'moral rebirth', forgiveness in order to save souls and the resurrection of 'dead souls'. This all under-scores the significance of the theme of 'renewal' in Dostoevsky's work. The themes of many of his works are Easter themes. The epigraph to *The Brothers Karamazov* is an Easter one.[123]

Zakharov also shows how the events of some of Dostoevsky's novels are threaded on points in the Orthodox Christian calendar, how these may have symbolic significance, and how even the names of some of his charac-ters (Nastas'ia = resurrection; Stavrogin = cross) echo this same complex of Orthodox ideas. Sonia (Sofiia) echoes the theme of the Divine Wisdom, which plays a particularly important role in Orthodox theology.

The spiritual experiences of Myshkin, Makar Dolgoruky, Markel, Alesha, also reflect the Orthodox emphasis on transfiguration. The recurrent image of the 'rays of the setting sun', from Dostoevsky's earliest work through to his last, and usually in situations of deep spiritual significance, echoes the Orthodox doctrine of the theology of light.[124]

And behind the belief of Zosima and Markel that 'everyone is culpable before everyone for each and for all' lies the idea of *sobornost'*. These are all emphases attributable not to Christian tradition in general but the Orthodox tradition in particular. As we shall see, it is perhaps not too fan-ciful to suggest that behind the reticence of some of Dostoevsky's characters in respect of God, and behind Jesus's silence in 'The Grand Inquisitor', lies the Orthodox tradition of apophatic theology with its stress on paradox and silence and the ultimate unknowability of the Godhead.

IV

Thirdly, our model is also to be distinguished from the view that Dostoevsky's novels are so deeply imbued with the Orthodox faith that they can only be read in the light of it.

It is necessary only to make a brief preliminary comment here by way of addendum to the previous section. There have, as we have seen, been important and influential commentaries on Dostoevsky by critics, Russian and non-Russian, with a basically uncritical attitude to the Orthodox tradition. While some (notably Leontev) have rejected him as a heretic, others have welcomed him enthusiastically into the bosom of Orthodoxy.[125]

The temptation to see Dostoevsky's novels, particularly the last, as a vindication of Orthodoxy, as a great work of religious metaphysics (Berdiaev),[126] as works deeply imbued with the Orthodox faith in all its fullness, as expressing a seamless Christian poetics, is encouraged by Dostoevsky's correspondence with Liubimov and Pobedonostsev (XXX, i, 63–65; XXX, 1, 120–22).[127] It is not necessary, in order to sustain such a reading, to claim that the richness of the Orthodox tradition is explicit in Dostoevsky's text. All that such a reading requires is an acceptance that Dostoevsky's ideal reader is committed to Orthodoxy as, it is alleged, Dostoevsky was himself. It is strengthened by the conviction (for which the evidence is ambiguous) that Dostoevsky knowingly made this assumption. Such readings acknowledge, of course, that many of Dostoevsky's principal characters are atheists and rebels (sinners), but account for this by reference to the alienation from God and the Russian soil that he saw all around him and that troubled him so deeply. This alienation may sometimes be expressed in divergent conceptions of Christianity that unfairly expose Dostoevsky to charges of heresy.

What such readings fail to take fully into account, however, is that this alienation troubled Dostoevsky not only in other people but also, and most particularly, in himself, and is directly expressed in the fabric of his text. He is depicting not only what he sees around him but also what he experiences within him.

It also fails to take into account the fact that many of Dostoevsky's readers, reared in the Orthodox tradition, had long ceased to be churchgoers, and that even for a significant proportion of those who continued in their religious observances, the tradition had become 'automatized', that is, it had lost its power over their conscious thought processes.

Moreover, Dostoevsky was most certainly not a theologian, least of all an Orthodox one. His knowledge and understanding of the Church Fathers was not especially profound in spite of his extensive course of concentrated reading in the 1870s.[128] It has been claimed that his knowledge of the Bible was impressive. By comparison with that of modern secular men and women, including many of his critics, there is no doubt that it was. But, according to Leskov, he was easily outscored in his knowledge of Scripture by a contemporary evangelical Protestant of his acquaintance.[129]

Together with the view that Dostoevsky's novels are so deeply imbued with the Orthodox faith that they can be read only in the light of it often goes the belief that the Biblical quotations and allusions with which his fiction is so liberally endowed give overwhelming preference to the Johannine texts, in accordance to the dominant role of these texts in the Orthodox tradition. By 'Johannine texts' is usually meant the Gospel according to St John, the first Epistle of John and the Book of Revelation, all of which are traditionally ascribed to the Apostle John. This view is reinforced by the knowledge that the greatest number of markings in Dostoevsky's own copy of the New Testament is to be found in these texts. Irina Kirillova has noted that in the Gospel of St John the number of markings is fifty-eight, in St Matthew, twelve, in St Luke, seven, and in St Mark, two. The Book of Revelation has sixteen markings. There is a direct correlation, she argues, between the Christological thrust of St John's Gospel, Dostoevsky's lifelong veneration of Christ and the number of markings.[130] There can be little doubt that she is correct in this view, but that is not the same thing as the assumption — which incidentally she does not make — that the Gospel and first Epistle of John play an overwhelming structuring role in the major novels. Nor is there any simple equation to be made between significant Biblical allusions in the novels and Dostoevsky's markings in his New Testament. I am here pushing the Book of the Revelation to the margins of the discussion for (leaving aside questions of authorship) the frequency of allusions to Revelation in *The Idiot* and *The Devils* has little to do with Dostoevsky's image of Christ and the Christian life, and much more to do with his intuition that Russia was rushing headlong towards some sort of apocalyptic disaster.

An examination of Biblical quotations and allusions in the novels actually shows a much more even spread of sources. Let us start with what most readers will regard as the major structuring passages in the first four of his five major novels. In *Crime and Punishment* this role is played by the story of the raising of Lazarus, read by Sonia to Raskolnikov, and does indeed come from St John's Gospel (John 11: 38–44). Moreover, it was also marked in Dostoevsky's copy of the New Testament[131] In *The Idiot*, Diane Thompson tells us, there are twenty six or so biblical allusions, the majority concerning the Crucifixion, followed by the Apocalypse, most of these occurring in Ippolit's 'Necessary Explanation'.[132] Thompson highlights Ippolit's invocation of two of Christ's most nature-defying miracles, the raising of Lazarus and the raising of Jairus's daughter. The first is to be found in John (11: 38–44) and, as we have seen, is marked in Dostoevsky's New Testament.[133] The second is in Mark (5: 21–42) and is not indicated. Undoubtedly, one of the most effective Biblical allusions in the novel is made by Radomsky when he tells Myshkin that although Christ may have forgiven the woman taken in adultery he did not tell her that she had done well and merited honour and respect (VIII, 482). The passage is to be found in John 8: 3–11, but is not marked in Dostoevsky's New Testament, although there are several other markings in this chapter. Myshkin's character and his account of his sojourn in Switzerland evoke many Biblical associations, though these appear to fall outside the scope of Thompson's calculation. Among them are the Beatitudes, from Matthew's account of the Sermon on the Mount (Matthew 5–7), and 1 Corinthians 13. The only part of the Sermon on the

Mount marked by Dostoevsky is the passage referring to adultery (Matthew 5: 27–29),[134] but 1 Corinthians 13: 1–11 is marked in pencil in the margin.[135] The emphasis on Jesus's preference for childlike attitudes, reflected in Myshkin and Dostoevsky's other saintly characters, is a feature of the Synoptic Gospels (Matthew, Mark and Luke) rather than of John.[136] Moreover, as Sarah Young has recently argued, the New Testament book that maps most exactly onto the spirituality of *The Idiot* turns out to be the highly controversial (from an orthodox point of view) Epistle of James.[137] In *The Devils*, the key to Stavrogin's moral disintegration seems to be the verse from Revelation (3: 16), 'So, because you are lukewarm, and neither cold nor hot, I am about to spit you out of my mouth.' This verse, together with those that precede and follow it (14–17), is marked in pencil in the margin and also with a stroke at the beginning and the end.[138] *The Devils*, like *The Brothers Karamazov*, has an epigraph. But whereas that of *The Brothers Karamazov* does come from John's Gospel (John 12: 24) the epigraph to *The Devils* is taken from the story of the miracle of the Gadarene swine told in Luke 8: 26–39 (the epigraph itself being verses 32–36) and is marked with a stroke before and after the quotation in Dostoevsky's New Testament.[139] Perhaps, however, the most significant passage from a Christian viewpoint is that which the Bible-woman, Sofia Matveevna, reads to the ailing Stepan Trofimovich from the Sermon on the Mount, none of which is marked in Dostoevsky's New Testament at all, apart from those verses, here irrelevant, referring to adultery (Matthew 5: 27–29 again). She then lights on the passage from Revelation about 'the lukewarm' and finally reads the passage from Luke about the Gadarene swine. *A Raw Youth* also has a number of Biblical quotations, but none of them is of sufficient weight to merit special consideration as a major structuring device.

These examples show that there is no exact correlation between markings in Dostoevsky's New Testament and significant Biblical quotations and allusions in these three (or four) major novels. We may go on to infer that even if the markings indicate those New Testament passages that Dostoevsky particularly treasured, they were not necessarily destined to furnish the dominant structuring principles for his novels. Significant Biblical quotations and allusions in the novels derive from a variety of sources, both from John and the Synoptics, and from other books of the Old and New Testaments. The Johannine Gospel and Epistle are not dominant either numerically or, in many cases, in terms of their importance for the fiction. This is true even where a character, for example Stepan Trofimovich Verkhovensky in *The Devils*, is experiencing an eleventh hour spiritual awakening and finds in a Biblical passage the key to understanding the events in which he has participated and which form the substance of the novel (X, 498). And we may pause at this point to note that his spiritual awakening is not to the fullness of the Orthodox tradition. Indeed the Bible woman, if not herself a Protestant, is a product of Protestant influence in Russia in the 1860s and 1870s. What we are surely witnessing, to repeat a phrase that we have previously used, are the shoots of a new faith, based on an openness to the Biblical word and shorn of all its institutional and ritual accretions.

But some readers will want to insist that the true measure of the thesis that the Johannine texts dominate Dostoevsky's Christian spirituality and that this feeds through into a vindication of Orthodoxy in his fiction, is his final novel, *The Brothers Karamazov*. It is not possible to give an exact count of Biblical references in this novel. This is partly because of possible disagreement over how to count multiple references to the same source (such as the numerous references to the Book of Job). It is partly because many references to the Gospels occur in more than one location in the New Testament (frequently in more than one of the Synoptic Gospels). Moreover, there are also numerous references to the Orthodox liturgy, and some of the Biblical references are to passages that feature prominently in it. Finally there are some misquotations and conflations of sources. With this caution, however, it is possible to indicate, in addition to references to Job, some dozen references to Genesis and half a dozen others to scattered sources in the Old Testament.[140] So far as the New Testament is concerned, the majority are from the Gospels (47 if one counts each incidence of references with alternative possible sources as one, 69 if one aggregates all possibilities). By far the greatest number is from Matthew (14 or 30), followed by John (nine), then Luke (seven or 17) and finally Mark (one or 13). Sixteen are from the Book of Revelation and the rest from The Acts of the Apostles or the Letters of Paul. Of the approximately 95 possible New Testament references only 11 correspond with markings in Dostoevsky's copy of the New Testament and only about half of the references to the Gospel of John itself are marked.

It is still possible to argue, however, that most of these references are of minor significance and that attention should be focussed on the key structuring passages. Most readers would agree that among these are the epigraph (John 12: 24) and Jesus's miracle at the wedding at Cana in Galilee (John 2: 1–11). Remarkably, only the former is marked in Dostoevsky's New Testament. But thereafter John's Gospel does not figure among the key Biblical passages at all. The principal references in Ivan's poem about 'The Grand Inquisitor' are to Mark 5: 40–42 (the raising of Jairus's daughter, unmarked) and to Matthew 4: 1–11 (Jesus's temptations in the wilderness, also, strikingly, unmarked; to be found, in a slightly different version at Luke 4: 1–13, likewise unmarked). In addition, Zosima in his testament makes special reference not only to Job but also to the story of Joseph and his brothers (Genesis 37–50, both also present in the Koran) and to that of the rich man and poor Lazarus (Luke 16: 19–31). The story of the rich man and poor Lazarus is also unmarked. Luke's, however, is the only Gospel that Zosima includes by name in the recommended reading in his personal testament: he exhorts his hearers to pay special attention to Jesus's parables, 'chosen mainly from the Gospel of Luke' and to Saul's speech from the Acts of the Apostles (XIV, 267). The thesis that Dostoevsky's markings are the key to *The Brothers Karamazov* may therefore be discounted. The theory that the Johannine scriptures offer the key (whether marked or not) is more defensible, but depends largely on the acceptance of the view that the novel should be read in the light of the epigraph and the miracle at Cana in Galilee. This slimmed down version, however, offers further support for my own thesis, namely that, having killed off the Orthodox tradition in the minds of most of his characters, Dostoevsky is letting us watch how the seeds burst forth in new life in the most unexpected ways and places.

Of course, an even more subtle argument might maintain that the question of the frequency and number of references to particular Biblical sources in Dostoevsky's text, or even in his copy of the New Testament, are quite beside the point: it is the ethos of the Johannine scriptures, in particular of the Gospel, that is to be found in his writing. The most obvious point of similarity lies in the emphasis that both John and Dostoevsky place on Christian love. But to say this brings us back again to a major point of difference, namely, that John's portrait of Jesus is of a mysterious stranger, a celestial being in human disguise, who came from above and was to re-ascend to heaven. He is the Son of God the Father in the full sense, and not just metaphorically. Unlike the Jesus of the Synoptics, the Jesus of the fourth Gospel is a lordly, superior, authoritative and transcendent figure. He speaks down to people and shuns equivocation. He is often not understood.[141]

Though love is the dominating factor in John's Gospel, it is seen not as an earthly practice, which may lead the individual towards belief in God and immortality, as it is for Zosima, but as defining the whole order of heaven and earth. The Father loves the Son and the Son loves the father; those who have faith in the Son love and obey him and are also loved by the Father and the Son and, moreover, they are called upon to love each other too. It was because God so loved the world that he gave his only begotten Son that whoever believes in him should not perish but have everlasting life (John 3: 16).

As we saw in the first essay, it is possible to find passages in Dostoevsky that reflect this view, but to say that it underlies his whole oeuvre is surely to stretch credulity too far. Indeed, the basic theology of John's Gospel, a theology that underlies Christian faith in the divinity of the Son of God, and provides source material for the doctrine of the Trinity that was later to become a defining doctrine of the Christian faith, is notable for its absence in Dostoevsky's fiction. As we have seen, it is just this otherworldly dimension, with its insistence on the vital historical reality of the Resurrection of Jesus ('I am the resurrection and the life' (John 11: 25)) as unique Son of God that Dostoevsky side-steps in his fictional texts. To say that he alludes to it is one thing; it is quite another to imply that his text expresses it directly, or even indirectly, least of all to imply that it is an underlying assumption. By and large, 'resurrection' seems to be a metaphorical concept in Dostoevsky, referring to a spiritual rebirth. It is certainly not so for John.

Moreover, there are important Biblical references in Dostoevsky's fiction to features of the Synoptic Gospels that are absent in John. One of these is the much remarked form of Zosima's testament. The way in which Jesus's sermons in the Synoptic Gospels are composed of short utterances and parables from different occasions has its parallel in the composition of Zosima's testament, and the Gospel writer's editorial role has its parallel in Alesha's, but this a characteristic of the Synoptic Gospels, not of the long, rambling, repetitious and often allegorical speeches of Jesus in John's Gospel.

We have already seen how the miracle of the casting out of demons and their transmission to the Gadarene swine (Luke 8: 32–36) serves as the epigraph and plays a key role in *The Devils*. The casting out of demons is one of the chief aspects of Jesus's function as a healer in the Synoptics, but it is completely missing from John. Even the performance of cures, perhaps the dominant feature of the portrait of Jesus in the Synoptics, loses its centrality in the fourth Gospel. Yet it is this aspect of Jesus's ministry that is highlighted in the legend of the Grand Inquisitor. While it could be argued that this portrait of Jesus is painted by the atheist Ivan and therefore should not be taken as indicative of Dostoevsky's own view, it remains the only extended portrait of a living Jesus that we are given in Dostoevsky's fiction.

V

Fourthly, my interpretation is also different from the view that atheism and Christianity are equally weighted voices in polyphonic discourse in Dostoevsky's novels. This view may be described, without any wish to give offence, as the vulgar Bakhtinian view. While Bakhtin stressed that in the polyphonic novel all voices have equal weight in the chorus, including that of the author, he did not deny that the author's organising role endowed it with a particular privilege. Moreover, whatever he wrote in his two books, he privately acknowledged in conversation that he had not done justice to what really mattered in Dostoevsky, namely the religious dimension.[142] All this is in a sense irrelevant, except that Bakhtin's name is sometimes invoked to support the view that Dostoevsky's novels consist of a dialogue of equals, atheists and believers, in which there are no ultimate victors or losers, a debate on which the reader is invited to cast his or her own vote, and in which the 'author' remains neutral.[143] While in one sense this is true — Bakhtin has correctly drawn attention to the 'unfinalizedness' of the Dostoevskian novel — it does not make sufficient allowance for development (the diachronic dimension) in Dostoevsky and particularly for the role of the overall structuring 'Easter' myth of death and renewal.

VI

It is also different from the view that Dostoevsky is a heretic. The charge that he was a heretic has to be considered quite seriously. It is a difficult accusation to refute. Once a thinker rejects the authoritative discourse of tradition and begins to seek to understand it and express it in ways that are inwardly persuasive, the chances of straying beyond the permissible are very real. As Kermode intimates, institutions generally seek to retain some degree of control over the interpretation of their sacred texts.[144] The seeds may mutate into forms that, in the view of the faithful, belie their ancestry.

Sergei Hackel, an Orthodox scholar who has made one of the most detailed and convincing analyses of religious motifs in *The Brothers Karamazov*, leaves no doubt that if Dostoevsky thought that Zosima and Alesha, separately or combined, faithfully express the Orthodox tradition, then Dostoevsky's understanding of that tradition was flawed. Even Alesha's great mystical experience is nearer to a cosmophany than a theophany (perhaps even 'cosmolatry'):

> Alyosha's experience is not necessarily nor yet obviously the fruit or the foundation of a Christian Orthodox commitment. His tears, prostrations, kissing of the earth and communing with the cosmos may still intrigue, impress or even move the reader with their innocent intensity. But despite the Christian cosmetics, which Dostoevsky has partially applied, they speak of little more than nature mysticism [...]
>
> The would-be prophet had attained his 'hosanna', his faith, 'through a great furnace of doubt'. Yet the doubt had not been left behind. It informs the arguments of Ivan, it gives Zosima's counterweight, that Western monk, the Grand Inquisitor, his haunting and lasting power. Dostoevsky thus had good reason to emulate the possessed boy's father in the Gospels and to pray, 'Lord, I believe; help thou mine unbelief' (Mark 9: 24).
>
> In the case of Zosima and Alyosha, who could have been, respectively, the proponent and champion of belief, the unbelief is not so far to seek as might have been expected. And in the case of either, but especially Alyosha, the reader is ultimately confronted with what A B Gibson has succinctly termed 'the combination of the sincerest piety with the apparent absence of its object.'[145]

There is much to be said for this view. Dostoevsky, as we have remarked, suppresses the role of sacraments and liturgy, even in the case of Zosima who is a priest. He introduces religious motifs with no strong tradition in Orthodoxy, for example bowing down and kissing the ground; institutions of a highly controversial nature within that tradition, for example the Eldership; mystical experiences with no distinctly Orthodox or even Christian content, for example Alesha's. He introduces emphases that are contrary to Orthodox doctrine (for example, the establishment by personal will-power of heaven on earth).[146]

That there are heretical motifs in Dostoevsky is as certain as that there are atheistic motifs. And these heretical motifs appear against a background in which explicit Orthodox dogma and Orthodox tradition is absent. If we are to judge the importance of Orthodoxy in Dostoevsky's fictional world by such criteria then theological inadequacy is the least charge he has to answer. But, as I have suggested, there is another more satisfying solution. It is only if we adhere to the view that all positive expressions of religion in Dostoevsky should represent Orthodoxy in its fullness that we shall be troubled by such a discovery.

VII

Finally, the model of death and resurrection is not compatible with the charge that Dostoevsky's treatment of Orthodoxy is better characterized as evasion than as vision. Hackel's article is entitled 'The religious dimension: vision or evasion? Zosima's discourse in *The Brothers Karamazov'*. The question is a genuine, not a rhetorical one, and the answer is not straightforward. Hackel comes down on the side of evasion. The passage quoted above concludes his article.

There certainly is evasion in *The Brothers Karamazov*, an unwillingness or incapacity to look the ultimate in the face: the avoidance of all but inescapable reference to God in Zosima's testament and little more than conventional reference elsewhere; Alesha's inability (through fear, and not because of any theological impediment)[147] to look at Jesus in his dream; avoidance of all reference to divine grace in 'The Legend'; avoidance of reference to innocent suffering and to Job's sense of abandonment in Zosima's account of Job (which is particularly odd in view of the fact that it is supposed to be an answer to Ivan); the expression of Alesha's great mystical experience in terms which have no Orthodox or even Christian content apart from a passing reference to the 'innumerable worlds of God', itself of dubious theological provenance. I shall not repeat the much-quoted passage here. Suffice to say that references to 'something as firm and unshakeable as this heavenly vault', 'some sort of idea', even 'someone' visiting Alesha's soul seem formulated more to avoid specific Christian associations than to reinforce them. Even Jesus's silence in 'The Legend' could be seen as evasiveness. Such evasiveness when characters are confronted with ultimate religious questions runs throughout the mature novels. Raskolnikov's spiritual rebirth is merely foreshadowed (the narrator evasively tells us the story would make another novel); Myshkin changes the subject when asked about his belief in God and declines to answer directly (thus opening himself up to the very charge that he levels against his interlocutor in his first anecdote); Myshkin's mystical experiences are not expressed in traditional Orthodox terms, but described as the highest synthesis of beauty and prayer, and they are experienced in an epileptic fit (cf. VIII, 186ff.). Shatov is no less evasive than Myshkin about belief in God, though he is keen to speculate about nations seeking their own God, about the Second Coming, about humanity's unremitting affirmation of life and denial of death, and about the possibility that the underlying principle is aesthetic or ethical (cf. X, 196ff.). This evasiveness is akin to what Bakhtin calls 'discourse with a loophole' — leaving open the possibility of changing the meaning of one's words, a form of unfinalizedness. Maybe it is on the brink of Orthodoxy; but maybe it reflects an ultimate scepticism about it.

There is also no doubt that Dostoevsky's use of Orthodox motifs is often accompanied by apparent evasion about the deeper reaches of Orthodox faith and practice. Sometimes one can even see a distancing taking place between his notebooks and his novels. Again it is Hackel who has pointed to this, in respect of the motif of transfiguration:

> Dostoevsky was evidently not ignorant of Orthodox teaching on the ultimate divinization of man, on man's striving towards theosis (*obozheniye*). In one of his notebook entries for Zosima's discourse he makes specific reference to it. In the Orthodox world, and in particular since the fourteenth century councils which upheld the teachings of Gregory Palamas, the light of Christ's Transfiguration on Mount Tabor had long been accepted as a model and an assurance of man's theosis. Hence the burden of Dostoevsky's fourfold notebook entry: 'Your flesh will be transformed (Light of Tabor). Life is paradise, the keys are in our keeping' (XV, 245). Yet the established text does not retain the first two statements, and the concept of life as paradise is thus deprived of an important gloss and validation.[148]

Ironically, it is in Ivan's poem about Jesus's return to earth that 'the sun of love shines in his [Jesus's] heart, rays of light, enlightenment, and power, stream from his eyes and, pouring over the people, shake their hearts with responding love' (XIV, 227). But when in Alesha's dream, as Zosima lies in his coffin, Zosima asks 'Do you see our Sun, do you see Him?' Alesha avoids the challenge with a whispered 'I am afraid. I dare not look' (XIV, 327).

I affirmed at the beginning of this section, however, that the model I am proposing for reading religious discourse in Dostoevsky's work is not compatible with the idea that Dostoevsky's treatment of Orthodoxy is better characterized as evasion than vision. Why is this?

The simple answer is that the metaphor of the death of Orthodoxy has already led us to expect that tradition as authoritative discourse will have lost its force, and that religious experience as inwardly persuasive discourse will have taken its place.[149] A positive reading of the evidence may lead us to the conclusion that the religious motifs which survive may be seen as the shoots, as yet tender, of a new faith, with its roots in the Orthodox heritage, but nourished by deep personal religious experiences. For an author whose private commitment to the Orthodox tradition was, it seems, obsessive, to write in this way is to take an enormous risk and not at all to shy away from the issue.

This brings me to my major point. What solid grounds are there for claiming that the text of the Dostoevskian novel is fertile ground for the resurrection of Orthodoxy rather than a graveyard in which its alienated children avert their eyes in embarrassment?

One can often gauge Dostoevsky's emotional commitment to a subject by the violence of his attack on it. This is certainly the case with Orthodoxy.

Whenever Dostoevsky's text is evasive on a religious issue, it is evasive with respect to something vital in the Orthodox tradition. We always know what is being evaded. The clue is in the Jesus of 'The Grand Inquisitor'. Jesus is silent (among other reasons) because he has nothing to add to what he has said already. In other words, the silence turns out to be not an evasive but an allusive silence. By saying nothing he is in effect saying 'I have said it all already; you know where to look without my saying it again.' It is not a vacuum that lies beyond the silence but an infinite richness of intertextual allusion. As Vladimir Lossky has written, 'The faculty of hearing the silence of Jesus, attributed by St Ignatius to those who in truth possess His word, echoes the reiterated appeal of Christ to His hearers: "He who has ears to hear, let him hear." The words of Revelation have then a margin of silence which cannot be picked up by the ears of those who are outside.'[150] The use of the word 'evasion' in the discussion above involves a value judgement; it assumes a secular reader who has ears to hear but does not hear. And of these there is in the real, twenty-first century world, an evident preponderance. However, the exclusion, or even the censorship, of the obvious, invites the attention of those with ears to hear. The invitations are everywhere to be found in Dostoevsky's text, but never more eloquently than where there is a glaring omission.

To change the metaphor, the Orthodox motifs in Dostoevsky's text may be seen to spring into new life when fertilized by the Orthodox intertext. If not, other shoots sprout, as generations of non-Orthodox interpretations bear witness.

If we ask where the critical silences are in *The Brothers Karamazov*, they point us directly to two Biblical texts: The Book of Job and St John's Gospel. Both books reject a mechanistic or literalistic approach to religion. It is not through rational discourse on the problem of suffering that God eventually addresses Job, but in his speech from the whirlwind. John too is antiliteralistic; he, and Jesus through him, constantly turn the literal into the metaphorical.

It is as though the main gaps in the spiritual text of *The Brothers Karamazov* exactly fit the main points of emphasis in Job and John. It is as if the silence was especially contrived to draw the reader's attention away from the text before him or her and onto the precursor text. One or two examples should be sufficient to make the point.

I have remarked elsewhere that the major defect of the Grand Inquisitor's presentation of the Gospel is that he ignores the doctrine of Grace;[151] that is to say, he argues that humanity is incapable of measuring up to the demands imposed by freedom, as though humanity, according to the Gospel, was required to do this without divine aid. To my remark, it might be objected that Orthodoxy has traditionally placed less emphasis than the Western Churches on the doctrine of Grace, but this hardly answers my point. Zosima also omits all mention of it in his discourse on hell. How could this not be conscious on Dostoevsky's part? We are not reduced to speculation here. The first chapter of John's Gospel contains the verse: 'For while the Law was given by Moses, grace and truth came by Jesus Christ' (John: 1: 17). This passage was actually marked in the margin in Dostoevsky's New Testament.[152] Moreover, Ivan Esaulov has shown how examples of divine Grace recur in his last novel.[153] This does not prove that the text ought to be read in the way I am suggesting. But it provides strong circumstantial evidence to support the thesis that such a glaring omission could not have been negligent or unconscious, or evasive in a negative sense.

Is it not even more extraordinary that in his gloss on the Book of Job, Zosima, who was meant, according to Dostoevsky himself, to answer Ivan's charges in 'Rebellion' and 'The Legend', entirely overlooks the problem of innocent suffering and God's eventual response in the voice from the whirl-wind? The latter omission is perhaps attributable to doubts about whether it squarely addresses the questions posed by Job's predicament. But Dostoevsky could not conceivably have been unaware that Job's situation, and that of his children, present the issue of innocent suffering, a suffering which God not only allows to happen, but even seems to authorize. Here again, the silence is deafening, and cannot have been an oversight. Reference to The Book of Job undoubtedly signposts the discussion in that Book as well as what is made explicit in Dostoevsky's text.

Finally, it is tempting, too tempting to omit from the discussion, to won-der whether the passage in which Alesha fears to look at the face of Jesus was written in the knowledge of the following story about St Serafim of Sarov, retold in the following century by Vladimir Lossky. A disciple of St Serafim says to his master that he does not understand how he can be firmly assured that he is in the Spirit of God.

> Father Serafim replied: 'I have already told you, my son, that it is very simple, and I have in detail narrated to you how men dwell in the Spirit of God, and how one must apprehend His appearance in us...What then do you need?'
>
> 'My need,' said I, 'is to understand this well!'
>
> 'We are both together, son, in the Spirit of God... Why lookest thou not on me?'
>
> 'I cannot look, Father, because lightning flashes from your eyes; your face is brighter than the sun and my eyes ache in pain.'
>
> 'Fear not,' he says, 'You too are now in the fullness of God's Spirit; otherwise you would not be able to look on me as I am.' (...)
>
> Encouraged by these words, I looked in his face and there came over me an even greater reverential awe.[154]

Whether or not this was so, we have seen that Dostoevsky omitted from the text of his novel explicit reference to a Transfiguration that was present in his notebook.

For Dostoevsky's world to be reborn (resurrected), dialogue with the Orthodox tradition, especially that of Scripture, is vital. Without that dialogue with the 'beyond-the-text' Dostoevsky's world remains much as Camus, or the critics of the Soviet period, saw it. It is this intertextual interplay which is the key to this interpretation according to the model we propose. Without it, the Orthodox motifs are no more than cultural colouring, the religious debates vain. With it, the reader can intuit and pursue a rich, sub-textual vein of religious discourse that gives life to the 'Easter' metaphors, which inhere the structure of the Dostoevskian text, without imposing itself.

At the end of the day, of course, such a reading remains optional. Silence always retains an ambiguity. It does not demonstrate the truth of the Orthodox tradition, nor does it imply that a reading without this dimension is entirely unsatisfactory. What I have tried to do is to show the plausibility of a reading that does justice to the structure of death and resurrection, which, Dostoevsky strongly hints, lies beneath his artistic vision, to the 'furnace of doubt' and the 'hosanna' of his own spiritual pilgrimage. If we see the shoots of a revitalized faith, they still, it must be admitted, remain young and frail even, some would say in the light of the ending of his last novel, infantile. Yet only such a reading does full justice to the text and remains faithful to all the varieties of religious and atheist experience to be found there.

The death and resurrection motif seen in this way and exemplified in the epigraph to *The Brothers Karamazov*, informs much of Dostoevsky's mature fiction. We find it underlying all four of his major novels, including *The Idiot*. It plays a structuring role within individual texts and frequently finds expression in scriptural allusions. Many Orthodox motifs appear in Dostoevsky's work, often in complex inter-relationships, which mark them off from more general Christian motifs. Culturally speaking, the Orthodox tradition plays a major, if not a dominant, role in Dostoevsky's fictional world. That Orthodoxy as Holy Writ is radically challenged in Dostoevsky is also easily demonstrated, as is his refusal to accept that the challenge is fatal to religious experience. More difficult to establish is that his texts should be read as evidence of reborn conviction, a conviction ultimately immune to the attacks of scepticism and reason. It is difficult to establish because it depends on our reading of his silences, and these silences, in a polyphonic context, are ambiguously signposted. But what from one point of view may be seen as evasion may be seen from another as allusion. The seeds of a rebirth of Orthodoxy in Dostoevsky are akin to what Mikhail Epstein in recent essays has called 'minimal religion', the shoots of a new religious consciousness emerging from the storms of atheism.[155] What I hope to have established is not that such a reading is obligatory, but that such a reading is plausible and, for what it is worth, that it accords with Dostoevsky's own literary ambitions. More than that the polyphonic text will not allow.

VIII

Even if we accept that the metaphor of the death and resurrection of Orthodoxy provides a viable model for the role of religion in Dostoevsky's world, however, that hardly does justice to the dynamic nature of religious experience and its structuring role in his text. The foregoing discussion has brought to light many features that it fails to explain. It remains to discuss whether it is possible to construct a dynamic model that will account for the connectedness of these various strands of religious and atheistic experience to be found there. In particular, such a model should account for the liminal nature of the extremes of religious experience as presented in Dostoevsky; their development along positive and negative lines through his saintly characters and his nihilists; and the way in which their open conflict gives rise to stalemate and subsequently to the birth of new forms of spirituality shorn of all but the pale shadows of the old religious traditions. A clue is to be found in a recent article by Mikhail Epstein that appeared in English translation in 1998. It is not about Dostoevsky. It addresses what it calls the phenomenon of post-atheism in Russia at the beginning of the twenty-first century, but its relevance will shortly become clear. The article is called 'From Apophatic Theology to "Minimal Religion"'[156] and I shall argue that what Epstein calls 'minimal religion' is very much what we find in Dostoevsky's text. Moreover, I shall suggest that much of the historical process that he traces over two centuries is to be found in embryo in Dostoevsky. Epstein begins by saying that what interests him is a new type of religious consciousness at the end of the twentieth century, or more specifically the coming back to consciousness of religious drives and instincts repressed into the unconscious during the Soviet period, when aggression, cruelty and destruction became official ideological doctrine.

But, according to Epstein — and this is where he becomes particularly relevant to our discussion — the suppression of religious consciousness during the Soviet period was not imposed by external sources alone: it was rooted in the very heart of the religious and theological tradition dominant in Eastern Christianity, and particularly in Russia. According to Pseudo-Dionysius the author of the *Areopagitica* (5th – 6th c. AD), God is more profound than any definition, image or name. To paraphrase Husserl, 'consciousness is always consciousness of something' while God is not 'something' and so escapes definitions offered by consciousness. In the words of Vladimir Lossky, 'all knowledge has as its object that which is, but God is beyond all that exists. In order to approach Him it is necessary to deny all that is inferior to Him, that is to say, all that which is [...] Proceeding by negations one ascends from the inferior degrees of being to the highest, by progressively setting aside all that can be known, in order to draw near to the Unknown in the darkness of absolute ignorance.'[157] Apophaticism, Lossky says, constitutes the primary characteristic of the whole theological tradition of the Eastern Church. According to Epstein, its most fundamental Russian manifestation was the suppression of theology itself, with its emphasis on the inexpressibility of God, and the source of Russia's ancient, enduring and centuries-long intellectual silence. Russia did, of course, produce important works in the field of liturgy, dogmatics and other disciplines, and religious thought experienced an upsurge in the second half of the nineteenth and early twentieth centuries, but theology in Russia has never been regarded as a particularly important function of faith. The shortest path to God was either through the incessant repetition of the eight-word prayer to Jesus or through 'inexpressible sighs'.

Epstein concludes that the apophatic tradition very clearly leads to the Russian nihilism of the nineteenth century and the Soviet atheism of the twentieth, in which negative theology becomes the negation of theism itself. God is transposed beyond the region of knowledge as such, and all predicates of being attached to the notion of God are rejected. This dark and unhealthy aspect of apophaticism has been part of Russian theology throughout its entire history, and the anti-intellectual stance of Orthodoxy may in some measure account for the atheistic inclination of Russian thought. It drove faith into the unconscious and cleared the way for the conscious cult of science, revolution and social ideals. The belief that there is no God thus has its roots in the ambivalence of apophatic theology itself that, by denying God any cognisable features, plunges us into the depths of non-knowledge-of-God, ultimately leading to indifference towards or simple rejection of God. It is in this sense that Soviet atheism can be regarded as the paradoxical development of apophatic theology: God is not only deprived of his attributes, but of the very predicate of existence itself. The difference is that in the one case the negation of God is but a step toward attaining God, while in the other it is the final point, at which reason stops and is petrified. Epstein does not argue, of course, that these issues play an overt role in the discussions of the Russian intelligentsia of the nineteenth and twentieth centuries. Indeed any conscious recognition of the problem is hard to find.[158] The implication of his argument is that this fatal disjunction was always present in the Russian mind at a subconscious level, in a way and to a degree that was obscured by theological developments in the West. It is an explanatory theory that cannot be proved or falsified; it can however be used to highlight some distinctive characteristics of the history of Russian spirituality.

Epstein pauses to note that the East has been the cradle of other religions embodying a negative infinity, Nirvana in Buddhism, Tao in Taoism, Brahman in Hinduism. In the East, negative forms of knowledge of God do not inevitably lead to atheism. Their nihilism, far from being a denial of religion, represents its profound essence and dignity. Christianity, however, differs markedly in that it affirms the positive manifestation of God in the image of his Son, who appeared in the flesh. Precisely because, for the Christian, God is revealed in the fullness of the human personality of Christ, the development of negative theology, thinks Epstein, was bound to lead to atheism.

However, this does not mean that atheism, in developing apophaticism to extremes, completely annihilates the religious principle. The paradox lies in the fact that while apophaticism contained the seeds of atheism, atheism retains the seeds of apophaticism. That is, atheism retains its own unconscious theology. *Apophaticism is a liminal phenomenon, through which faith crosses into atheism, while atheism itself reveals the unconscious of faith.*[159]

Once suppressed, Epstein continues, religion makes its presence felt in indirect ways, just as for Freud repressed sexuality can betray itself in distorted forms. Epstein lists a number of examples from the Soviet period: the creation of idols, the adulation of leaders and their images, state worship of many kinds, as well as regressions into forms of primitive tribal rituals. Russian culture of the Soviet period teems with unconscious revelations of religious intentions.

In post-Soviet Russia, the spiritual vacuum created by Soviet atheism gave rise, in the 1970s and 1980s, to a new type of post-atheist religiosity that Epstein calls 'poor' or 'minimal' religion. It had no clear denominational characteristics, manifesting itself as an indivisible sense of God. Minimal religion thus became the next stage of apophaticism after it had crossed the threshold of atheism and reclaimed its religious content. According to Epstein, the atheistic negation of all religions thus gave rise to a 'minimal' religiosity, negating all positive distinctions among historical religions. Since Soviet atheism was a historically new phenomenon, post-atheist spirituality was even more of a novelty.

In fact post-Soviet Russia exhibits a number of tendencies. Firstly, there is a return to pre-atheist beliefs. Traditional religions — Orthodoxy, Catholicism, Islam, Buddhism, Judaism — are regaining their status. Secondly, there is a return to neo-paganism and the ancient cult of nature, often mixed with elevated ecological sentiments. Thirdly, there is a mixture of the two in which Orthodoxy doubles as a religion of the Heavenly Father and an ancient cult of Mother Earth, and in which Orthodoxy is destined to protect Russia against foreign contamination and heresies. The new paganism also features the cultivation of magic, extra-sensory perception, parapsychology, spiritualism and other beliefs going back to animism and fetishism. Finally, there is minimal religion, without an order of service, dogmas, holy books or specific rituals.

Epstein is here setting out, in the well-established tradition of the Russian intelligentsia, a meta-historical account of developments in the field of Russian spirituality. Its perspective is therefore *diachronic*. But, whether he is aware of the coincidence or not, he has also accidentally identified and theorized the whole range of religious phenomena of Dostoevsky's world, the vital difference being that in Dostoevsky they appear *synchronically* and before, and in anticipation of, the events of the Soviet period. For in Dostoevsky's world, we see religious faith and atheistic nihilism side-by-side and seemingly bound to each other by invisible threads. There are also notable examples of repressed spirituality expressing itself in distorted form in his fiction. Kirillov's messianic delusions in *The Devils* are a striking example. The combination of Orthodoxy with the cult of Mother Russia can be discerned in his companion Shatov, not to mention the several occasions when characters bow down reverentially to kiss the ground and shower it with their tears. Indeed, like his Slavophile contemporaries, Dostoevsky was himself obsessed by the idea that one could not be a true Russian without being Orthodox. Above all, we see the reappearance of religious experience in minimal form, in primitive form, and in distorted forms that incorporate pagan, reductive, heretical and apocalyptic elements. Traces of the Protestant and Catholic traditions, and of Christian socialism, are also to be found, as are the values of a shallow modern secularism. In this context it is hardly surprising that readers have found it possible to map aspects of Buddhism and Islam onto the spirituality of Dostoevsky's fictional world as well, not to mention the concerted attempts of Soviet Marxists to claim him as their own. One important feature of the spiritual map (both ours and Dostoevsky's) that Epstein does not mention is what Philip Goodchild has recently called 'the dominant contemporary global piety' whose organizing principle is 'the self-regulating market',[160] in other words the substitution for religious piety of a piety directed towards the transcendent principle of money, financial speculation (gambling) and its accumulation (what Dostoevsky calls 'the Rothschild idea').[161] Perhaps most interestingly of all we can trace moments in the course of the narrated events where the individual stands on the edge of the abyss of nothingness, and even occasionally on the threshold between the abyss of nihilism and the fullness of religious experience. As Tikhon tells Stavrogin, 'The complete atheist stands on the last step but one before perfect faith' (XI, 10). Moreover, we can also identify aspects of Dostoevsky's narrative technique that facilitate the depiction of such a world. It is this combination of forms of spiritual awareness within the one text that so confuses those readers and critics able to conceive of religious experience in Dostoevsky only in traditional Christian terms. For the first time, perhaps, it is possible to see the whole range of spiritual experience in *The Brothers Karamazov* in its interconnectedness and to give full weight to the fact that although Dostoevsky projected a novel in which Orthodoxy would be vindicated and atheism refuted, its realisation was to take place in a future novel, which he never wrote. If we bear this in mind, it is perfectly possible to accept that Dostoevsky himself may have turned to the fullness of Orthodox tradition for his personal salvation while, as novelist who accepted the multifaceted spiritual reality around him, intuiting the interconnectedness of these phenomena within the 'apophatic semiosphere'. Within this context, a claim like that of Orlando Figes, that 'Dostoevsky's whole life can be seen as a struggle to combine the teaching of the Gospels with the need for social justice on earth, and he thought he found his answer in the "Russian soul"',[162] may be seen as a response not to the fullness and richness of Orthodoxy but to the whole range of phenomena in the spiritual atmosphere around him:

I am now speaking not about church buildings and not about sermons; I am speaking about our Russian 'socialism' (and, however strange it may seem, I am taking this word, which is the very opposite of all that the Church represents, to explain my idea), whose purpose and outcome is the establishment of the universal and ecumenical Church on earth insofar as the earth is capable of containing it. I am speaking of the ceaseless longing, which has always been characteristic of the Russian people, for a great, general, universal union of brotherhood in the name of Christ. And if this union does not yet exist, if the Church has not yet been fully established, not merely in prayers alone, but in fact, then the instinct for this Church and the ceaseless longing for it, sometimes almost unconscious, is still undoubtedly to be found in the hearts of our people in its many millions (XXVII, 18–19).

The thought that the concurrence of these phenomena may be facilitated by the peculiar characteristics of apophatic theology in Russia is a fascinating one. If it has any historical validity, then this may perhaps be ascribed to the coincidental appearance in Russia of the European Enlightenment and the re-establishment of a monastic tradition based on apophatic theology at the end of the eighteenth and beginning of the nineteenth centuries. However, ultimately it is not a question of whether or not Epstein is right in a historical sense, but of whether or not he provides a viable dynamic model for the phenomena that he purports to theorize, and of whether or not it helps us to understand Dostoevsky. I think that we shall find that it does.

ESSAY IV

Dostoevsky's Deconstructive Anxiety

I

A Perilous Threshold

In his contribution to Pattison and Thompson's recent book, Henry Russell cautions the reader:

> Lest apophatic knowledge be misunderstood [...] for its mute step-brother deconstruction, it is important to note that human inability to refer with full truth to God is a result of God's perfection which we, as sinful creatures, cannot know. Language about God refers then to a plenitude, which it cannot contain, not to an absence.[163]

In drawing attention to this vital distinction Russell, perhaps unintentionally, highlights the ease with which one may be confused with and slip into the other, not only conceptually but also, depending on the mood of the experiencing subject, experientially. In other words, the silence at the core of apophatic religion may be interpreted or experienced either as a fullness or as an absence, as glorious plenitude or as desolate abyss, as a God-centred locus of meaning or as total chaos and meaninglessness. As we have seen, Dostoevsky experienced this himself and understood the slippage very well. Similar experiences may be observed in the experience of his individual characters, and also among them. As Thompson points out,[164] characters as unlike each other as Myshkin and Ippolit quote the same phrase from the Book of Revelation, 'there will be time no more' (Rev 10: 6), the one in his epileptic ecstasy, the other in suicidal despair. This dual experience is not a modern discovery. It was known to Job, to Jeremiah, to the Psalmists, even perhaps to Christ himself on the Cross (Matthew 27: 46; Mark 15: 34), and must be a possibility for any religious vision in which God (or Being) is conceived as the wholly other. Within the traditions of twentieth century European theology and philosophy of religion, comparable positions have been taken up by such seminal figures as Karl Barth, for whom God is wholly inaccessible to human thought, but has broken into the world and revealed himself in Christ, and Martin Heidegger, for whom God has fled, but for whom the experience of dread before nothingness is a key step in the quest for Being and the God that is to come.[165] The articulation of the problem in Dostoevsky's work has some very modern features.

Traditional analyses of the ideological and religious dimension of Dostoevsky's fictional world often focus on its relationship to the polemics of the day, to the debates between the Slavophiles and the Westerners, for example, in which Dostoevsky's fiction, like that of his contemporaries Turgenev, Leskov and Tolstoi, played such an important role. Others recognize that its significance is considerably wider, and attempt to define its place in the whole development of Western philosophy or of Christian theology. Such studies have played a major part in establishing Dostoevsky's credentials as a writer of world stature. Nothing that follows is intended to diminish their importance.

It may readily be agreed that Dostoevsky's fiction contains examples of all the types of spiritual and ideological consciousness listed towards the end of the preceding chapter, apart, of course, from those relating directly to the Soviet episode. Most of them have already been thoroughly examined in critical literature, sometimes individually and sometimes in conjunction with an overarching theme or a broader critical analysis. Perhaps it will therefore suffice to refer to some of these studies here, and to give illustrative examples, rather than to rehearse them all in detail. On Dostoevsky and Orthodoxy, and indeed other forms of Christianity, there are too many well-known examples to require enumeration. I have already referred and given references to a number of these in earlier chapters. On the apocalyptic strain in Dostoevsky, it is perhaps sufficient to refer to the work of W J Leatherbarrow[166] and David Bethea.[167] In fact it was this aspect of his sensibility that made Dostoevsky so popular among West European writers in the period around the First World War. Richard Peace is generally credited with being the first to draw attention in English to the importance of the role of the Old Believers and Russian sectarians in Dostoevsky's novels.[168] Michael Futrell is the author of a well-known article on Dostoevsky and Buddhism.[169] Harriet Murav has written eloquently of the role of holy foolishness in Dostoevsky's work.[170] Further important studies are listed in the bibliography at the end of this book. My purpose here is not to rewrite these studies, but to establish a new model for reading their dynamic interrelationship.

My thesis is that Dostoevsky does not merely depict a variety of religious experiences, and is not merely engaged in polemic with the leading thinkers of his day, but that at a deeper and more dynamic level, all these phenomena derive from the ambiguity of that apophatic theology which permeated the air in which he drew his breath. Although some of these phenomena are reflected in the work of some of his contemporaries, in none of them is their whole range and depth expressed as they are in Dostoevsky, whose intuition seems, in this respect as in others, to have outreached that of his peers and most of his successors. Its crucial test will be our ability to demonstrate that some of the most critical spiritual experiences in his work exist on the threshold between the fullness of religious experience and the emptiness of nihilism. As Mikhail Epstein says, as we noted above, 'apophaticism is a liminal phenomenon, through which faith crosses into atheism, while atheism itself reveals the unconscious of faith'.[171]

It is perhaps worth pausing to repeat that this book makes no attempt to show that Dostoevsky was a deconstructionist *avant la lettre*, though what follows may have implications for such a reading and even seem to legitimize it. Instead, it makes the subtly but vitally different point that Dostoevsky, very early in his career, was intuitively aware of aspects of writing that much later became the focus of attention for twentieth century post-structuralism and that, far from celebrating this, it caused him deep anxiety. However, rather than suppress them or avert his gaze, he seems compulsively drawn to such features, to the extent of modelling and remodelling the structure of his works in order to afford himself, and the reader, the best possible view of them. This deconstructive anxiety pervades his whole oeuvre, and this is possibly because, whatever conventional literary models may have inspired him at any time, he was compulsively drawn to consider their implications for what he called the 'accursed questions' of human life and death. Though this anxiety is not unconnected with his depiction of Russian nihilism and with his place in the development of modern existentialism, it goes much deeper and permeates even the narrative structure of his work.

We may also pause to take a closer look at the tradition of apophatic theology itself. Vladimir Lossky offers a well-known account of the apophatic tradition and its origins in the writings of the Pseudo Dionysius, who distinguishes two possible theological ways. The one, cataphatic theology, proceeds by making affirmations about the nature of God. It may lead to some knowledge of God, but it is an imperfect way because God is by his very nature unknowable. The other way is that of apophatic or negative theology, which leads us ultimately to total ignorance. God is beyond existence, so that to approach him it is necessary to deny all that is inferior to him, that is to say, all that exists. By progressively setting aside all that can be known, one may draw near to the unknown in the darkness of ignorance, wherein He who is beyond all created things has his dwelling. The mysteries of theology are finally laid bare in a darkness of silence beyond the light of created things. Apophatic theology is a way towards mystical union with a God who is incomprehensible to us.[172] The paradox of apophatic theology, therefore, is that one may only come close to an experience of the fullness of the divine presence through an encounter with the silent darkness of total ignorance. The stakes are high. The famous New Testament passages that stand at the very centre of Johannine theology, 'The light shines in the darkness, and the darkness did not overcome it' (John 1: 5) and 'This is the message we have heard from him and proclaim to you, that God is light and in him there is no darkness at all' (1 John 1: 5), were, perhaps surprisingly, not marked by Dostoevsky in his copy of the New Testament. Perhaps they were too well known to him to need underlining. Lossky points out that unknowability does not necessarily entail agnosticism or refusal to know God. Theology must be not so much a quest for positive notions about the divine being as an experience that surpasses all understanding. It will never be abstract, working through concepts, but contemplative, raising the mind to those realities that pass all understanding.[173] This tradition, affirms Lossky, 'constitutes the fundamental characteristic of the whole tradition of the Eastern Church.'[174]

There is no evidence that Dostoevsky himself systematically explored the apophatic or negative approach to the experience of the divine, let alone that he came to an experience of deconstructive nihilism through such an exercise. However, it is entirely possible that a religious environment dominated by the apophatic tradition made him particularly susceptible to that slippage between the two to which Russell[175] and Epstein have both, in their different ways, drawn attention. The evidence of *The Idiot* suggests that Dostoevsky linked the negative side of the tradition to the Old Believers. Rogozhin, in whose dark, gloomy house the reproduction of Holbein's painting of Christ's body in the tomb hangs, is associated with them. Rogozhin confirms that his father regarded the Old Belief as nearer the truth and had a special respect for the sect of the Castrates (VIII, 173). As Richard Peace says, the religious significance of Rogozhin in the novel is clear: he is the dark side of the Russian religious temperament.[176] Much later in the novel, Myshkin reveals that his own passionate conviction, that belief in God cannot exist in anyone who has renounced his native land, was first suggested to him by an Old Believer (VIII, 453). We are evidently dealing chiefly with intuitions rather than with conscious thought processes. What we can say with certainty is that Dostoevsky and some of his characters are profoundly aware of the dark side of Russian religious traditions and are frequently drawn to those areas of belief where the dark side (heresy) meets the authentic side (Orthodoxy). Such a meeting place is that of messianic Christianity with Russian nationalism. As Margaret Ziolkowski has shown, such nationalism, which she discerns in Zosima in *The Brothers Karamazov*, sits uneasily with what she, following Fedotov, calls the kenotic tradition in Russian spirituality.[177] Since it played such an important role in his anti-European polemics, Dostoevsky's belief that Roman Catholicism's espousal of rationalism led directly to Protestantism and hence to atheistic socialism has been widely remarked and documented, but less commonly noted is his awareness that a similar evolution could be seen in the Russian soul. As Myshkin says in his tirade at his 'engagement party', 'It is quite easy for a Russian to become an atheist, much easier than for anyone else in the whole world! And Russians do not simply become atheists, but actually *believe* in atheism, as though it were a new religion, without noticing that they believe in nothingness. Such is our thirst for belief! "Whoever has no firm ground under his feet, has no God either." That's not my own expression. I heard it from an Old Believer merchant that I met on my travels' (VIII, 452–53).

Even though his theological understanding may at that age have been minimal, Dostoevsky was acquainted with apophatic spirituality from his earliest years, through his professed knowledge of the Russian monasteries. It is against this background that his own spiritual development must be seen, though it is only with his preparatory work on *The Brothers Karamazov* and his brief visit to the monastery of Optina Pustyn with Vladimir Solov'ev in the summer (26–27 June) of 1877 that he can be said to have made anything approaching a study of the monastic tradition, itself a product of the renewal of hesychasm in the Russian Church in the late eighteenth and nineteenth centuries, at the very time that the values of the European Enlightenment were taking root in the Russian educated mind. Sergei Hackel, while giving an account of the various books on the monastic tradition that Dostoevsky possessed, and which he probably acquired during his brief visit, warns us against assuming that he read them all with deep understanding.[178] Yet, Dostoevsky clearly had a grasp of the inner tensions in the monasteries. It has even been argued that Ferapont was based on an historical personage placed in Optina Pustyn by the Russian Church authorities to undermine Father Leonid, who was Elder there from 1829 to 1841.[179] In harmony with the hesychast tradition, Leonid placed a particular emphasis on humility and passive suffering.

With these considerations in mind, we may begin with Dostoevsky himself, for if we can trace the phenomenon back to the experiences of the real author it creates a presumption that similar phenomena in his work are more than a product of the reader's tendency to free-associate. It is worth recalling again the passage in his letter to Fonvizina of January 1854 that is quoted so often for so many different purposes (XXVIII, i, 176).

The letter is often the focus of disputes as to whether Dostoevsky was essentially a child of doubt and unbelief to the end of his life, as he predicted at this time, or whether he recovered his Christian faith in its fullness, as he would have liked it to be believed. The key passage tells us something else, however, which is perhaps even more important: it was in moments of the deepest spiritual affliction that he often found the greatest spiritual comfort. It can hardly be doubted by any sympathetic reader of his fiction that a slippage in the other direction also sometimes took place. He often found himself on the threshold between total despair and a vibrant hope. This was no theoretical formula or pious repetition of conventional religious dogma. Nor was it a conscious exercise in apophatic theology. It was, he protests, what he actually experienced himself. It is no surprise, then, to find that this threshold experience has its roots in a mystical experience, and that this mystical experience was felt most intensely in his epileptic fits. We know from what Dostoevsky told other people that such experiences could fill him with ecstatic joy. 'For several moments,' he told his colleague the philosopher Strakhov, 'I experience a happiness that is impossible under ordinary circumstances, and of which most people have no comprehension. I feel a complete harmony within myself and in the whole world, and this feeling is so strong and affords so much pleasure that one could give up ten years of one's life for several seconds of that ecstasy, perhaps one's whole life.'[180] However, we have to look to his fiction for a complete account of this experience and we find it of course in *The Idiot*, in Myshkin's account of his own epileptic fits, which he describes as harmony and beauty brought to the highest point of perfection, giving a previously undreamed feeling of completeness, proportion and reconciliation; an ecstatic and prayerful fusion in the highest synthesis of life, in which he understands the saying that time shall be no more. Yet stupor, spiritual darkness and idiocy are inextricably linked with this 'highest synthesis of life'. They precede it and they follow it. This ecstatic experience is not presented as an Orthodox Christian experience, or indeed as a Christian experience at all. Indeed an explicit connection is made with the Prophet Mohammed. It goes beyond theology and dogma, and bypasses divine revelation in the person of Christ. Myshkin is quite prepared to grant that it may be a symptom of illness. However, the experience is of such marvellous intensity that, illness or not, he would give his whole life for it (VIII, 188–89). This is the only description in Dostoevsky's work of a mystical experience that embraces both religious ecstasy and spiritual darkness, though Myshkin has come very close to it in his empathy with condemned men in their last moments of life on the scaffold, reflecting Dostoevsky's own traumatic experience of December 1849. However, as we have seen, Kirillov shares Myshkin's epileptic aura. He too momentarily feels eternal harmony in all its fullness, and has a joyful sensation of the whole of nature and truth for which he would give his whole life; but it is an experience alien to a physical life in which people are tormented by pain and fear, and Kirillov sees it as his quasi-messianic mission to sacrifice himself in order to demonstrate that if God does not exist then everything is a matter of the self-will of the individual who can conquer pain and fear in the most significant way possible, by taking his own life (X, 470). Together with Myshkin, Kirillov is the best example in Dostoevsky's fiction of what it is like to live on that perilous threshold between belief and unbelief. Unlike Myshkin, it appears,[181] Kirillov lives on this threshold and falls into the abyss of nihilism. He assures Petr Verkhovensky that God is necessary and so must exist, but at the same time he knows that he doesn't and can't exist, and that a man with two such ideas can't go on living. One man in a million simply won't put up with the torment and will take his own life. According to Kirillov, Stavrogin too was consumed by such an idea: if Stavrogin believes in God then he doesn't believe that he believes; if he doesn't believe, then he doesn't believe that he doesn't believe (X, 469). And Ivan Karamazov's Grand Inquisitor reverses Dostoevsky's repeated affirmation that the image of Christ burns so brightly in him that even if the truth were outside Christ, he would prefer to remain with him than with the truth. Alesha asks Ivan what happens to the old man after Jesus has kissed him on his aged lips and departed. Ivan replies, 'The kiss glows in his heart, but the old man remains with his former idea' (XIV, 239).

Kirillov exemplifies in his own person several aspects of the spiritual map drawn by Epstein. The most obvious is that he expresses the intolerable experience of living on the perilous threshold between belief and non-belief, eventually opting for the negative, nihilistic side of the apophatic heritage. He also exemplifies ways in which the religious tradition finds distorted expression when nihilism triumphs, for his messianic self-image undoubtedly derives from this tradition. Thirdly, he illustrates the particular consequences for Christianity (as opposed to other Eastern religions) of the search for nothingness. As Epstein remarks, Christianity is unlike the other religions of the East that seek a negative infinity, in that it finds its focus in 'the positive manifestation of God in the image of His Son, sent in flesh and blood to expiate the sins of man.'[182] Kirillov, like Ippolit before him in *The Idiot*, draws a picture of a dead, human Jesus, stripped of his divinity in a world without God. The pictures drawn by Kirillov and Ippolit of a deluded and powerless Jesus show how the image of Christ withers when it is no longer founded on an experience of the divine energies. Elsewhere in Dostoevsky's fiction, one glimpses either the positive or the negative aspect in isolation. The principal exponent of the atheist denial of God is Ivan Karamazov, in his poem on the Grand Inquisitor, where he refers to Satan tempting Jesus in the wilderness, as 'the dread and intelligent spirit, the spirit of destruction and non-being' (XIV, 229). Insofar as this derives from Russian Orthodoxy's characteristic tendency towards apophaticism, the affinity originates, of course, not in academic study or theological training, but in Dostoevsky's own psychopathology. It is a psychopathology that maps so well onto the apophatic tradition, as glossed by Epstein, that it can scarcely be doubted that at some level a connection was made, if only in the context of what Avril Pyman calls the Orthodox semiosphere.[183] The reticence and evasiveness of Dostoevsky's religious characters (Myshkin, Shatov, Zosima and Alesha) with respect to belief in God is wholly in keeping with this tradition. We do not know how far Dostoevsky was conscious of the coincidence; nor do we know how far his experience was facilitated by an unconscious absorption of the tradition, but that there is a striking coincidence is plain.

There are also experiences in Dostoevsky's fiction that to one degree or another partake of nature mysticism and, taken as a whole, these exhibit the same ambiguity. A notable example is that of Makar Dologoruky in *A Raw Youth*, who recalls a summer visit to the Bogorodsky Monastery. The context, as is often the case with Dostoevsky, might lead the reader to assume that it expresses an Orthodox spirituality, and the intermittent use of traditional Christian language shows that it has indeed grown in Orthodox, or perhaps sectarian, soil; but it is unclear how far this language is essential to the message and how far it simply reflects the medium of expression:

Everywhere there is inexpressible beauty! Everything is silent, the air is light; the grass grows (may God's grass continue to grow), a little bird sings (may God's little bird go on singing), a baby gives forth a cry (may God be with you little fellow, may you grow in happiness, little man!) And for the first time in my life, it seemed, I had grasped it all inwardly [...] Everything on earth is good, my dear child! [...] And that it is a mystery only makes it better; it fills the heart with awe and wonder and this awe gladdens the heart. 'All is in Thee, O Lord, and I am in Thee; have me in Thy keeping!' (XIII, 290).

In a parallel example, in *The Devils*, Maria Timofeevna makes the connection between nature mysticism and Orthodoxy that Epstein includes in his list of post-atheist phenomena:

In my view, God and nature are the same thing [...] The Virgin is the great mother earth and in that there is great joy for humanity. And every earthly sorrow and every earthly tear is a joy to us, and when you have filled the earth beneath you with tears a foot deep, you will immediately rejoice for it all (X, 116).

Still, we do not have to look far in Dostoevsky for experiences in which this mysterious mystical sense of oneness with nature is replaced by a sense of total alienation. It will not surprise us to find it in Ippolit, who demands to know what Myshkin's sunrises and sunsets and blue skies, in which every tiny gnat takes part in the banquet and chorus and has its place in the festival that has no end, has to do with him, when he alone is excluded from it (VIII, 343). But we may momentarily be more surprised to find Myshkin himself using similar images and haunted by similar questions; indeed it seems to Myshkin that Ippolit has borrowed his own words:

What sort of banquet was it, what sort of great, endless festival, which had drawn him for so long, since he was a child in fact, and which he could never join? Every morning the same bright sun rose, every morning there was a rainbow on the waterfall; every evening the highest snow-capped mountain, in the distance, at the edge of the sky, burned with a purple flame; every tiny gnat that buzzed around him in the hot ray of the sun was a participant in this great chorus: it knew its place and was happy; every blade of grass grew and was happy [...] only he knew nothing, understood nothing, neither people nor sounds, a stranger and outcast to everything (VIII, 351–52).

Yet the same Myshkin, on a different occasion, speaks words that seem to anticipate those of Makar Dolgoruky, significantly perhaps, shorn of the traditional religious language:

I just don't know how anyone can pass by a tree and not be happy at seeing it. To speak with a person and not be happy that you love him.

Oh, I simply cannot put it into words, but there are so many beautiful things at each step, things that even the most dissolute man would find beautiful. Look at a child, look at God's dawn, look at the grass, how it grows, look at the eyes that look at you and love you…(VIII, 459).

The duality in the contentless ecstasy and despair of Myshkin's epileptic fit thus seems to be echoed in the way in which he perceives the natural world.

It is said of Myshkin that he has proclaimed that 'beauty will save the world' (VIII, 317), and a link between the aesthetic and religious spheres is repeatedly made in the major novels. Shatov identifies the 'aesthetic principle' with 'the seeking of God' (X, 198) though he has, on his own admission, not yet found God. In a letter to V A Alekseev in 1876, Dostoevsky wrote 'Christ bore within himself the ideal of beauty' (XXIX, ii, 85). Many more such passages could be quoted to support the view that Dostoevsky saw a close connection between the experience of beauty and the experience of the divine. Indeed it is already there in his letter to Fonvizina. It is therefore not surprising to find in his discussions of beauty other echoes of his discussions of religion. In 1861 he had written, in an article on Dobroliubov and the question of art,

The need for beauty is greatest when a person is at odds with reality, in a state of disharmony, of conflict, when he is living most intensely, because a person lives most intensely when he is seeking, aspiring towards something. There then arises in him a completely natural desire for everything that is harmonious, for tranquillity, and in beauty is harmony and tranquillity (XVIII, 94).

But it is in Dmitry Karamazov that the reader feels the connection most intensely. In a famous passage he tells us that 'beauty is a frightening and horrifying thing! It is frightening because it is indefinable, and it cannot be defined because God has set us nothing but riddles. Here all shores meet, here all contradictions live together' (XIV, 100).

The best known, and most often quoted, example of religious ecstasy is of course that of Alesha Karamazov, who after his vigil at his Elder's bier, emerges into the open air (XIV, 328).

This experience is often seen as a continuation and confirmation of the preceding scene at Zosima's coffin, which is imbued with Orthodox Christian motifs. Yet it has to be remembered that although Alesha comes fresh from that encounter, he has also very recently experienced the full impact of his brother Ivan's statement of cosmic rebellion, with which he in part concurs, and Ivan's powerful poem about the Grand Inquisitor. Against this dual background what will strike us again, and even more forcefully than before, is that Alesha's mystical rapture, intense though it is, is expressed in terms that seem to avoid all Orthodox associations, all mention of God, all mention of the image of Christ. Alesha experiences 'something firm and unshakeable', 'an idea', 'someone' visited his soul. Whatever we may make of this, it has all the hallmarks of what Epstein identifies as a post-atheist, minimal religious experience, born of the irreconcilable clash between the light of faith and the darkness of unbelief. So far as we are told, Alesha has no countervailing experience of spiritual darkness, and perhaps we should not make too much of the stars that shine from 'the abyss'. We know that Dostoevsky had such a future in mind for him, but that future remained to be written on the author's death. However, Alesha had surely glimpsed the abyss through his brother's eyes. At all events, what we see here is not Orthodoxy in all its fullness, but the shoots of a new spiritual consciousness which may grow into Orthodoxy; it has emerged from the clash of Orthodoxy with metaphysical nihilism and could equally well, in a different context, lead to a different sort of spirituality altogether.

Zosima confronts the experience of stark unbelief and offers a recipe for converting it into faith, when Lise's mother comes to him to confess that she dare not even think of God, and is deeply troubled by the question of a life after death, a thought that unnerves her to the point of suffering, fright and terror. Perhaps she will die and find nothing. How can she be convinced? 'By the experience of active love [...] and the avoidance of lies' replies Zosima and adds, 'I predict that at the very moment when you see with horror that in spite of all your efforts you not only have not come nearer your goal but are more distant from it, you will at that very moment [...] suddenly reach your goal and clearly behold the miracle-working power of the Lord' (XIV, 51–54). This is perhaps what the English nineteenth century hymn-writer J G Whittier means in his lines about Jesus sharing with the believer 'the silence of eternity interpreted by love'.[184]

If characters such as Ippolit, Kirillov or Ivan's Grand Inquisitor exemplify the dark pole of nihilistic dread confronted by death, then Zosima's dying brother Markel best exemplifies the transition from the negative to the positive pole. When he first learns that he is not expected to live through spring, and is gently exhorted by his mother to observe Lent and take communion, he is angry and swears at God's Church. But then a wonderful change takes place in him. He does as his mother bids, and becomes joyful; he lets his nanny light the icon in his room (previously he would have blown it out), tells his mother that life is paradise, but we do not want to know it; if only we would acknowledge it, there would be paradise all over the world. He tells the servant that we must all serve each other, tells his mother that we all are guilty before everyone and that if everyone will forgive him that will be paradise. He even begs the birds' forgiveness and declares that there is so much of God's glory in the birds, trees, meadows and sky, while he alone has dishonoured everything. Here, confronted by death, Markel senses God's energies all around him, in the sacraments, in the icon, in nature, in his relations with other people. Unlike Ippolit, Kirillov and the Grand Inquisitor, he has found tranquillity and joy in the face of his own physical extinction. The image of Christ as such is still absent from his discourse, but Markel seems to have stepped over the perilous threshold onto the side of the angels.

The experience by the same individual of the desolation of the abyss and an intuition of the fullness of the divine presence does of course have a long tradition and is not unique to Dostoevsky or indeed to the theological traditions of the Eastern Church. It is not even unique to the Hebrew–Christian tradition, as the evolution of St Augustine's religious awareness from Manichaeism to Christianity amply demonstrates. St John of the Cross's *Dark Night of the Soul*, which sees the inner darkness of abandonment by God as a necessary stage on the way to purification, makes copious references to the Old Testament, notably to the Psalms and to the Book of Job. The Book of Job was, as we have seen, of enormous importance to Dostoevsky virtually all his life. In a letter to his wife from Bad Ems in 1875, he had written, 'I am reading the Book of Job, and it is bringing me to a state of morbid ecstasy; I stop reading and walk for an hour around the room, almost in tears' (XXIX, ii, 43).[185] It also plays an important part in Zosima's religious worldview. It is therefore the more remarkable that none of Job's cries of despair and dereliction appear in Zosima's testament. Perhaps by this time in his life, Zosima is in denial of such experiences. Perhaps by this stage in his life, this was also true of Dostoevsky — in his personal life — but not, as we have seen, in his fiction.

II

The Underground as the Site of Deconstructive Anxiety

If the source of Dostoevsky's positive values was that Russian Orthodox tradition in which he was nurtured as a child, his nihilistic anxieties also seem to have accompanied him from an early age, and they soon came to constitute a fundamental counter-principle permeating his work. Until 1866, and the writing and publication of *Crime and Punishment*, there is no attempt in his novels to present the fullness of Christian faith (and Diane Thompson has shown us how flawed even these presentations can be).[186] The theme of resurrection from the dead is of course present in *Notes from the House of the Dead* (1860), in which Dostoevsky presented in fictional form his experiences as a convict in the fortress of Omsk, but here it is associated as much with the release of the narrator from prison and with the natural world (the coming of Spring, the release of the wounded eagle), as with the brief account of the religious services during Holy Week. Dostoevsky's intention to map out a Christian Golden Age in *Notes from Underground* (1864) was frustrated by the censor, and no remnant of it remains, unless, as we have speculated, it would have echoed his words on the death of his first wife. However, the opposite extreme of nihilistic despair finds various forms of expression. It was in

Notes From Underground that Dostoevsky first attempted a philosophical formulation of this nihilistic despair. Traditional criticism connects this work either with contemporary polemics (Chernyshevsky and utilitarianism) or with its anticipation of modern existentialism, (Nietzsche and Kierkegaard offering the most striking parallels). Both approaches are entirely convincing in their own terms, but neither satisfactorily teases out the radical nihilism in the story, unless a connection is made with the postmodernist developments of Nietzsche's thought. Nathalie Sarraute, in writing of Dostoevsky in the context of modern literature, tells us that 'the time has long passed when it is possible for a Proust to believe that "in pushing his imagination to the limits of which his powers of penetration are capable", [he might] hope to reach that ultimate ground on which truth, the real universe, and our authentic impressions are founded. Having experienced multiple deceptions, everyone now knows that there is no ultimate ground. It has been discovered that "our authentic impressions" are multi-layered, and that these layers pile up to infinity.'[187] This is almost exactly the problem that vexes Dostoevsky's Underground Man in 1864:

> Where are the primary causes on which I can take my stand, where are my foundations? Where am I to get them from? When I exercise my powers of thinking, each of my primary causes pulls along another, even more primary, in its wake, and so on *ad infinitum*. This is the very essence of every kind of consciousness and thought. It must be another natural law (V, 108).

Almost, but not exactly, for the question of whether there is some ultimate ground beyond our reach remains unresolved. There is reason to believe that Dostoevsky saw a connection (with hindsight perhaps) with his much earlier second novel *The Double* (1847) for he saw its hero, Goliadkin, as his 'major underground type' (XXI, 264). In 1875, nearly thirty years after writing *The Double*, a period covering almost the whole of his creative life, he wrote in an unpublished preface to *A Raw Youth*:

> As for the underground and *Notes from Underground*, I take pride in the fact that I was the first to bring out the real man of the *Russian majority* and was the first to expose his deformed and tragic side. His tragedy consists in his consciousness of his own deformity. [...] I alone have brought out the tragedy of the underground, consisting of suffering, self-punishment, of consciousness of the ideal and of the impossibility of achieving it and, most of all, of the clear conviction of these unfortunate beings that everyone is in the same boat and that consequently there is no point in trying to reform. [...] The underground, the underground, the poet of the *underground* — the feuilletonists have repeated this refrain as though it were something I should be ashamed of. The little fools. It is my glory, for it is the truth. [...] The cause of the underground is the destruction of faith in general laws. '*There is nothing sacred*' (XVI, 329–30)

We shall never know *exactly* what Dostoevsky meant by 'the underground', and perhaps he never knew exactly himself. Vladimir Tunimanov has rightly warned us that these words were written many years after the writing of *Notes from Underground* (even longer after *The Double*), and cannot be taken as authoritative.[188] The obvious and most usual answer is that it describes the state of mind of his hero, who increasingly withdraws from the world of everyday reality in which he feels impotent into a world of paranoid fantasy or even hallucination, which eventually swallows him up. Undoubtedly, this was a crucial part of what Dostoevsky had in mind, but the text of *Notes from Underground* contains an even richer seam, suggested in his concluding words: 'The cause of the underground is the destruction of faith in general laws. "*There is nothing sacred*"'. In other words, this is not just a problem of integration into society or of inner division and wholeness: more fundamentally, the hero has entirely lost his faith in truth and ultimate values, and this is the underlying cause of his psychological state. The Underground Man yearns for the practical man's faith in hard reality, but cannot find it. He 'knows' that there is something better, but cannot identify it. He lives in a world that has, he believes, lost its sense of the holy and with it any sense of an ultimate reality, truth, meaning or good. It is this idea that continues to haunt Dostoevsky's world, and the thoughts of his intellectual heroes, throughout the major novels that followed and which causes them to take matters into their own hands and seek intrinsically destructive solutions. Thus Raskolnikov projects himself as a potential Napoleon with the right to transgress human laws and to deny human morality, but breaks down under the strain, realising that his theory is built on sand; thus Myshkin bemoans the fact that in the modern age people are no longer guided by a governing idea (VIII, 433) and eventually experiences a complete breakdown of his mental faculties. The idea is expressed again in Dostoevsky's notebooks for *A Raw Youth*, 'The lack of a common, guiding idea, which has affected all levels of education and all levels of development [...] This link has been lost, this guiding thread, this certain something that was supporting everything' (XVI, 68). Or, as Dostoevsky wrote in a brief article on modern youth in his *Diary of a Writer for 1876*, 'Ideas fly in the air, though always according to laws; ideas live and spread according to laws that are too difficult for us to grasp' (XXIV, 51).

　　Thematically and structurally, the issue can really be said to take wing in *The Idiot*. To complain that people are no longer guided by a governing idea is at one level merely a comment about social and ideological fragmentation. Seen in the context of the modern European mind, however, it can be reformulated as saying that they have lost faith in God, or, in Derrida's subsequent language, the transcendental signifier. If there is a religious message in this novel, it is that no amount of saintly behaviour, or religious imagery, or acts of benevolence will avail, if that central factor is missing. Ippolit, with his image of a desolate, deluded Jesus on the Cross, or those who contemplate Holbein's picture of Jesus taken from the Cross with sinking hearts, express this in its strongest form. But even Myshkin, very significantly, draws back from making his belief in God explicit. And the result is either the creation of one's own earth-bound set of values (perhaps more than one in contention) or increasing anarchy. It is entirely appropriate that the narrator is made to experience and express this predicament himself, now attempting to impose one set of genre conventions on his narrative, now another, but eventually losing confidence in any of them and rushing onwards towards an apocalyptic climax. Starting his narrative boldly in the guise of an omniscient narrator with full confidence in his hero, he progressively, in fits and starts, loses his grip both on narrative plot and on his hero himself, yielding both to the mercies of the other characters, each with their own agenda.

But it is in *The Devils* that the issue becomes really central. Stavrogin recognizes no central idea, no transcendental signifier. He seems to believe that we have to create our own system of values and does it himself at several reprises, but without gaining any permanent foothold. As we have seen, it is said that when he believes, he does not believe that he believes and, when he does not believe, he does not believe that he does not believe (X, 469). En route, however, he converts Petr Stepanovich Verkhovensky, Kirillov and Shatov to different value systems, bequeathing to them at the same time his absence of belief in a transcendental signifier. In the light of Ivan's poem on 'The Grand Inquisitor', in Dostoevsky's last novel, we may perhaps be tempted to see the philosophies of Verkhovensky, Kirillov and Shatov as embodiments of the three satanic principles rejected by Christ in the wilderness: authority, mystery and miracle. Kirillov comes nearest to the pure metaphysical nihilist, for whom the absence of God brings him to a state of desolation. His picture of Jesus on the Cross is similar to Ippolit's, though perhaps even more bleak, and he preaches that if it is not God's will, then it is our will, which we must express in its purest form, in his own case by suicide, that is by self-annihilation. Young Verkhovensky expresses a cynical political response; for him power and control are the vital things, subject to no moral constraints whatever. Shatov, of course, expresses the Slavophile creed, that so appealed to Dostoevsky himself, but with one vital omission: he too cannot 'yet' bring himself to declare his belief in God. Perhaps it is Verkhovensky senior who comes closest to such belief, in his dying hours, too late to influence anyone positively, after a lifetime spent undermining such an outcome. But even his revelation seems to depend on a highly questionable identification of the Christian God with the 'eternal and infinite Idea', derived not from the Orthodox tradition but from German idealist philosophy (X, 506).

And it is, of course, in *The Brothers Karamazov* that the issue is made explicit, not by the representatives of Orthodox Christianity but by the chief representative of metaphysical nihilism, Ivan Karamazov, in his declaration that if there is no God and immortality, then everything is permitted. (If there is no transcendental signifier then there is no ultimate sanction for human values.) We shall note that the narrative anarchy that prevails in *The Idiot* and *The Devils* has been reduced in *The Brothers Karamazov*. The narrator retains a fairly stable and consistent gaze. He does not get bogged down in questions about his role as narrator or his proper point of view. He claims to be an eyewitness to some of the public events, but not to be a participant in the central drama or in any way to be implicated in the action (though of course if we are 'all responsible for everything' that must apply to him too). He may make little attempt to disguise his personal sympathies and antipathies in his choice of language, but he reserves his judgement on the central religious and philosophical issue, preferring, when he expresses a view at all, a psychological approach.

As indeed, in the last resort, does Dostoevsky himself, who did not attempt to resolve the issue in any text that has come down to us. If, indeed, he continued to hold that 'even if it could be proved that the truth were outside Christ he would choose to remain with Christ rather than with the truth', that does nothing to resolve it. While there can be little doubt that at times he thought that he had found a solution, there can be equally little doubt that the spectre of unbelief repeatedly came back to haunt him. The way in which this affected his fiction can perhaps best be exemplified in relation to *The Idiot*.

III

The Self-adjusting Novel: Dostoevsky's 'Idiot'

Whatever role Dostoevsky, or his readers, may assign to the positive religious sub-text, there can be little dispute that it is the negative pole that dominates his narrative and motivates most of his most memorable characters. Dostoevsky did, however, make one attempt to write a novel in which the centre of gravity was a Christ-like figure. *The Idiot* continues to perplex us. Most modern critics agree that it breaks all the rules and contains flaws that in a lesser writer would be seen as signs of gross incompetence. Full of inconsistencies in characterization and plot, with false beginnings and unmotivated events, threatening at times to lose its way and collapse into incoherence, it nevertheless remains one of the acknowledged masterpieces of the novel.[189] Gary Saul Morson might dispute the word 'nevertheless'. Perhaps it succeeds precisely because it rejects the Aristotelian concept of poetic structure, at every turn frustrating and confusing the reader or critic nurtured in this tradition, and at the same time setting up a new, and equally valid, model of experience, in which we intuitively recognize genius. Morson has proposed 'tempics' as a generic name for this new model.[190]

Stressing that in *The Idiot* we experience events in progress, not events recapitulated with hindsight once they have fallen into a teleological pattern, and that this reflects Dostoevsky's own creative process, Morson recognizes it as a high-risk strategy. Morson's is an inspired idea. The question he fails to address in his path-breaking article, however, is what makes the difference between brilliant success and dismal failure in the realisation of tempics, the difference one might say between an *Idiot* and a *Raw Youth*.

We shall not be able to answer this question fully in a few pages. A satisfactory answer would have to take into account the countervailing Aristotelian impulse, which Robin Feuer Miller has so persuasively mapped out in her classic study.[191] After all, as Robert Jackson reminded us more than thirty years ago, there is also a 'quest for form' in Dostoevsky,[192] a striving to contain 'tempics' within a 'poetics' or at least to find the right balance between them. Using Roland Barthes' metaphor, we may say that Dostoevsky's novels manifest an urge to present experience both as seen from the top of the Eiffel Tower and as seen in walking through the streets of Paris.[193] *The Idiot* manifests this programme (for Paris read St Petersburg) by advancing briefly and tentatively along various traditional thorough-fares (using the Gothic map, the apocalyptic map, the map of the novel of manners and so on) and then running into blind alleys or entirely uncharted territory, suddenly emerging into new novelistic space which (at least at first) may seem strangely familiar or reassuringly weird. It is not clear how far the narrator, our guide, is working from instinct, or trusting his experi-ence to steer him across new terrain, or entirely bemused. His lurches late in the novel into discussions of the problems of writing novels and about ordinary people (VIII, 383–84) suggest a desperate grasping for familiar points of reference. Yet whatever may happen in the novel on the level of the narrator, and whatever anguish the real author may have experienced in drafting his narrative in his notebooks, our intuition tells us that on the level of the implied author (the imaginary authorial mind that would be able to account for the whole text, independently of what the real author intended or the fictional narrator actually says) the narrative finally succeeds in finding its natural balance.

In this brief section, I wish to examine an additional and strangely neglected factor: the degree to which Dostoevsky's last minute inspiration of making his hero a 'perfectly beautiful man' not only involved abandon-ing all his previous drafts for the novel, being, as Dostoevsky himself acknowledged, an unprecedented project in world literature, but also defied the natural balance of the Dostoevskian novel, as experienced on the level of implied author. In other words, it was precisely because he had taken the risky and unprecedented step of making his 'perfectly beautiful man' the centre of attention and of the action, and that this had, against all the odds, succeeded so well in Part I, that Dostoevsky was at a complete loss to know how to continue and what existing model to follow, and still needed to entertain, explore and juggle all the possibilities he could think of, including those suggested by current events. His surviving notebooks provide overwhelming evidence that this was actually the case. We may speculate that he entertained the Gospels as a model, and indeed Myshkin's fate in St Petersburg has sometimes been compared by critics to Jesus' crucifixion in Jerusalem.[194] But the challenge of developing the plot towards some kind of personal 'resurrection' was one with which Dostoevsky clearly had great difficulty within the confines of nineteenth century realism. A novel with a perfectly beautiful man at its centre was not only a daring project; it was one that seriously challenged the laws of gravity obtaining in Dostoevsky's own imaginative world. It was as though Dostoevsky had had the sudden inspiration of trying to write a novel 'upside down' or 'on its side' and, that, once he let go of it, he found it constantly trying to right itself, just as a Kelly doll (a *nevaliashka* or *van'ka-vstan'ka* in Russian) tries to resume an upright position as soon as the pressure holding it down is released. What we then witness is the process by which the component parts of the novel — characters, events, narrator — dart around trying to establish new relationships and alignments by a process of trial and error, until eventually a version of the familiar Dostoevskian model emerges and the plot is free to work itself out with a sudden rush of energy in the normal way. We should expect to witness this process in its most energetic form in the notebooks, as indeed we do, but in *The Idiot* we also witness it to an unusual degree in the novel itself. If I am right, underlying the Dostoevskian novel at the level of implied author, is a self-stabilising, transformational system that would be instantly recognisable to a structuralist critic, with one very important caveat: unlike the traditional semiotic model of the structuralists, it is not sealed off from external influences. The importance of this caveat is made plain by Morson's work on tempics.

So far I have been talking metaphorically. What evidence is there to support such a thesis? The first thing to do is to reach agreement on what constitutes the Dostoevskian model in question. We are not dealing here, it seems to me, with types of plot in the conventional sense, but rather with dynamic models of human relationships and perceptions of human experience that draw plots and sub-plots into their field. Fortunately, Dostoevsky gives us a clue, and he does so in the passage that is perhaps the most often quoted in the whole novel, and that I have paused on before. Ippolit says:

> 'You can be certain that Columbus was happy not when he actually discovered America, but during the process of discovering it. You can be certain that his happiest moment of all was perhaps exactly three days before he discovered the New World, when his mutinous crew almost turned the ship back to Europe in despair [...] It is life that matters, life alone — the continuous and everlasting process of discovery, and not the discovery itself' (VIII, 327).

Let us translate this into a statement about the Dostoevskian novel: 'You can be sure that the Dostoevskian novel achieves its natural balance not when it focuses on a realisation of the ideal, but when it presents the process of discovering it. You can be certain that it achieves its natural balance when, though actually on the verge of making the discovery, its rebellious and sceptical characters (its mutinous crew) are on the point of rejecting all possibility of it. It is life that matters, life alone, the continuous and everlasting process of discovery, and not the discovery itself'. If there is any truth in this translation, then it is easy to see that Dostoevsky was flying in the face of nature (his own nature as a novelist) in placing a 'perfectly beautiful man' (the New World discovered) at the forefront and centre of his new novel. What we then witness is that nature reasserting its rights and wreaking its revenge. However, it will not do simply to state this thesis. Some convincing demonstration of its plausibility and consequences is required.

The creative history of the novel can itself be advanced in support of the argument. The extensive surviving notebooks show that Dostoevsky's original idea revolved around the usual mutinous crew. As Edward Wasiolek says, 'The heroine of the first plan is already in essential gesture the Nastasia Filippovna of the final version: pursued by General Epanchin, Gania, Rogozhin, Totsky and the Idiot, and attracting and rejecting throughout the novel both Rogozhin and the Idiot [...] The Idiot's passions are violent, he has a burning need of love, a boundless pride, and out of pride he means to dominate himself, conquer himself. He takes delight in humiliation'.[195] The idea of a saintly Myshkin emerged abruptly only at the very last minute, in the seventh plan, and with it the notion that he would restore Aglaia's humanity, exercise an influence over Rogozhin and rehabilitate Nastas'ia Filippovna (IX, 252).[196] As Wasiolek points out, even in the early drafts Dostoevsky had held out the prospect that in the end the hero would be saved by love, much as Raskolnikov had been in *Crime and Punishment*,[197] but that hero, like Raskolnikov, had been conceived as proud and inwardly divided, a representative of the mutinous crew. The notion of a hero who already embodies the ideal, attractive though it was, was clearly incompatible with the model outlined above. Dostoevsky's second problem was that none of the characters who seem to be most closely involved with Myshkin and most likely to form the central plot-line, was a suitable spokesman or spokeswoman for life's mutinous crew. Nastas'ia Filippovna and Rogozhin, though certainly mutinous, were insufficiently cerebral and articulate for the purpose, Lebedev articulate but insufficiently serious, Gania altogether too shallow, though each of them is either pushed into the background (first Nastasia Filippovna, then Rogozhin) or into the foreground in new roles (Gania and Lebedev). Dostoevsky seems to experiment with Rogozhin as the spokesman at the beginning of Part II, and the experiment turns out to be partly successful and partly a failure, for the motif of Holbein's picture of Christ taken from the Cross, a copy of which Rogozhin owns and which stops Myshkin in his tracks with its faith-destroying potential, is preserved and taken up again, while its owner (Rogozhin) is made to relinquish intellectual ownership to Myshkin and Ippolit, especially to Ippolit, in whose confession it becomes a central image (VIII, 338–39). It is the medium through which the centre of gravity of the novel eventually passes from Myshkin to Ippolit, and the note is struck, let it be noticed, very shortly after Myshkin's return to St Petersburg or, speaking in biographical terms, within two short chapters of Dostoevsky's apparently floundering introduction to Part II. To get himself out of his narrative predicament, he thus makes use of a powerful and dramatic autobiographical experience, which challenges the very basis of his hero's Christian world-view, an experience that seeps into the texture of the narrative and crucially re-emerges at a vital later point in Ippolit's confession.

In fact Ippolit was not, as some critics appear to think, a last minute, gratuitous intrusion into the plot. After considerable difficulty and delay, Dostoevsky got the first two chapters of Part II to his publisher in the third week of April 1868, but his notes for 12 March already show Ippolit reflecting on how even a man like Rogozhin, who lives life with all his strength, seems to understand his situation, and pondering on why the world is so constructed that some are condemned to die, whether it is possible to love for just two weeks and whether it would be possible to commit murder in the time that is left to him (IX, 223).[198] The Ippolit of the notes is already planning that public confession and 'suicide at sunrise' which eventually he is to attempt in Part III, Chapter 7 of the novel, and reflecting that perhaps he does not understand Christ at all (IX, 224). And it is perhaps significant that among notes apparently made on the same day Dostoevsky had jotted down enigmatically: 'About Christopher Columbus' (IX, 221).

What this shows is that in the first stages of his rethinking, when his thoughts were in turmoil, but neither he nor the novel were yet ready for it, Dostoevsky was already feeling the need of Ippolit as intellectual ballast to restore the novel's natural balance. The notes show him continuing to experiment with the Aglaia–Myshkin–Nastasia Filippovna triangle, exploring, it would seem, every possible outcome, some of which involve Rogozhin; then devising the episode of 'Pavlishchev's son,' which was to precede Ippolit's confession in the final version; and then back to the motivation for the love triangle and indications that Myshkin is to run a children's club. There are notes about Myshkin's personality and the importance of showing him in action, with the famous 'Prince Christ' jottings (IX, 246, 249, 253). There are indications that there is to be a discussion about Russia. There are reflections on the plot and on the possibility of parallel plots, and occasional mentions of minor characters. By 15 April, Dostoevsky had decided to use mysterious events during Myshkin's absence in Moscow to motivate subsequent developments. The absence had been extended from three weeks in an early jotting to six months (IX, 216, 255). But it is fairly obvious that Dostoevsky still conceives of the novel revolving round a love story (even if it is a Dostoevskian one involving a fair degree of manipulation and nastiness) and that it lacks intellectual articulation of the note of cosmic anguish that had characterized *Crime and Punishment* and was in due course to characterize *The Devils* and *The Brothers Karamazov*. Notwithstanding Robert Lord,[199] Dostoevsky had denied himself the possibility of giving this role to the saintly Myshkin. It is in his notes for 11 June that Ippolit and his death resurface briefly (IX, 275).

In the novel itself, Ippolit had begun to emerge in Part II as a powerful if marginal character. It is therefore of significance that Dostoevsky's brief, surviving drafts for Parts III and IV devote so much space to him. And here comes the surprise. For Dostoevsky, the development of Ippolit was not just authorial self-indulgence of a kind that could have been well excised. In a note for 15 September, he wrote, 'Write tersely and powerfully about Ippolit. Focus the whole plot on him' (IX, 280). Earlier in the same sequence, he had referred to him as 'the main axis of the whole novel', having a hold even on the prince, though he is aware that he can never dominate him; being an indispensable image to Aglaia, dominating Rogozhin and dominating and inciting Gania (IX, 277–78). If Ippolit is the main axis of the whole novel and the centre of the plot, this is neither plot in the normal sense nor in the sense in which Dostoevsky has been exploring all its possible twists and turns in his drafts. If we are to take this note seriously, we have to grant that Dostoevsky is talking about another sort of structure, in which people and events are dominated by emotionally powerful images of human experience and manipulated and incited, as we see in the novel itself, into accepting an image of the world in which the ultimate forces are unremittingly hostile to all human ideals and uplifting illusions, which threatens to undermine Myshkin's commitment to Christian compassion and is all too plausible as a backdrop to the narrated events. A novel that begins with a 'positively beautiful man' at its centre ends with a twisted rebel (a ringleader of the mutinous crew) as its 'axis'. Thus the novel ends the 'right way up', thanks to Ippolit, and the motif which enables the transition from the one to the other is that of public execution, first introduced by the prince himself in Part I, taken up by Lebedev with his prayers for the Countess du Barry and interpretation of the Apocalypse early in Part II, and developed in chapter four of the same part through Rogozhin's copy of Holbein's picture of Christ taken from the Cross. The rest of the novel shows the values implicit in these cosmic images gradually insinuating themselves into the fabric of the drama of romantic liaisons, and subverting them.

Gary Saul Morson writes of the passages containing Ippolit:

> So brilliant are these passages that the novel would be seriously impoverished if they were removed. And yet, had they not been written, one would not notice that they were missing, a test that, from Aristotle on, indicates something that does not belong.[200]

Yet Morson is surely making a false equation here. We may agree with his first sentence, and even with the view that we would not notice if they were missing, but with every respect to Aristotle, that does not mean that they do not belong. It is not just that we, the readers, would be the poorer for not having them. The novel itself would, if I am right, lack any full and adequate articulation of its spiritual centre of gravity. These passages may be capable of standing on their own. But the novel is not capable of standing without them, without, that is, leaving a void at its very core. Of course Dostoevsky was quite capable of leaving voids at the cores of his novels, and of exploiting them for artistic purposes, as he does with the key period Myshkin spends in Moscow between Parts I and II of this very novel, but he was evidently aware that this one was so vast that it would present the reader with an insurmountable challenge.

None of this means, as some may be tempted to infer, that such negative images represent the 'true meaning' of the novel, or the 'ultimate truth' of Dostoevsky's metaphysics. On the contrary, Myshkin's presence continues, even when he is again in the grip of his illness, to purvey that combination of innocence, compassion and idealism, which is at once his glory and his downfall. Nastasia Filippovna herself is the source of one of the most idyllic scenes in the novel, in which Christ sits with little children (VIII, 379–80). And, as Erik Egeberg rightly points out, even Ippolit, who maintains that he has hated the prince for five months, admits that he may love him (VIII, 322):

> His feelings towards the Prince are indeed ambiguous and oscillating, but Ippolit accepts his invitation to spend his last days among the people and trees of Pavlovsk. The last days of Ippolit also testify, by the way, to the fact that Prince Myshkin's initiative might have been successful.[201]

Egeberg goes on to speculate that when Lebedev says that 'the Devil equally rules humanity until a temporal limit, unknown to us' (VIII, 311), he may be expressing Dostoevsky's own view that the contemporary world was doomed but that an undefined future might bring salvation. The New World, in other words, may be just over the horizon. The particular role that Ippolit is made to play in this novel may also be seen as an anticipation of Dostoevsky's subsequent confession that his own 'Hosanna' had emerged from 'an immense furnace of doubt' (XXVII, 86). This experience of a rebirth of Christian faith through a searing doubt leaves its mark not only on the personal experiences of his individual characters, but even more importantly, on the very shape and dynamics of his novels.

As we shall see in more detail later, it was a lesson that Dostoevsky did not forget in the creation of his next and last major saintly hero, Alesha Karamazov. In making him the son of Fedor, and the brother of Dmitry and Ivan, even, apparently, of Smerdiakov, and making him share the limelight with them, he avoided the problem that he had encountered in writing *The Idiot*, and, in particular, his difficulties in proceeding beyond the end of Part I. Yet the reader may feel thankful that he did write *The Idiot* in this way. To live through, with Dostoevsky, a topsy-turvy novel in the process of righting itself is a magnificent artistic experience. And it would have been a very much lesser work, and very much less discussed, if he had opened it in any other way.

Whatever irregularity *The Idiot* may manifest on the level of the narrator's text (the plot), is amply compensated for by its balance on the level of implied author, where its meaning ultimately resides. Perhaps this is the way to explain both the novel's frequently observed imperfections and also its widely acknowledged success. On the level of implied author, as I have tried to show, the religious significance of the text is to be found not in an Orthodox sub-text, but in the shoots of a new spirituality appearing in a text that seems designed, though ultimately in vain, to suppress it altogether. For the centre of gravity of Dostoevsky's novels remains a world in which direct access to divine truth is impossible, in which the source of ultimate values and truths remains beyond human reach, in which his characters live (whether they are conscious or it or not) on the cusp of the fullness of faith and the abyss of nothingness, and in which most of them either try to disguise this by a life based on this-worldly preoccupations and pieties, or else risk in their quest for God slipping into that black hole of nihilism, which is the atheist equivalent of hell. Thompson is right to find the novel lacking as an expression of Orthodoxy but perhaps wrong to be depressed by its overall spiritual tenor, for the shoots of minimal Christianity have not been choked. The fact that they seem frail as the novel closes merely emphasizes that in reality they have been frail, but not impotent, all along.

IV

Bracketing Out the Referent: The Undecidability of Dostoevsky's Text

We have seen how the fateful meeting point of faith and unbelief is reflected in Dostoevsky's own experience and also in that of some of his major characters. I have argued that it is actually the negative aspect of this duality that dominates the structure of his major fiction, originating in his early work. Since this early work owes an acknowledged debt to his reading of Gogol, in whom folk superstition, with its terrifying images of the devil and his agents, dominates the narrative, and to the European traditions of the Gothic novel and the supernatural horror stories of Hoffmann, this bias evidently found reinforcement in the popular reading of the 1840s. Yet, notwithstanding constant references to the devil and the diabolical, it is not the supernatural that overwhelms the world of Dostoevsky's mature fiction. It is rather the threat of an ultimate nothingness, of a reality that evaporates before one's gaze. This vision merges with Dostoevsky's perception of the 'unreality of St Petersburg', of which one famous account is to be found in *A Raw Youth*:

I can't express my impressions properly, because it's all fantasy, that is, poetry, or consequently rubbish; all the same I have been and still am troubled by one completely nonsensical thought, 'There they all are, rushing hither and thither, and perhaps it's all someone or other's dream, and there's not a single real person there, not a single actual deed. Whoever has been dreaming will suddenly wake up — and everything will suddenly disappear.' But I've let myself get carried away (XIII, 113).[202]

Yet this deconstructive anxiety is not merely a thematic motif in Dostoevsky. It is embedded in the narrative techniques that he uses, from the very first to the very last. For the narrative structure of Dostoevsky's novels is so constructed as to facilitate slippage between the view that there is a higher truth beyond human knowledge and the contrary view that beyond the infinitely receding layers of knowability there is nothing at all. In this brief concluding section I shall try, without lingering too long on examples, to point to some of the ways in which this effect is achieved.

As one of Aldous Huxley's characters in *The Genius and the Goddess* says:

'The trouble with fiction…is that it makes too much sense…Fiction has unity, fiction has style…' He leaned over and touched the back of a battered copy of *The Brothers Karamazov*. 'It makes so little sense that it's almost real.'[203]

In a letter to V S Solov'ev of 16 (28) July 1876, Dostoevsky quoted the famous line from Tiutchev's poem *Silentium* ('a thought, once uttered, is a lie'), this time not to make a point about reality but to draw attention to strategies authors deploy in representing their perception of reality, and about the effect these have on the reader:

If the most celebrated minds, Voltaire, for example, had, instead of using allusions, hints, innuendoes and elisions, suddenly decided to declare everything, to suddenly reveal their deepest secrets and their inner being, you can take it from me that they would not have had a tenth of the effect. On the contrary, people would have laughed at them. In fact people generally dislike final words, 'uttered' thoughts, affirming that *a thought once uttered is a lie* (XXIX, ii, 102).

When a writer expresses his vision directly, he reduces the effect on the reader by a factor of ten. Readers do not like 'final words': they quote Tiutchev back at you. This is but a preliminary hint of one of Dostoevsky's narrator's major strategies, a strategy, it might be claimed, that makes the apophatic principle a principle of narration in general. Much might be and much has been said about the role of narratorial silence in Dostoevsky's final novel. No attempt will be made to rehearse it in full in this book. Dostoevsky's narrator in *The Brothers Karamazov* is notoriously reticent about the moment of parricide itself; even about whether the murder is in fact a case of parricide, except in the moral sense in which all the sons are culpable by thought or omission: Smerdiakov's relationship to Fedor Karamazov is never put entirely beyond doubt. For that matter, the reader's confidence in the whole, apparently reliable, narrator is subtly unsettled — typically for Dostoevsky — by one of his minor characters, the Defence Counsel at Dmitry's trial, who accuses the Prosecutor of taking hold of individual facts and making his own novel out of them (XV, 156). By way of reply, the Prosecutor accuses the Defence Counsel of doing the same thing (XV, 174). The reflective and attentive reader cannot entirely escape the reflection that this is exactly what Dostoevsky's narrator is doing too.

Dostoevsky had long ago learnt the advantages of eschewing clear explanations of mysterious events or personality traits. To some extent this discovery may have been forced upon him by the suppression of the passage on the Christian Golden Age in *Notes from Underground* or the chapter 'At Tikhon's' in *The Devils* (which he decided never to restore). Yet *The Idiot*, where no such external pressure was exerted, exemplifies the technique supremely well, through the narrator's professed uncertainties about the key period that Myshkin spends in Moscow between the events of the first and second parts of the novel and progressive loss of control over the development of the plot. The relativisation of the narrative point of view vis-à-vis 'what really happened' is one of the principal techniques that Dostoevsky uses to trap the reader in a web of words whose relationship to 'reality' always remains ambiguous.

There is, of course, a sense in which fiction always, and by definition, brackets out the referent (the 'reality' beyond human discourse). Even where it takes its inspiration from real-life people and events, as Dostoevsky's novels often do, it knowingly transforms them into fiction, thereby breaking the link with 'real-life' models. Even where the narrator purports to be chronicling real life, we know, in fiction, that this is but a pretence. What Dostoevsky does additionally, and from the very beginning of his career, is to bracket out the author as well, or at the very least to blur his identity. Of Dostoevsky's thirty-four published works of fiction only eight even purport to be told consistently by an impersonal omniscient narrator, that is, the real author, and only one of the five major novels for which he is world-famous. Even this (*Crime and Punishment*) was originally drafted in the first person and retains many of the characteristics of a first person narrative.

From the very beginning of his career to its end, Dostoevsky seems to resort to every trick available to him, and some that might be considered illegitimate, not only to bracket out the real author (himself) from his fiction, but also to confuse the reader about where both reader and author stand in relation to the narrative, by relativising or arbitrarily shifting the narrative point of view. His first novel (*Poor Folk*) was written as an exchange of letters between hero and heroine. In *The Double*, ostensibly told by an omniscient narrator, the narrator's point of view is drawn inextricably into the orbit of its emotionally and mentally disturbed fictional hero. His next tale is an exchange of letters between two male characters ('A novel in nine letters'), and although the next two ('Mr Prokharchin' and 'The Landlady') are ostensibly told from the point of view of an impersonal omniscient narrator, the narrator's voice is either drawn into the hero's consciousness or the narrative itself is so fantastic as to raise serious doubts about its reliability. 'The Landlady', in fact, brings together three characters, all of whom are emotionally disturbed and seem to confuse reality with fantasy, and all of whom claim to give a reliable account of events. The reader is left totally baffled. Whatever other significance this unsuccessful story may have in the development of Dostoevsky's fiction, there can be no doubt that it was conceived, and realized, as an experiment in the juxtaposition of unreliable narrators. 'A Weak Heart', The Honest Thief', and 'A Christmas Party and a Wedding' are all told by fictional first person narrators, while interference between the voices of the narrator and character, typical of Dostoevsky's other tales of the 1840s, is to be found in 'Someone else's wife and a husband under the bed.'[204] 'White Nights' is told in the first person by a fictional hero, the unfinished novel *Netochka Nezvanova* by a fictional heroine; *The Little Hero*, *Uncle's Dream*, *The Village of Stepanchikovo and its Inhabitants*, *The Humiliated and the Oppressed* and *Notes from the House of the Dead* all have fictional first person narrators (the last introduced by a fictional author). Whereas 'A Nasty Story' and *The Eternal Husband* have impersonal omniscient narrators, Dostoevsky's first major work, *Notes from Underground*, is again narrated by its hero. *The Crocodile*, though narrated by an omniscient narrator, is a highly fantastic tale whose 'realism' resides in the setting and narrative style rather than the plot. *The Gambler* is told by a neurotic hero and the narrative point of view of *Crime and Punishment*, although ostensibly omniscient, remains close to that of its hero for the greater part of the text. The narrative point of view of both *The Idiot* and *The Devils*[205] shifts about so much that the voice of the narrator in both novels has been the subject of repeated scholarly and critical studies, while *A Raw Youth* is again told in the first person by a fictional hero who has a strong emotional investment in giving form to his disordered experience, and eventually admits defeat. 'Bobok' is again a first person narrative by a fictional character, 'A Boy at Christ's Christmas Party' and 'The Peasant Marei' are first-person narratives by a novelist–diary writer, 'A Gentle Spirit' and 'The Dream of a Ridiculous Man' are first person narratives by fictional heroes and *The Brothers Karamazov* (though you might never guess it to read much standard criticism) is a first person chronicle by a fictional non-participant inhabitant of the town where the events take place, whose point of view is far from objective. All this could be put down to literary experimentation, but why this kind of highly risky and repeated experiment? What is the point? One way of answering this question is to say that Dostoevsky compulsively distances himself as author from his narrative voices in ways that almost always raise questions about the trustworthiness of the narrative itself and often raise questions about its coherence. To close one's eyes to such features, or to see them as flaws, may facilitate naive readings, or readings in terms of the 'implied author', but it wilfully neglects in pursuit of an illusory coherence one of the most important features of Dostoevsky's work, namely his obsessive avoidance of anything that might be mistaken for a stable, objective representation of a reality 'out there'. Even when his narrator makes claims of this sort (of objectivity and of the sifting the evidence), as he does in *The Devils*, his stance is so inconsistent as to undermine his own claims.

Whatever Dostoevsky's conscious reasons for experimenting with narrative voice throughout his career and frequently slipping from one convention to another within the same work of fiction, the effect was to undermine the integrity of the narrative voice in every possible way and to invest it with an ambiguity that increases what Roger Poole calls the undecidability of his texts. By 'undecidability',[206] Poole means a resistance to what he calls 'blunt readings',[207] that is readings that seek to reduce the text to a single meaning. Although Dostoevsky has attracted many such readings, some of them expressed with a great deal of passion, and their authors have inevitably seen rival blunt readings as mistaken, the very existence of so many competing and at first sight highly plausible blunt readings gives us reason to pause and reflect. Such reflection leads to the conclusion that while many of them are defensible, indeed highly attractive, they still leave some important aspect of the text unaccounted for. Dostoevsky's texts are in this sense not simply polyphonic in Bakhtin's sense, that is they are not simply vehicles for many contending voices: more importantly, they allow us to read the text through the eyes of these different speakers in such a way that much of the narrative is reducible to their points of view, but never quite, and this 'never quite' leads us on to explore the viability of other readings suggested by the elements that refuse to be assimilated. This is no less true of Dostoevsky's last novel, *The Brothers Karamazov*, which can be read equally persuasively from Ivan's or Zosima's points of view, but in neither case without qualification. This unassimilable part of the text is what Derrida has called the *supplément*, and we can see it working better than anywhere in Dostoevsky's second short novel, *The Double*, one that he was later to regard as a failure and immature, but the basic idea of which he was always to regard as one of his most important discoveries (XXVI, 65).

On the surface we are faced with a hero (Goliadkin) who meets his own double in the government department where he works, and who feels more and more persecuted by him until he eventually goes out of his mind. But we find in *The Double* a narrative in which both narrator and hero are subject to dissolution, in which both the author–narrator and real-life are bracketed out, and from which no single 'truth' emerges. Whatever strategies we, as readers, employ to find a single overall meaning we can never find any satisfactory answers to questions like: is there really a double out there or is he partly or wholly a figment of the hero's imagination; if there is really someone out there, does he really resemble the hero as much as the hero thinks, and is he really persecuting him; if we have reason to doubt the reality of the hero's perception of the double, can we rely on that of the narrator, who seems to get drawn into the hero's field of vision? What is really going on; where do we as readers stand? Where does the author stand? Though we may try various hypotheses, like a succession of critics down the years, there is always something left in the narrative that seems to elude and falsify it, some imperfection in the underlying rationale of the fiction, as traditional criticism would have it. Every hypothesis seems eventually to crumble, leaving a meaningless void, as though, to use Dostoevsky's own metaphor, it were someone else's dream. And that the narrative is as a consequence replete with anxiety no sensitive reader would doubt.[208] This is the nature of the underground, and it is a phenomenon to which Dostoevsky returns again and again in his fiction throughout his career.

In a brief but brilliant article written as a tribute to the French Dostoevsky specialist Jacques Catteau, William Mills Todd III[209] makes some acute observations about *Notes from Underground*, from which we may take lessons for all Dostoevsky's work. He reminds us of Jakobson's communication model, comprising the roles in any speech event of context, addresser, message, addressee, contact and code. Jakobson suggests that imaginative literature renders message, addresser, addressee and reference ambiguous, split, or double-sensed,[210] to which Scholes has added that we sense literariness when any of these six factors loses its simplicity and becomes multiple or duplicitous. Mills Todd's originality lies in his claim that *Notes from Underground*, Dostoevsky's most intricate work, complicates each and every one of these communicative elements: all are duplicitous. The addresser, he claims, is at least trebly a fiction: a creation of Fedor Dostoevsky; his own fiction as a dreamer who has created a life for himself; and a creation of the romantic fictions he reads. The addressee is likewise duplicitous: are the 'gentlemen' to whom the fiction is addressed, real or invented? And is the real addressee these 'gentlemen' or the narrator himself? If so how does this project the real reader? The context (or referent) of the text is likewise ambiguous. It claims cognitive value yet revels in literary fabrication, and the narrator constantly warns the reader that he is lying. Likewise with the spatial and temporal coordinates: St Petersburg is presented as abstract and premeditated, and 'the underground' is at once a psychological, a political and a physical metaphor. One could add to this that it is also a philosophical and religious metaphor. Finally the codes in which the narrative is presented vary according to the narrator's 'performative goals', from the code of social romanticism to that of the realistic exposé, to which one might add that of 'the confessional'. The only point at which I should want to take issue with Mills Todd is in the formulation of his introductory sentence, which reads, 'However much his readers have taken him to be a prophet, philosopher, journalist and political thinker, Dostoevsky's vocation was imaginative literature, the art of writing.'[211] This surely contains a false opposition. It is precisely on such literary devices that the deconstructive aspect of Dostoevsky's philosophy is based.

If we move on directly to the major novels, we find that *The Idiot*, as Robin Feuer Miller[212] has shown, is told by a narrator who not only shifts from apparent omniscience to the relative knowledge of the chronicler of events, and from that to the stance of novelist struggling to make sense of his material, until eventually he seems to run out of patience with his hero and rush on towards the dénouement, almost out of control, but who also, in telling his tale, adopts at one point the style of a sympathetic narrator, at another that of the comic novelist of (ill-) manners, at another of the Gothic novelist, at another of a Dickensian humourist. While the change in tone may be accounted for by a change in the nature of the material (that is, by positing a narrator who adopts the voice that seems most appropriate), the shifts from omniscience to the point of view of a chronicler with limited vision and from this to the struggling novelist (whatever the biographical explanation) leaves the attentive reader feeling dizzy and confused. Once again our attention is drawn to the conventionality of the medium, and our uncertainty about 'what is supposed really to be going on' is aggravated. *The Idiot* is an extreme case of narratorial confusion, but *The Devils* is not far behind. Although I have argued elsewhere[213] that the inconsistencies of narrative point of view in this novel are ultimately reconcilable on psychological grounds, it still remains the case that we are left with a shifting narrative point of view that, while it constantly appeals to objective criteria for the evidence it presents, is nevertheless that of an involved participant. This participant narrator, while he participates on the very fringes of the action, observes, or fantasizes, a great deal of it, and in this respect he is typical of the narrators of Dostoevsky's last three great novels, ostensibly keeping their distance while imaginatively deeply involved.

Notwithstanding the reservations we have noted above, it has often been remarked that Dostoevsky's last novel has a fictional narrator who provides a stable point of view untypical of Dostoevsky's major fiction. We shall return to this and related issues in the next chapter. Relatively stable it may be, but here Dostoevsky uses another limiting technique: his narrator's dominant point of view is that of common sense. One of the most disconcerting aspects of *The Double* was that it had no common-sense yardstick against which the reader could measure the veracity or plausibility of the various possible accounts of what was actually going on. By the time he had reached maturity Dostoevsky was evidently aware of this and, however unstable the narrative point of view may be, the narrator, and through him the reader, can usually manage to identify the point of view of common sense. In *Notes from Underground*, the narrator repeatedly projects this point of view onto the reader. In the major novels it is often a minor character who plays this role: Razumikhin in *Crime and Punishment*, Radomsky in *The Idiot*, the narrator, fitfully, in *The Devils*. In *The Gambler*, interestingly enough, this role was allocated to the Englishman, Mr Astley. But the point of view of common sense is narrower than fantastic realism. The narrator of *The Devils* therefore abandons common sense when dealing with the most dramatic and 'fantastic' episodes in his story and adopts the tone of a Gothic novelist, like his predecessor in *The Idiot*. The narrator of *The Brothers*

Karamazov, however, rarely transcends common sense. Though he has detailed privileged knowledge of private scenes, such as Ivan's long conversations with Alesha or his devil, the source of which he passes over in silence, his tone of voice remains commonsensical throughout.

However, common sense is not to be confused with authority regarding an ultimate truth. If Dostoevsky had wished to give this impression in his last novel, there was an obvious way of achieving it, a way that his great contemporary Tolstoi employed in both his great novels, the second of which, *Anna Karenina*, was to appear in the same decade in which Dostoevsky planned and published *The Brothers Karamazov*. That was of course, the way of the omniscient narrator. Dostoevsky consciously chose not to employ this mode of narration and, although the narrative point of view is relatively stable, he uses other ways to stress the multi-layered character of discourse and to stress the inaccessibility of an ultimate truth beyond discourse. One way, as was usual with Dostoevsky's narrators, was subtly to suggest the imperfections in his own knowledge in the course of his narration. But another, more significant perhaps, was to distance himself at many removes from the immediate source of his narrative, where that source might be taken to convey the underlying meaning of the text as a whole. Such is the case with Ivan's legend of the Grand Inquisitor, or Zosima's testament. The legend, never written down, is told in prose summary by one character to another and the whole episode is then retold by a narrator whose source for the detail is never stated. Moreover, allusions to history and to ancient texts and traditions, including the New Testament, combine to suggest that the legend itself is far from being an originary text, but could in principle be traced back layer upon layer into the mists of the past. Without expressing it in this way, this is what critics who attempt to interpret it in the light of, say, medieval traditions, seem to be assuming. In the case of Zosima's testament, we are told that he never actually expressed it in continuous form, but that Alesha made notes and what we read is the narrator's edition of Alesha's notes. But once again, the allusions to anterior texts are so rich and numerous that the cultured reader or critic finds it impossible to be sure of the character or identity of an originary text. Put in simple terms, the debate over whether or not Zosima is Orthodox or heretical derives from this uncertainty.

V

The Dissolution of the Subject

Huxley's character's comment on *The Brothers Karamazov* finds a parallel in a conversation initiated by Sologdin in Solzhenitsyn's *First Circle*:

> 'Well, to take an example, how are we to understand Stavrogin?'
> 'But there are already dozens of critical studies on the subject!'

'They're not worth a penny. Believe me, I've read them. Stavrogin! Svidrigailov! Kirillov! How can anybody understand them? They are as complex, as incomprehensible, as people in real life. We rarely understand a person straight away, and never right through. Something always pops up to surprise us. That's why Dostoevsky is such a genius! And literary critics imagine they can hold his characters up to the light and see right through them. It's so ridiculous!'[214]

It has to be admitted that Western literary critics have been somewhat subtler in their analyses of Dostoevsky's characters than some of those Soviet counterparts of whom Sologdin was no doubt thinking. Nevertheless, it can scarcely be denied that Dostoevsky's characters, even some of his minor ones, do stick in the mind as well-defined personalities with their own distinctive character traits. If one adds to this the success that some critics have had in applying psychoanalytic techniques to his characters, a process seemingly underwritten by Freud himself, then Sologdin's claim may seem excessive. On the other hand, when one contemplates the disagreements, both subtle and occasionally extreme, about individual characters, then one may begin to see why he, and Solzhenitsyn's character, came to this conclusion. At the end of the day the psychological approach to Dostoevsky's characters turns out to be quite compatible with such a view. As Frank Seeley wrote many years ago, the problem of personality in Dostoevsky's fiction is twofold, hinging on the questions of self-respect and identity. Dostoevsky's 'little men and women' (*malen'kie liudi*) are engaged in a desperate and unending struggle to disentangle their own image of themselves from the world's image of them as a preliminary to achieving an attitude to themselves independent of the world's attitude. For the major heroes and heroines, however, the question is rather different. It is at the centre of the personality, rather than at the interface with other people, and can be simply expressed in the question 'Who am I?'[215] In both cases we are dealing with images and perceptions whose relationship with an underlying reality is guaranteed only by the strength of the emotions and passions that infuse them. Any final year undergraduate who has seriously grappled with the question of Raskolnikov's motives for committing a double murder, or with Myshkin's elusive and subtly changing personality, will instantly recognize that here too we are dealing with laws that are ultimately too difficult for us to grasp. We are given too much information, too many clues to too many possible explanations for us ever to be content with any one of them. As Philip Rahv wrote even longer ago, 'Dostoevsky is the first novelist to have fully accepted and dramatized the principle of uncertainty or indeterminacy in the presentation of character.'[216]

At first glance it may seem as though Seeley and Rahv are at odds, the one saying that Dostoevsky's characters have a definable core and definable problems, the other stressing the opposite. But what they have in common is a perception of what Bakhtin called their 'unfinalizedness'. Lest we, the readers, or Dostoevsky's characters themselves, should settle too easily into a definite image of the individual personality, Dostoevsky deploys a range of techniques to decentre their personalities and keep us permanently unsettled. I have examined some of these in a previous book. Here I shall not repeat what I argued there at length, but a brief summary will allow me to draw this chapter to a conclusion.

Much has been written about inner conflict in Dostoevsky's characters, often drawing on the problematic concept of the 'double'.

R D Laing, in his book *Self and Others*,[217] begins with an analysis of Raskolnikov from the point of view of his confusion of dream, fantasy, imagination and waking perception, but then he moves on to show the deeply unsettling and confusing effect on him of his mother's letter, which places him in a position that could be termed 'false', 'unfeasible', 'untenable' or 'impossible', because Raskolnikov's mother defines him in it in two incompatible ways: as a Christian who could never accept his sister's voluntary sacrifice to help him on his way, and also as a brother, who should be grateful to her for her sacrifice to enable him to get on in a world that does not recognize Christian values.

I argued that this is but one of many strategies that Dostoevsky's characters deploy to 'drive each other crazy', to dissolve their confidence in their own images of themselves. Usually the process is unconscious; sometimes it is conscious but with unforeseen and unintended consequences; sometimes it is perfectly conscious, and its consequences are the intended ones, as in the case of Porfiry Petrovich's interviews with the suspected murderer. Whether conscious or not, the process often indicates a desperate attempt on the part of the subject to force the object into a mould that accords with a particular view of himself, or herself, and the world, a view that is itself under threat and urgently requires reinforcement. Thus Raskolnikov tries to destroy Sonia's faith in God, a faith that is beginning to have an unwelcome effect on him, and will eventually lead to his confession, while Sonia in her turn is also subtly subverting Raskolnikov's view of himself as a Napoleon figure and his apparent confidence that he is beyond the morality of ordinary beings. Thus, while Dostoevsky's characters are constantly trying to break down the other's self-image, they are vulnerable to this process themselves. The subject is constantly subject to the processes of dissolution and reformation. Equally to the point, I argued that similar processes of mutual deconstruction and reconstruction are at work in the relationship between the reader and the text, and that similar strategies may be identified in this process.[218] For present purposes, it may be sufficient to underline that these decentring processes, which embrace characters, narrators and the Dostoevskian text itself, derive from a view of the world without a transcendent truth, in which patterns and fixities of whatever kind are no more than superficial assemblages of signs, more often than not of genre conventions. This is the world in which Dostoevsky's characters and narrators seem to live and whose fragility and possible illusoriness constantly haunted him. This, in the end, is the world of Fantastic Realism.

ESSAY V

Religious Polemic in Narrative Form: The Brothers Karamazov

I

If the theses advanced in the preceding chapters are correct, then the evidence should be found in Dostoevsky's last novel. We should look there not only for what Epstein calls minimal religion, but also for signs that such phenomena tend to proliferate in a situation where the extremes of religious faith and atheistic conviction appear to have reached stalemate. We should also look for evidence that these extremes have a common origin in the nothingness where cosmic despair or an experience of a transcendent reality may equally be found.

When Epstein talks of minimal religion, of course, he has the Russian context specifically in mind, and he seems to use the expression to denote any manifestation of religion that falls short of a complete expression of Russian Orthodoxy. It could be argued that all manifestations of religion in *The Brothers Karamazov*, including Zosima's faith, and the conception of God against which Ivan rebels, fall into that category. The concept is an extremely broad one and, as we shall see, it encompasses many varied expressions of religious sensibility. Moreover, the expressions 'minimal religion' and 'minimal religious experience' are often used outside the Russian context simply to mean an experience of a transcendent reality unencumbered by all but the most rudimentary of interpretative traditions. In the pages that follow, we may have to distinguish Epstein's sense from the more usual sense. However, we shall also find instances of interpretative traditions unencumbered by any experience of the transcendent (Grigory and arguably Ferapont), or the rejection of such traditions by people with no such experience (old Karamazov, Smerdiakov, Rakitin, Miusov, Kolia, perhaps even Ivan, though his case is more complicated). Among these, the basis for rejection differs considerably, ranging from the sophisticated enlightenment views of Miusov, to the more modern views of Rakitin, their caricature in the young Kolia Krasotkin, and the crude, autodidactic literalism of old Karamazov or Smerdiakov. Most important perhaps are the examples of experiences of the transcendent facilitated, but thereafter only lightly touched, by the interpretative tradition (for example, to differing degrees, Zosima's and Alesha's). It is quite difficult to categorize all these, especially since there is so much dialogic overlap and interaction between the characters. Perhaps it is not necessary to do so.

Any modern reader coming to *The Brothers Karamazov* for the first time is likely to be struck not only by the quantity and variety of religious discourse in Part 1 of the novel but also by the way in which it is set forth in dialogue. There are two important things to note about the nature of the dialogue. One, for which we are indebted to Bakhtin, is that the narrator's voice carries only relative weight, and is itself of variable reliability, a point on which the narrator himself repeatedly insists. We have already noted that the Counsel for the Defence accuses the Prosecutor of making up his own novels (XV, 156), that the Prosecutor replies in kind (XV, 174), and that this may lead the reader to wonder whether the narrator is dropping us hints about his own account: after all, he is writing a novel too. He repeatedly warns us that he is being selective in the material he presents. It may be of interest to consider what principles determine his selectivity and any realistic reading of his narrative must grant that, like his predecessor in *The Devils*, he slips very easily from the stance of chronicler to that of creative novelist, for example in his detailed description of private scenes, like Ivan's encounter with his devil. At the very least, we are confronted with an irony that threatens the credibility of the narrative.

The Counsel for the Defence bases his case on the principle that although the overall picture strongly suggests Dmitry's guilt, not a single piece of evidence will stand up on its own (XV, 153). Perhaps that is also how we should see the novel's own relationship to 'reality'. In reflecting on this, we may perhaps be reminded of Father Paissy's, at first seemingly conflicting, advice to Alesha that, although science has disposed of all religious claims one by one, it has overlooked the broader picture (XIV, 155). Is it the broader picture or the accumulation of individual details that we should trust? In the first case, the broader picture, though factually mistaken, seems to bring us nearer to the reality of Dmitry's moral guilt. In the case of religious truth, it is also on the broader picture, we are told, that we should fix our gaze, though we are left uncertain of its ontoiogical status. In *A Raw Youth*, Dostoevsky had quoted two lines from Pushkin: 'an illusion that elevates us is dearer to me than an infinity of low truths' (XIII, 152).[219] The question of whether, and where, the reader should seek the broader picture or take his or her cue from the significant detail is one that haunts literary criticism too. We can only bear in mind that there may be problems here for any reading of the religious dimension of *The Brothers Karamazov*.

The other thing to note about the nature of the dialogue, as I suggested in the previous chapter, is that the characters who participate on the level of the narrated text frequently try to provoke each other, often succeeding, into speaking or acting out of character, or into admitting things that they would prefer not to acknowledge. Disagreements over whether Ivan is 'really' an atheist or an agnostic hinge on our perception of when he is telling the truth; when he is merely being provocative, or is allowing himself to be provoked; whether and how often he changes his view; what his 'bottom line' is, or if indeed he has one. With hindsight, we may recognize that it is this uncertainty and variability that lays the foundation for the fierce debate between religious faith and metaphysical rebellion that surfaces in Part 2. But in doing so it presents not a duel between two fixed, impermeable positions (Zosima's and Ivan's), but a wide spectrum of unstable and interacting religious and antireligious phenomena. In reading Part 1, it may not yet be clear to the reader whether this discourse should be seen principally in terms of characterization or whether it will have an independent role with its own internal dynamic; whether it belongs solely to the surface structure or hints at the deep structure of the text.

Yet, as we have seen, it is arguable that the varieties of religious experience, practice and discourse encountered in *The Brothers Karamazov* have a dynamic relationship with each other, and that this relationship has its origin in that silent threshold where the choice between religious faith and atheistic despair occurs and where the individual stands over the abyss. So, perhaps, the detail and the broader picture are not after all incompatible. Perhaps it is a question of how we read them. It is for this reason that in analysing the religious phenomena in the novel, I shall pay special attention to their dialogic development and presentation.

The most common way of reading the religious dimension of *The Brothers Karamazov* is, of course, to see it in terms of the juxtaposition of the philosophies and quality of life of the Elder Zosima and Ivan Karamazov. There are good reasons for this, one of them being that this is more or less what Dostoevsky said that he intended. Seen in this light, the novel confronts the spiritual depths of Orthodox piety with the intellectual critique of a rebellious young atheist (or radical agnostic), which has seemed to many readers to encapsulate the essence and drama of the confrontation between religion and the scientific enlightenment of the modern age.

Looked at from the point of view of plot-development, Ivan's philosophy, based on the premise that if God and immortality are illusions then 'everything is permitted', seems crucial, since it rationalizes the act of parricide and consequently allows the plot to unfold. Such illusions, for Ivan, are not uplifting, but the gateway to moral nihilism. Many readers associate Ivan's philosophy not only with the act of parricide itself, but also with the 'murder of God' (the heavenly Father) in human minds. The influence of Nietzsche and Freud on the modern mind has tended to reinforce such readings. Ivan himself considers that once you accept this premise then egoism to the point of evildoing should be acknowledged as the most necessary, the most rational and most noble course of behaviour (XIV, 65).

Looked at from another point of view, the perspective of Zosima is of more fundamental significance to our reading of the novel (that is, at the level of ideal author rather than narrator), since it articulates the order against which Ivan rebels, and seems to hold out the possibility of renewal. As Dostoevsky mused to himself in one of his notebooks: 'The scoundrels ridiculed me for my *ignorant* and retrograde faith in God. The dolts never dreamed of such a powerful denial of God as I put in the Inquisitor and the preceding chapter, to which the whole novel serves as an answer. It is not as a fool or a fanatic that I believe in God. And they wanted to teach me and laughed at my immaturity. Yet in their stupidity they never dreamed of a negation as powerful as the one that I have been through' (XXVII, 48).

There is another, broader, way of reading Ivan's dictum. If indeed '*everything* is permitted' then this includes not only murder and other vicious deeds, but also a whole spectrum of beliefs and conduct, not excluding a life devoted to active love, such as that advocated by Zosima. The views of Fedor Pavlovich Karamazov, Smerdiakov, Rakitin, Zosima, Father Paissy, Miusov, Ivan, Dmitry, Khokhlakova and many others, even of the narrator, are all given equal rights in Ivan's world, if not conceded equal rationality. All are permitted. Lies are permitted; but so is integrity and so is the creation of a philosophical position in which one does not actually believe oneself, as appears to be the case with Ivan's article on Church and State, perhaps even with his poem on the 'Grand Inquisitor', and was certainly the case with Stavrogin in *The Devils*. In other words, the implications of Ivan's dictum bring us very close to a post-modernist position, and to that of Nietzsche from which it may be said to derive, to a world in which there is no ultimate truth and in which we have to constitute our own systems of meaning. Many of the disputes about *The Brothers Karamazov* are reducible to the question: whose novel is it, Zosima's or Ivan's?

There is a strong case for saying that it is Ivan's, as a consequence of the characteristic internal balance of the Dostoevskian novel, in which the mutinous crew sets the tone. Add to that features of its narrative structure that are seemingly designed to subvert any idea of a stable meaning and the powerful emotional impact of Ivan's contribution, of which Dostoevsky was himself all too aware, and readings such as that of Albert Camus are all too understandable. But Ivan does not have a single, stable philosophy. Frank Seeley has identified four stages of Ivan's thinking, presented out of chronological order in the novel. Two of these, chronologically the first and the last, are presented by Ivan's devil, but since Ivan's devil is Ivan's projection, there are grounds for taking them seriously. The first is the legend of the philosopher who refused to believe in a future life; refused for a thousand years to accept the penalty imposed upon him for his unbelief, and finally, after walking a quadrillion kilometres in darkness, became convinced that two seconds in Paradise was worth a walk of a quadrillion quadrillions to the quadrillionth power. This 'legend' belongs to Ivan's teens and represents an early stage in his thought, in which Ivan believes that science has all the answers, and values it above his direct experience. At this stage in Ivan's life, faith only just barely overcomes the arrogance of science and reason, but it still just does so. The second stage, about five years later, is represented by the legend of the Grand Inquisitor. This legend is composed about a year before Ivan tells it to Alesha. For this reason — that Ivan's thought has already moved on when he tells the legend to Alesha — there are subtle discrepancies between it and the previous chapter ('Rebellion') in which Ivan rebels against the innocent suffering of children. The Grand Inquisitor, says Seeley, rebels against Christ's teaching out of love and compassion for humanity: the happiness of humanity is his objective. In the later 'Rebellion', Ivan revolts against the order of the universe itself, out of love and compassion for little children: justice, without which life is not worth living, is his objective. Between these two outpourings, the article on the ecclesiastical courts appears to have been written. Perhaps it should be seen as an appendix to the poem about the Grand Inquisitor, for it advocates an order in which the state is subordinate to the Church. It has to be noted, however, that it is an Orthodox Church seen as a beneficent institution, not the demonic Roman Catholic Church of Ivan's poem. Finally, there is the philosophy of the 'Geological Upheaval', which has often provoked comparisons with Nietzsche's doctrine of Eternal Recurrence. This represents the final stage of Ivan's thought, in which science and human will take the place of belief in God and immortality and move towards the realisation of a heaven on earth created by humanity itself. It is worth noting this final stage, because it moves beyond and countermands the nihilistic philosophy with which Ivan is normally associated.

Here then is Ivan, from age 18 to 24, poised over a dark abyss of nothingness and unbelief, at first allowing a glimmer of faith a brief entry, but then banishing it and subsequently evolving in several stages his own all-too-human systems of meaning, 'projecting', as Seeley says, 'new fantasies in desperate attempts to light up the darkness beyond'.[220]

We can see him as a precursor of twentieth-century existentialist angst, as a proto-socialist, or as a forerunner of postmodernist deconstruction, but we can also see him hovering perilously over that abyss identified by Mikhail Epstein as characteristic of the apophatic heritage, where the consciousness of nothingness can lead either to despair or to faith. We might perhaps even wonder whether what is visible on the surface in Ivan is present in a more diffused form in those around him. It has recently been argued that even Smerdiakov is capable of seeking theosis.[221]

II

Religious Dialogue: Preliminary Skirmishing

Against this background, we may see Part 1 as introductory. The narrator is surprisingly careful to be even-handed. While he makes no secret of his likes and dislikes among the characters,[222] he sometimes allows characters whom he clearly dislikes (Rakitin, for example) to make the most percipient comments. Though his personal sympathies are clearly with his 'hero' Alesha, with whom the novel begins and ends, and he takes religious experience very seriously, he does not commit himself overtly to Alesha's point of view. The narrator, if in fact he should be seen as a man of faith rather than as a man of wide sympathies, appears to be what we should today call a liberal Christian, attempting to be fair to a variety of religious attitudes and experiences.

These attitudes include the psychological interpretations of the narrator himself, the vulgar literalism of old Karamazov and Smerdiakov, what old Karamazov calls 'unbelief through negligence', the secular liberalism of Miusov and Rakitin, the commitment of faith and the living of a life of active love of Alesha and Zosima, the poetical paganism of Dmitry, the uneducated and superstitious piety of Grigory and Marfa, the radical agnosticism or atheism of Ivan and the careerist motivation of Rakitin. Through Zosima, we see examples of faith healing, telepathy or precognition, as well as prophetic gestures. There are allusions to the Russian tradition of the holy fool, references to martyrs for faith, to hagiography, to sectarianism, to folk religion, to Christian socialism, even the claim that religion is a theatrical sham. There are explanations by the narrator of the strengths and weaknesses of the institution of Elders. And, at the heart of it all for some of the characters, lie the despair, torment and suffering of the soul without belief in God and immortality.

As is characteristic of Dostoevsky, this panorama is not set forth in clear and systematic form. It emerges in an often loosely structured, even chaotic dialogue in which the relationship between characters is tense, where some are intent on causing anarchy and embarrassment and others desperately fear it, and where mutual trust is entirely lacking. While Zosima repeatedly exhorts the Karamazovs and others not to tell lies, some of those present suspect him and the other monks of living a lie themselves. Sometimes, when one character reports the views of another, the reader has no reason to doubt the report; sometimes he or she has very good reason, perhaps because of the track record of the speaker, of an inherent duplicity or implausibility, or because doubt is cast by another speaker in whom the reader may have more confidence. Sometimes the other character is present to respond; sometimes he or she is absent. Sometimes the issue is clarified, more often it is left shrouded in ambiguity.

As if to underline this ambiguity, religion first appears in the book as a function of Fedor Pavlovich Karamazov's buffoonery, as he declaims Scripture after his first wife's death. There is much more of this to come, including his brief disquisition on whether or not there can be hooks in hell if hell has no ceiling, and his blasphemous outburst in front of the Elder and the assembled company. Then, shortly after our introduction to old Karamazov, we meet the sophisticated Miusov, described as an enlightened metropolitan, a cosmopolitan, a life-long European and liberal of the 40s and 50s, with his sceptical view of Zosima. There follows the uneducated folk beliefs and superstitions of the peasants Grigory and Marfa and, by way of contrast, the first reference to Ivan Karamazov's article on the ecclesiastical courts and to Alesha's being a novice in the local monastery. The negative representation of religion is not limited to Ivan and his Inquisitor.

Even Alesha is not quite what he seems at first sight. The narrator explains that he was not a mystic or a fanatic but a realist, and that he had become a novice because he had concluded that God and immortality exist and that the monastery seems to offer the only path from worldly wickedness to a life of love. If he had concluded that God does not exist then he would, equally rationally, have become an atheist and a socialist. In addition to an account of Alesha's religious motivation, we are told of his memories of childhood emerging as specks of light against the darkness — the icon, the slanting rays of the setting sun, his mother pleading for him to the Mother of God. But, by way of contrast, the narrator tells of the untutored religious superstitions of Alesha's father and Grigory, his guardian. Grigory shows Alesha his mother's grave with its inscription and four-lined verse from old cemetery lore, while old Karamazov suddenly takes 1,000 roubles to the monastery to have a memorial service said for the soul of his first wife (not the one who has just died). Far from being religious, the narrator tells us, the man had probably never put a five-kopeck candle in front of an icon in his life. When Alesha suddenly announces that he wants to enter the monastery, his father tells him sentimentally and unconvincingly that it will be an opportunity to pray for 'us sinners'. There follows his ridiculous excursus about the devil's hooks, linked with his claim that it will be easier to go to the other world knowing for certain what it is like.

Old Karamazov's discourse on religion, although it is in a sense sheer buffoonery, has its serious side too. Like Smerdiakov's, yet to come, it effectively ironizes and deconstructs pedantic and *literalistic* interpretations of the Christian tradition. For this reason, the narrator's insistence that Alesha is a realist is doubly significant. Miracles, he tells us, will never confound a realist, for whom faith is not born from miracles but miracles from faith. St Thomas believed not because he saw the risen Christ, but because he wanted to believe. Here the narrator gives his first hint that he sees religious faith in terms of psychology. 'Realism' in religious faith is clearly not the same thing as literalism.

In the description of Elders and the institution of Eldership, and of Zosima's place in the monastery, which concludes the first book of the novel, the narrator employs a kind of double-voiced discourse or *style indirect libre*. He indicates a genuine desire to understand by using appropriate religious language, while at the same time remaining uncommitted. Indeed, the first reaction to the Elder that we are shown is that of Miusov; it is not at all favourable, and the narrator at first seems to share Miusov's reservations. However, this view does not go long unchallenged. Zosima demonstrates a highly developed emotional intelligence in his handling of old Karamazov's buffoonery, in particular his invented anecdote about Diderot and the Metropolitan Platon, and continues to do so in receiving a string of female visitors to his cell. These include Khokhlakova and a 'shrieker'. Again the narrator adopts a dispassionate, secular attitude. He gives a naturalistic account of the way that such shriekers have been cured the moment they are brought to the chalice, refers to the common view that it is simply a pretence to avoid work and the medical view that it is a disease particularly characteristic of Russian women, but he prefers a psychological explanation, holding that healing is caused by a shock provoked by the expectation of a miracle. Zosima next comforts a grieving mother by reference to the words of a saint of old, and corrects another for thinking of praying in the spirit of folk-religion for a missing son, as though he were already dead. He tells her to pray to the Queen of Heaven and assures her that her son is surely alive and will soon come home or write to her. He tells another woman that God will forgive her if she truly repents, however great the sin she has committed. Love, says Zosima, is such a priceless treasure that you can redeem the whole world with it.

The notion of psychologically induced illness and recovery due to spiritual healing is also applicable to the case of Lise Khokhlakova, who first appears with her mother in this chapter. It is questioned by the little monk from Obdorsk, and Zosima is not yet willing to speak of cure, only of improvement. By contrast to the narrator, he attributes this to the divine will.

Here then we have, presented in the course of the narrative, a bewildering variety of examples of the cultural and spiritual environment in which the religious drama of the novel is played out. The narrator clearly has his own views about the characters, and they tend to favour those who adopt a positive view of life and display spiritual maturity. Yet, while faithfully describing events that have a religious colouring, he shows a disposition to question the more traditional religious explanations and to prefer naturalistic explanations of faith and miracles. It is quite unexpectedly, and again through a secondary character, that readers find themselves plunged into the very heart of the religious drama.

III

Ultimate Questions Introduced

Lise's thirty three-year-old mother has a profounder problem than the others who visit Zosima. She says she lacks faith in life after death and dares not even contemplate the question of faith in God. It causes her acute anxiety, suffering and even terror. Zosima believes in the genuineness of her anguish. She imagines a person of lifelong faith finding nothing when she dies. Zosima says one cannot prove anything about these things, but it is possible to be convinced by the experience of active love, and this will lead to belief in God and in the immortality of the soul. This has been tested and it is certain, he says. Like the narrator, Zosima here seems to adopt a

Jamesian religious pragmatism, placing emphasis on the psychological route to faith and on empirical evidence of its efficacy. The one thing that would cool Khokhlakova's active love for humanity is ingratitude, she says. In response, Zosima quotes a doctor who confessed to him once that the more he loved mankind in general the less he loved people in particular, and vice versa. Zosima praises her sincerity and tells her to avoid lies, especially lying to herself, and to avoid contempt, both of herself and others. He contrasts active love in life with love in dreams. 'I predict that at the very moment when you realize with horror that, despite all your efforts, you not only have not come closer to your goal but seem to be farther away from it than ever, at that very moment — I predict this to you — you will suddenly arrive at your goal and will clearly behold the wonder working power of the Lord, who all the while has loved you, and all the while has mysteriously guided you' (XIV, 54). Here is Dostoevsky's Columbus image again, but also the sudden discovery of God, or by God, at the moment of deepest despair, the mysterious revelation of religious truth at the heart of apophatic silence, an echo of Dostoevsky's own experience that the truth of religion shines more brightly in moments of affliction (XXVIII, i, 176). It is on this axis that the spiritual issues of the novel will hinge.

It is Miusov (another secondary character) who develops the contrary view. Ivan, he says, sees belief in immortality not as a consequence of a life of active love, but the other way round. In the chapter 'Why should such a man live?' Miusov tells another anecdote about Ivan: he apparently once said that there exists no law of nature that man should love mankind, and that if this has occurred in the past it is solely because of belief in immortality. If belief in immortality were to be destroyed, not only love but any power to continue the life of the world would dry up, nothing would be immoral any longer, everything would be permitted, even cannibalism. Ivan holds, as we have already seen, that for anyone without belief in God and immortality, egoism should not only be permitted, but also acknowledged to be necessary, the most reasonable and most noble consequence of his situation. Dmitry asks him to confirm that he believes this. Ivan confirms: there is no virtue if there is no immortality. The Elder responds: 'You are blessed if you believe so, or else most unhappy' (XIV, 65). In all probability, he adds, Ivan does not believe either in the immortality of his soul or even in what he has written about the Church and the Church question. Ivan says maybe not, but he wasn't exactly joking either. The Elder replies that a martyr too may like to toy with his despair, also from despair as it were, just as Ivan does. The question is not resolved for him, and therein lies his great grief. If it cannot be resolved in a positive way, then it cannot be resolved in a negative way either: Ivan should be thankful that he has a lofty heart capable of being afflicted by such a torment.

Here we have the core of the novel's religious drama: a lofty heart in torment on the threshold between faith and total despair and unbelief, in which the question of the existence of God and immortality awaits resolution.

Zosima's answer is of course to pursue a life of active love and faith will follow. The two routes are stated dramatically by Ivan and Alesha in the later discussion in the presence of their father, who asks Ivan, is there a God or not? Ivan says there is not a God. Alesha says there is. Ivan says there is no immortality either, not of any kind. There is complete zero. Alesha says there is immortality and that immortality is in God. Fedor Pavlovich considers how much faith, how much energy has been spent on this dream through the ages, and asks Ivan who then is laughing at humanity? It must be the devil says Ivan, and instantly denies that there is a devil either. However, he asserts that there would have been no civilisation at all if that belief had not been invented. Old Karamazov, though he may well be making this up, adds that even Zosima does not believe in God (XIV, 124), and that he once said to a visiting Governor that he believes but he doesn't know in what. For Alesha, Ivan has a stormy soul, there is a great and unresolved secret in him; he is one of those who needs to resolve their thought. In other words, Alesha too sees all too clearly the profound spiritual drama at the heart of the novel. The key to Ivan is not the endless philosophising to which so much attention has been paid — this is only secondary — so much as the agonising secret that torments his soul and will not let him go.

Some characters may plumb the ultimate questions, but there are others who continue, it seems, to live on the surface, and these are no less important to the interpersonal dialogue, to the panorama of religious discourse and to the unfolding of the plot. Rakitin, for example, is an acute psychologist. He has the whole Karamazov family neatly summed up, and thinks he has Zosima summed up too. Unlike Ivan in his present mode, but not unlike the Ivan of the 'Geological Upheaval', he believes that mankind will find enough strength in the notions of liberty, equality and fraternity to live for virtue without belief in the immortality of the soul. But Rakitin is spiritually shallow and has not experienced the anguish of Ivan's or Dostoevsky's spiritual pilgrimage.

Grigory is hardly more spiritually profound, but he has a superstitious fascination with the dark side of the Russian folk religion. Ever since the death of Grigory and Marfa's six-fingered baby, Grigory has read the *Chetii-Minei* (the lives of the saints) silently to himself; he loves the Book of Job and has obtained from somewhere a copy of the words and sermons of 'Our God-bearing father, Isaac the Syrian', understanding almost nothing, but valuing the book perhaps all the more for that. He has also begun to take an interest in the sect of the Flagellants (*khlystovshchina*) who exist in the neighbourhood, and has been deeply affected by though not converted to them. A singular event has left an imprint (*pechat'*) on his soul. As if by design, on the day of the birth of their six-fingered baby (which he sees as a sign of the devil), his wife thought she heard the sound of a baby crying outside in the bathhouse: it was Lizaveta giving birth to the child of whom Fedor Pavolovich is reputedly the father. When she died soon afterwards, Grigory and Marfa saw it as the hand of God, and took the baby in.

Here we have a sort of peasant mysticism mixed up with superstition. Zosima has already reproved one of his visitors for indulging in folk religion. But true peasant spirituality, we are told, is something different. Ironically it is Smerdiakov, yet another secondary character, who gives voice to it. In a later chapter, Grigory tells the story of a Russian captured by Muslims who refuses to convert and is flayed alive. There follows a dispute with Smerdiakov as to whether it would have been a very great sin for him to have recanted. Smerdiakov adopts the approach of rational literalism, somewhat more refined than old Karamazov's but of the same school. Since his own faith is already insecure (as proved by the fact that mountains do not move when he commands them), his expectations of heaven are not very high anyway, so he could not truly be said to be foreswearing his faith if he were to recant in such a situation. In any case the very idea of recanting is equivalent to doing it, so when the idea passes through his mind he is already not really a Christian any more, so he can't be accused of renouncing Christ, since he has nothing to renounce, and so on. Old Karamazov calls him a stinking Jesuit. Smerdiakov posits that perhaps two hermits exist whose faith would move mountains, and old Karamazov retorts that that very thought is typical of Russian folk religion. Alesha agrees. Smerdiakov himself, however, is impervious to religion or to literature. It is clear that he makes two cardinal mistakes in what old Karamazov calls his jesuitical casuistry. Firstly, he mistakes myth for literal historical fact and secondly, on this assumption, he tries to draw rational inferences from it. For example, he wanted, at the age of twelve, to know where the light shone from on the first day, if God created the sun, moon and stars on the fourth?

However, the most striking form of spirituality to assail the reader before the close of Part 1 belongs to Dmitry. It is true that he uses conventional religious language to support an oath, swearing 'as God is holy and Christ is the Lord', but apart from this there is nothing Orthodox at all about his philosophy of life. Even his beliefs in a miracle of divine Providence and that God knows his heart and sees all his despair (maybe he'll kill his father, maybe he won't) is not distinctively Christian. In fact Dmitry quotes Schiller's 'Ode to Joy'. He says he hardly thinks of anything but man's fallen state, but doesn't know what it means to 'make a compact with the earth evermore.' Life is a riddle. Sensuality brings him joy. Beauty is a fearful and a terrible thing, fearful because it is indefinable. Here shores converge and all contradictions live together. Too many riddles oppress man on earth. He can't bear it that a man should start with the ideal of the Madonna and end with the ideal of Sodom. It is even worse when someone already has the ideal of Sodom in his soul and does not deny the ideal of the Madonna burning within him. Man is too broad. For the vast majority, beauty lies in Sodom.[223] Beauty is not only fearful, but also mysterious. The devil is struggling with God, and the battlefield is the human heart (XIV, 98–100).

That these last words of Dmitry should strike a familiar note with readers with a Christian background only points to the catholicity of the religious subtext, for Dmitry evidently shares the deep existential anxiety that troubles Ivan and, as later becomes clear, Alesha.

As we have seen, there is a school of Dostoevsky criticism that holds that the true religious subtext is the Orthodox tradition in its fullness. Yet it is striking that in these introductory chapters no one, not even Zosima, acts as spokesperson for that tradition or appeals to its authority. Zosima, and his office of Elder, are presented as tangential, even as objects of suspicion to Orthodoxy. It is said, though not confirmed, that Zosima does not know what God is. He certainly holds that religious truths are incapable of proof. He makes no reference to the sacraments or to the veneration of icons as windows to a higher world of the spirit. Instead he tells his hearers that it is by leading a life of active love for one's neighbour that one will come to believe in God and immortality, just when one thinks that one is as far as possible from that conviction. He understands the soul tormented by unbelief and the spiritual value of such torment on the journey of faith. He advocates repentance and prayer; he warns against lying and contempt; he foresees personal joys and tragedies and bows down before suffering, but for every reader who sees these words as the flowers on the tree of Orthodoxy, another will perceive them as expressive of a more primitive form of Christianity in which ritual, dogma, hierarchy and tradition are secondary and inessential accretions, not far in spirit perhaps from the author of the Letter to the Ephesians. Later we shall be told about Zosima's reading and the importance that it has for him, but the only character in Part 1 whose reading includes the classics of Russian Orthodoxy, including the Book of Job, is the peasant Grigory, who does not understand them. It remains to be seen whether the later parts of the novel support one interpretation to the exclusion of the other.

Finally, Part 1 not only illustrates many divergent varieties of religious discourse and sensibility, some of which will be developed in later parts of the novel. It also contains important hints as to how the debate will be conducted. We have seen how Rakitin attempts to deconstruct Zosima and the life of the monks by positing deception and mystification on their part and how old Karamazov and Smerdiakov engage in a vulgar deconstruction of a debased, literalistic Christianity. In Part 2, we see Ivan doing something similar, but on a much more sophisticated level. Stewart Sutherland[224] has argued persuasively that the Christianity that Ivan attacks is in fact a debased form rooted in radical misconceptions.

IV

Pro and Contra, Stage One

The second part of the novel is framed by the Elder Zosima, or more precisely by the expectation and the realisation of his death. It includes the famous chapters 'Rebellion', 'The Grand Inquisitor', 'From the life of the

Hieromonk and Elder Zosima' and 'From talks and homilies by the Elder Zosima', and presents in a number of unforgettable ways, and through diverse literary genres, the religious issues for which the novel is famed, giving a mythical identity to the time and location (what Bakhtin would have called the chronotope) where the parting of the ways occurs: the wilderness where the Jesus of the Gospels meets Satan and makes his choice between the devil and his divine calling.

It opens with Zosima's feeling the nearness of death and with references to the Church's sacraments. He now makes confession (*ispoveduetsia*), receives communion (*prichastitsia*) and the rite of holy unction (*soborovane*) begins. Then he takes his leave of the monks. It is a prolegomenon to what we shall shortly read in his testament. He seems to want to speak for one last time before his death, to say all that he had not said during his life. He wants to share his joy and ecstasy, enjoining the monks to love one another and to love God's people. Monks are not holier than those who live in the world. They are in fact lower than them; that is why they originally entered the monastery. A monk must acknowledge that he is not only lower but is also guilty before everyone, on behalf of all and for all: only then will the ultimate goal of unity be achieved. This recognition is the crown of the monk's path and that of every one on earth. Only then will hearts be moved to a love that is infinite, universal and insatiable. Zosima is here elaborating on his previous injunction to live a life of active love, but here he also reminds his hearers that as a precondition it is necessary to acknowledge one's personal guilt for everything and for all. Repentance must come first. There is no need to be afraid of one's sins, provided that one is repentant and does not place conditions on God. He enjoins his hearers not to be proud before the lowly or the great, not to hate those who reject, disgrace, revile and slander them, not even atheists, teachers of evil, materialists, whether they are good or wicked. They should pray for those for whom there is none to pray, and for those who do not wish to pray, and they should add that they do not pray out of pride, for they are the lowest of all. They should teach the gospel untiringly and abstain from usury. The narrator tells us that some wondered at Zosima's words and saw darkness in them, but everyone expected something remarkable to happen when he died.

The authority of his words is seemingly reinforced when Alesha leaves the cell to receive a letter brought by Rakitin from Khokhlakova: Zosima's prophecy to the peasant woman who has not heard from her son has come true, and he has written to say that he is coming home. Within an hour the 'miracle' becomes known to the whole monastery, though Father Paissy, typically, urges caution on the grounds that there may be a natural explanation. We are never told who is right but, since it is in harmony with the narrator's position, we are left with Father Paissy's explanation in our minds.

Although the first section of Part 2 begins with the dying Zosima, and introduces the main features of his Christian faith, this is embedded in further dramatic manifestations of deviant religious belief and practice, breaking up and delaying the juxtaposition of Zosima and Ivan, and further complicating the reader's picture of religion and the life of the monastery. The chapter is actually entitled 'Father Ferapont' and concludes with Father Paissy. It is important not to overlook either of them, for they are both significant figures in the gallery of monks. The first is a multi-faceted caricature, taking to grotesque extremes characteristics that elsewhere in the novel are given positive value. Among these are the tradition of the holy fool (elsewhere associated positively with Alesha and Zosima), the spiritual value of silence (which we shall consider later), fasting, the mysterious prophetic gesture and a very loose relationship to monastic rules (Zosima). But Ferapont, aged seventy-five or more, is all those things that Alesha is not. He is not a realist; he is a fanatic; moreover, he is an egoist and a showman, and highly judgemental. He is a great faster and keeper of silence, and is strongly opposed to the institution of Elders. He rarely appears at the liturgy, but sometimes spends the whole day in prayer. If he speaks, he is curt, eccentric and almost always rude. He often utters a single strange saying and refuses an explanation. Ignorant people hold that he is in communion with holy spirits and converses only with them, which is why he is silent with people. He asks the little Obdorsk monk if he has noticed all the little devils around, claiming that when he was up at the Superior's at Pentecost last year, he saw one sitting on a monk's chest, hiding under his cassock, with only his little horns sticking out; another monk had one peeking out of his pocket, looking shifty-eyed, because he was afraid of him; another had one living in his stomach; and there was one who had one living on his neck, clinging to him, and he was carrying him around without even being aware of it. As he was leaving the Superior's, says Ferapont, he looked again, and there was one hiding from him behind a door, a yard and a half tall or more, with a long, thick brown tail, the tip of which accidentally got stuck in the doorjamb, whereupon Ferapont seized his chance and suddenly slammed the door shut and pinched his tail. He started squealing and struggling, and Ferapont crossed him with the triple sign of the Cross. The little devil immediately dropped dead on the spot, like a squashed spider. He must still be rotting and stinking in that same corner, but no one sees, or smells a thing. The Obdorsk monk asks whether it is true that he is in constant communion with the Holy Spirit. Ferapont answers that the Holy Spirit flies down in the form of a bird. He distinguishes between the *sviatyi dukh* and the *Sviatodukh* (XIX, 154), which Pevear and Volokhonsky translate as 'The Holy Spirit' and the 'Holispirit'.[225] The latter can fly down in the form of a swallow, a goldfinch or a tomtit. He speaks in human language. For example, today he told him that a fool would visit him and ask improper questions. He points to an elm, which at night becomes Christ on the Cross. He fears that he may be grabbed and 'taken up' like Elijah. The Obdorsk monk is more inclined towards Ferapont than towards Zosima, owing to his liking for fasting. Of course his words are absurd, he thinks, but the Lord knows what is hidden in them and they are no stranger than those of other holy fools. Ferapont's idea of monastic life and of Christianity is the obverse of that of Fedor Pavlovich Karamazov and of Smerdiakov and, other things aside, it provides another example of a debased religion, thus alerting the reader again to the possibility that the objections to Christianity that he or she is shortly to encounter may themselves be predicated on a misconception.

Why Ferapont? Why does there have to be such a character in the novel? Why here? It is possible to discuss his effect within the unfolding drama and even to commend his contribution to the rich tapestry of monastic life. But within the novel's religious dispensation he plays a very special role. More than any other character he drives home the point that Zosima is challenged not only by Ivan and what he represents, but also from within his own tradition. Ferapont may be a caricature, but he is not sheer invention. What he caricatures presents a real threat to the claims of religious experience for our serious attention, precisely because he takes to extremes features that elsewhere in Dostoevsky are given positive value. As Keith Ward says in a different context, 'Religious experience is [...] about a personal apprehension of spiritual reality [...] But to make an accurate assessment requires maturity, self-confidence, self-knowledge and sensitivity. Some people have lots of these qualities, some conspicuously lack them, and some are immature, self-deceived, fearful and deeply prejudiced. If religious apprehension were like personal knowledge, one would expect that religious experiences would range from wildly fantastic projections of personal inadequacies to positive and life-enhancing transformations of personality by encounter with a wider and deeper personal reality'.[226] While Zosima clearly belongs to the latter category, Ferapont equally clearly belongs to the former. As well as throwing Zosima's positive characteristics into relief by his appearance at this crucial point in the narrative, he presents a radical challenge to the claims of religion, as subversive in its way as that of Ivan.

The passage relating to Father Paissy is relatively brief. Here Paissy tells Alesha what we noted in our introduction to this chapter, that science has taken away everything that was once considered holy, but that it has taken the parts and missed the whole. It has been unable to create another higher image than that of Christ. And whatever scientists have attempted, the result has been only monstrosities. The same might be said of Ferapont and the little Obdorsk monk. Alesha realizes that he has found a new friend in Father Paissy and readers may sense that they may have found a lodestone to guide them through the tangle of religious phenomena that reside in the monastery.

Zosima now calls for Alesha and tells him that he should be with his family. He promises he will save his last word on earth for him. Following his Elder's injunction, Alesha does in fact call on his father, who tells him that it is inappropriate for a decent man to go to his paradise, if there really is such a place. He says that a man falls asleep and doesn't wake up and that's all there is to it. Remember him in his prayers if he wants to, if not, may the devil take him. That's his philosophy. Ivan spoke well yesterday though he doesn't have any learning or education and it is by being silent that he gets by.

The next important allusion to the religious theme again comes quite unexpectedly, this time in a conversation between Alesha and Lise, in which Alesha says he is a monk but maybe he doesn't even believe in God himself (XIV, 201). He proposes seriously to marry Lise in eighteen months time. It is not clear how far what Alesha says echoes Zosima's reported admission that he does not know what God is (XIV, 124) or Ivan's forthright denial of his existence. Nor is it clear exactly what either of them means by what he reportedly says, but what is clear is that there is a very thin line for them all between belief and unbelief and that the slippage between them is all too easy. This same slippage is evident in Ivan's discourse with Alesha.

For, after these introductory scenes, and several chapters that advance the plot in other ways, the reader plunges straight into the ideological heart of the novel. Ivan knows that for the Karamazov type at least there is a way of lessening the existential despair of nothingness. He tells Alesha that the Karamazov thirst for life will be stronger than the horrors of human disillusionment for the first thirty years of his life, after which its effect will cease. Meanwhile, it is with his guts that he loves Europe (though he knows it is a graveyard) and the sticky little buds. Alesha says he understands perfectly. Everyone should love life more than its meaning. The first half of life consists in loving life, the second in resurrecting one's dead.[227] Father means to go on until he is 80. Ivan refers to young men in a tavern talking about the universal, eternal (*mirovye, vekovechnye*) questions: the existence of God, immortality. Those who do not believe in God talk about socialism and anarchism, about transforming the whole of humanity according to a new order, but it's the same thing from the other end. Now Ivan changes his tune. If Alesha is toying with the idea that God does not exist, Ivan is toying with the opposite idea. He says that at his father's yesterday he said that there is no God, just to tease Alesha. Now he invites him to imagine that he does accept God. The wonder is not that God exists; it is that such a wise, holy notion could creep into the head of such a wicked creature as man. He has decided not to think about whether man created God or God created man. He wants to declare to Alesha what sort of person he really is, so that he will not hypothesize. He declares that he accepts God pure and simple. But if God exists, and if he created the earth, he created it in accordance with Euclidian geometry and created human reason with a conception of only three dimensions of space, though there are scientists who go further than that and doubt that the whole universe was created in accordance with Euclid. Ivan says that if he does not understand even that then how can he understand about God? He cannot resolve questions that are not of this world. He advises Alesha not to think about whether God exists or not. Such questions are quite unsuitable for creatures with Euclidian minds. So he accepts God willingly, with his wisdom and his purpose completely unknown to us; he believes in the order and the meaning of life, in eternal harmony, in which we are all supposed to merge, in the Word for whom the universe is yearning, who himself was with God and is God and so on. He accepts God, but he does not accept this world of God's. He has a childlike conviction that the sufferings will be healed and smoothed over and that ultimately, when the world ends, something will be revealed that is so precious that it will satisfy every heart and justify everything. But he does not accept it. Alesha asks him to explain why he does not accept it.

Following a section in which Alesha says that perhaps he does not believe in God, Ivan says in effect that perhaps he does. Both seem to agree, though it is Alesha who actually says it, that people should love life more than its meaning, though this contrasts starkly with the whole tenor of the legend of the Grand Inquisitor with which Ivan is shortly to regale his brother. However, the reason for the parting of their ways is soon made clear and it resides in the efficacy of Zosima's central principle. Alesha says there is plenty of Christ's love still in mankind. Ivan says that that it is impossible to love one's neighbour up close, only abstractly. One can love innocent little children. If they suffer it is for their fathers' sins, because they are innocent. No animal could possibly be as cruel as a man. If the devil does not exist, then man has created him in his own image and likeness. Ivan recalls the story, told in a pamphlet sent out by some 'Lutheranizing high society philanthropists',[228] of one Richard who repents and experiences the grace of the Lord, and is then executed in a brotherly fashion in Switzerland. There is a beast hidden in everyone. Some people particularly like torturing defenceless children. When Alesha hears the story of the general who set his dogs on a child, he agrees that he should be shot. Ivan has taken children only to make his case more obvious; he has narrowed down his theme on purpose. Life is absurd. He cannot agree to live by it. He needs retribution. Otherwise he will destroy himself. He wants to see with his own eyes the hind lie down with the lion and the murdered man rise up and embrace his murderer. He doesn't want heavenly harmony. The price is too high. He returns his ticket of admission. It isn't that he doesn't accept God; it is that he returns the ticket to him. Alesha says that that is rebellion. Ivan replies he is sorry to hear that, because one cannot live by rebellion. Alesha agrees that if he was asked to design a world with the object of making people happy at the grand finale, and the price was the unrequited tears of just one small child, he wouldn't do it. He also agrees that people could not remain happy forever in the knowledge that they owe their happiness to the unjustified blood of a tormented child. But there is a being, namely Christ, who has the right to forgive all because he gave his innocent blood for all and for everything. It is on him that the structure is built, not on the sufferings of a tortured child. Ivan says he had not forgotten about that. He would like to tell him his *poema*.

V

The Chronotope of the Wilderness

The 'Legend of the Grand Inquisitor', as it is usually called in critical literature, has been retold so many times that it may be thought unnecessary to do
it again here. However, I do so not only for the benefit of the reader who is
unfamiliar with the literature, but in order to underline the ways in which the
Epstein model is anticipated in this chapter and the ones that follow. Ivan
begins his account by referring to medieval poems and plays, European and
Russian, in which saints, angels and all the powers of heaven appear on earth.
In his poem, it is Christ who will appear, though without speaking. Fifteen
centuries have passed since he gave his promise to come in his Kingdom.
Jesus passes silently among the crowds who have gathered. An irresistible
force draws people to him. He passes among them with a smile of infinite
compassion; just touching him has the power of healing. In response to their
pleas, he cures a man blind from birth and raises a dead girl, just as he did in
the Gospels. But when the Grand Inquisitor appears, such is his earthly power
that they instantly make way for him and let him arrest Jesus. He visits Jesus
in his cell and tells him to be silent, for there is no more that he can say. He
has no right to add anything.[229] Everything has been handed over by Jesus to
the Pope. The Grand Inquisitor adds that Jesus does not even have the right
to proclaim one of the mysteries from the world from which he has come, if
by doing so he would add to what has already been said and deprive people
of the freedom for which he stood so firmly. People are now convinced that
they are completely free, but they have laid their freedom at the feet of the
Church, which has vanquished freedom in order to make people happy. Man
was a rebel and rebels can't be happy. Jesus had plenty of warnings when he
was on earth. 'The dread and intelligent spirit, the spirit of self-destruction
and non-being' spoke to him in the wilderness. His three questions were the
real miracle. In essence, the first was the proposition that if you turn stones
into bread and feed people they will follow you like sheep. Feed them first,
then ask virtue of them. Some may follow you for heavenly bread, but there
will be millions who will not be strong enough to forgo earthly bread for the
sake of heavenly bread. They will understand that freedom and a plentiful
supply of earthly bread for everyone are inconceivable. People seek something indisputable to bow down to, something that everyone will agree to
bow down to and worship. The loaves would have served this purpose.
People have made gods and called upon everyone else to come and worship
them, abandoning their own gods or suffering death. So it will be to the end
of time. Even when gods have disappeared from the earth, men will still fall
down before their idols. Mistakenly, in the view of the Grand Inquisitor, Jesus
rejected earthly bread in the name of freedom and heavenly bread.

But the mystery of man's being is not just in existence. It is in what he
lives for. Without a firm idea of what he lives for, man will not consent to

live and will sooner destroy himself. Jesus seems to have forgotten that peace and even death are dearer to men than free choice in the knowledge of good and evil. Instead of the unchangeable law of old, humanity had henceforth to decide for itself, with only Jesus' image before it as a guide. The burden was too great. But did it not occur to him that, oppressed by so great a burden, humanity would eventually reject that image and that truth? That was inevitable once it was abandoned to so many anxieties and insoluble problems. Jesus himself laid the foundations for the destruction of his own kingdom. There are only three powers on earth capable of conquering and forever enthralling the conscience of these feeble rebels: miracle, mystery and authority. Jesus did not throw himself from the pinnacle of the Temple, because he knew that he would have immediately tempted the Lord and have lost all faith in him. He rejected miracle. But humanity seeks not so much God as miracles. Humanity will go and create miracles for itself, including the miracles of quacks and the magic of women. But Jesus wanted love that is free, not people enslaved by miracles. He behaved as though he had ceased to be compassionate because he asked too much of them. People will tear down temples and drench the earth with blood, but finally they will realize that although they are rebels they are feeble rebels. They will realize in despair that he who created them rebels did it to laugh at them. They will know that this is blasphemy, and that will make them even more unhappy. Jesus suffered so much for their freedom yet they are in a state of turmoil, confusion and unhappiness. Revelation foresees 12,000 from each tribe taking part in the first resurrection, but what about the rest? If Jesus came only for the elect, there is a mystery here. So the Church has the right to preach a mystery too. It is not the love, the free choice of people's hearts that matters, but the mystery that they must obey blindly. The Church has corrected Jesus' deed and based it on miracle, mystery and authority. Is it not loving humanity in doing this? Why has Jesus come to interfere now? The Church is not with Jesus but with the devil. That is its secret. It has been with him for eight centuries (that is, from 755 AD when the secular power of the papacy was established in Italy). The Church will eventually conquer the earth like the Caesars. That was the last gift of Satan: someone to bow down to, someone to take over the individual conscience and a means for uniting everyone into an anthill. Universality has always been man's dream. If Jesus had accepted Caesar's purple, he would have founded a universal kingdom. So the Church took Caesar's sword and followed not Jesus but Satan. There will be centuries more of lawlessness and free reason, but in building their Tower of Babel without the Church, people will end up in cannibalism. Eventually people will come and beg the Church. It will offer the cup inscribed with the word Mystery. Then and only then will the kingdom of peace and happiness come. Meanwhile, many of Christ's elect will raise their free banner against him. Of the rest, some will destroy themselves, some will destroy each other, others will crawl at the Church's feet and beg to be saved from themselves. It will teach them not to be proud, and that they are feeble. They will become timid and cling to the Church in fear. It will arrange their lives like a children's game, with children's songs, choruses and innocent dancing, allowing them to sin too. Everyone will be happy, liberated from the torments of personal and free decision. Everyone will be happy except for the hundred thousand who govern the million. Beyond the grave they will find only death, but the Church will entice them with a heavenly reward.

The Grand Inquisitor says that he too has dwelt in the wilderness, where he ate locusts and roots; he too has blessed freedom, and was preparing to join Jesus' chosen ones. But he awoke and decided not to serve madness. The Catholic Church has corrected Jesus' teaching. He is confident that the crowd will rush tomorrow to heap hot coals around Jesus when he has him burnt at the stake.

Alesha protests that that is not at all what Orthodoxy means by freedom and that Ivan's poem is actually in praise of Jesus. Not even Rome, not even the Jesuits, are as bad as Ivan paints them. His Grand Inquisitor is just a fantasy. Ivan grants that he is a fantasy. Alesha adds that Father Paissy once said to him something along the same lines, 'but not like that of course'. Ivan regards that caveat as important and adds that there must be people like his Inquisitor who loved mankind all his life, but are tormented by great sadness, knowing that the rest of God's creatures are set up for mockery. Alesha concludes that Ivan's Inquisitor doesn't believe in God. At last he has understood, says Ivan. That is his secret. He deceives them in the name of the great ideal of human happiness and that is the source of his suffering. Alesha exclaims that maybe Ivan does not believe in God after all. The poem ends when, silently, Jesus kisses the old man on his lips without a word. That is his whole answer. The kiss burns in the old man's heart, but he holds on to his former idea. Ivan is not going to the Jesuits, however. What does he care? He will wait until he is thirty and then smash the cup on the floor. He does not renounce yesterday's 'everything is permitted' that Alesha has remembered, and Dmitry has rephrased. Alesha then kisses Ivan on the lips in imitation of his poem. He says he will come back to see him when he is thirty, before he smashes the cup, and then he runs back to the hermitage.

A profusion of articles and even books has been written on this episode in the novel. There are just two points to be added here. The first is to reiterate that the wilderness in which Jesus encounters Satan and is tempted is that mythical location (what Bakhtin would call the chronotope) where the parting of ways between the certainty of faith and atheistic despair occurs and where Jesus made his fateful choice to go with God rather than Satan. In the same mythical location, the Grand Inquisitor and, it would seem, Ivan make the opposite choice. The second point, however, is more complex. Throughout Ivan's narrative we not only catch echoes of previous dialogue, but are also made aware of the overlap between Ivan's and Alesha's perceptions and important elements of instability in both. A further reading of the text may be necessary to locate all of these, for most readers seem to think that where Alesha expresses agreement with Ivan it is because he is momentarily caught off guard by of the power of Ivan's rhetoric or possibly because he shares Ivan's 'Karamazov nature'.

However, we have been told long ago that Alesha has become a novice solely because he is convinced of the existence of God and immortality and that he sees the monastery as offering the only available path from worldly wickedness to a life of love; if he had reached the opposite conclusion, he would have become an atheist and a socialist, like Ivan. Perhaps the main difference between the two brothers, after all, is that they did reach opposite conclusions. However, the text is littered with statements by both, and also by Zosima, all of them, by the nature of the narrative structure, reported rather than direct, that suggest that they all have reservations about their respective positions, and can easily slip over into that of the other. Moreover, not only are these statements often unreliable guides to a basic position, they even make the reader question whether there is a basic position. For example, when Alesha says to Lise that although he is a monk perhaps he doesn't even believe in God, what are we to infer from this? Is this an untypical moment of doubt? Or are we to infer that in Alesha's view, at the time he speaks, it is all right to be a monk, even a Christian, and not to believe in God? Is this a lapse into unbelief or is it a clumsy way of affirming the unknowability of the Godhead, in accordance with the apophatic tradition? And is old Karamazov uncharacteristically telling the truth when he reports that Zosima has said that he does not know what God is? After all, that might be consistent with the apophatic tradition as well. And is not Ivan's insistence that his Euclidian mind prevents him from solving the question of God's existence or non-existence very similar to the apophatic view that it is impossible to reach the knowledge of God by way of positive definition? Most critics prefer to solve such problems by assuming that Alesha and Zosima have a firm Orthodox faith and seeing apparent departures from it as lapses, or personal idiosyncrasies, or misreporting. But much more important perhaps is the fact that religious discourse in the novel, even that of Zosima, constantly escapes the straitjacket of Orthodoxy, and refuses to be tied down to accepted dogma, while Ivan, notwithstanding his professed atheism (which he partly retracts, at least for the sake of argument), is capable of saying that he accepts God willingly, with his mysterious purpose; it is his world that he does not accept. The two brothers again come very close when Alesha agrees with Ivan that the price of eternal harmony is too high if it requires the unrequited tears of just one innocent child. Alesha, of course, sees the love of God in the incarnation and the Passion of Christ, though significantly he does not spell out the detail, while Ivan appears unconvinced. Finally, the two brothers seem to run close again when Alesha recalls Father Paissy saying something along the lines of Ivan's idea that the fact that his tale of the Grand Inquisitor is a fantasy does not reduce its value. We are not told exactly what Father Paissy has said, let alone what he meant. Perhaps he meant something akin to Dostoevsky's quotation from Pushkin, or to his assertion that he would choose to remain with Christ even if it could be proved that the truth lay elsewhere. What we are given is a whole series of agreements and disagreements that indicate all too clearly the potential for slippage between Ivan's and his Grand Inquisitor's points of view (on the one hand) and Alesha's and Zosima's (on the other). At the end of the day, the important distinction is perhaps not between those who are Christian and those who are atheist, but between those who are deeply aware of the disjunction between them, and of the moment of choice, and those who simply play with religious ideas (like Miusov, Rakitin, old Karamazov or Smerdiakov), engage in religious posturing (like Ferapont) or fall prey to superstition (like Grigory). It is only the former who may exercise the true freedom that, according to Ivan, Christ offers.

VI

Zosima's Life

Alesha's account of Zosima's testament, that occupies Book 6, is designed to introduce the necessary stability into this highly unstable mix, or to put it in poststructuralist terms, to reintroduce a logocentric notion of truth into a world in which, as Derrida would put it, 'there is nothing outside the text'. Yet it is a 'truth' that is mediated through several fictional texts. Ostensibly, we are hearing Zosima's words, yet the narrator is at pains to tell us that Alesha wrote it all down from memory some time after the Elder's death and that he may have added bits from other conversations. In any case, reports suggest that the Elder did not narrate his life as a continuous, uninterrupted narrative as he lay on his deathbed, but was often interrupted or had to rest. Later the narrator tells us that he has preferred, in recounting what followed, to use Alesha's notes, which differ from the conversation in many ways. The reason he gives is that Alesha's account will be briefer and less tedious. There is an implication here that he could have recounted the conversation verbatim if he had wished to, though he also gives the impression that he knows of it only at second hand, using such expressions as 'according to later reports'. Nor do we, as readers, know whether the narrator has edited Alesha's text in some way. As I have argued elsewhere, we are in the presence of a truth that comes to us through a process akin to the game of Chinese Whispers,[230] no less in the case of Zosima's testament than in that of Ivan's legend of the Grand Inquisitor. However, the composition of the two is different. Zosima's testament, while the latter parts take the form of homilies, or perhaps a Pauline letter, begins with autobiographical notes, some of which include overt dialogue. It is true that the recollection of this dialogue is shaped by its significance for the speaker's spiritual development, but it is also true that this spiritual development is perceived as having taken shape through dialogue, unlike Ivan's, which seems to be the result of lonely introspection.

When he enters the Elder's cell, Alesha is surprised to find Zosima sitting cheerfully in his chair. Fathers Iosif and Paissy, Father Mikhail (superior of the hermitage), Brother Anfim (a simple peasant monk) — Zosima's closest friends — are also there. About 40 years ago, when Zosima first became a monk and belonged to a poor, little-known monastery in Kostroma, he had travelled with Anfim over Holy Russia. They travelled for many years collecting donations for the monastery. Zosima greets Alesha and tells him to find Dmitry and to stop him doing something terrible. Yesterday he had bowed down to his future suffering: he had read something in his face, which seemed to bespeak his fate. He tells Alesha that everything is from the Lord and quotes John 12: 24 'Except a corn of wheat fall into the ground and die, it abideth alone: but if it die, it bringeth forth much fruit', the minimalist passage that Dostoevsky used as the novel's epigraph. He says that Alesha reminds him spiritually of his elder brother, Markel, without whom he might never have become a monk.

The story of Markel is important not only by virtue of his influence on Zosima but also as a further distinctive example of minimal religion, and the first one that comes close to the purer type of minimal religion that we discussed at the opening of this chapter, a minimal religion, that is, unencumbered by an interpretative theological tradition, in which aspects of Orthodox ritual are important not in themselves but as a gateway to a higher state of spiritual consciousness. Zosima relates how his mother begs his dying brother to observe Lent and to take communion, but he simply swears at God's Church. On the Tuesday morning of Holy Week, he starts keeping the fast and going to Church, for his mother's sake. Then he takes to his bed, confesses and receives communion at home. Suddenly he becomes joyful and utterly changed in spirit, even letting his childhood nanny light the icon in his room. He begins to preach that life is paradise, that we are all in paradise, but do not want to know it. If we did want to know it, there would be paradise, the world over, tomorrow. He says that he is not worthy to be loved and served by others. We should all serve each other. Each of us is guilty for everything and before everyone. He begins to ask the birds for forgiveness, declaring that he alone has dishonoured everything and did not notice the glory and beauty of it all. All this remains indelibly imprinted on Zosima's heart.

Following this episode we soon learn of Zosima's own first minimal religious experience at the age of eight and, interestingly, it too is associated not with the theological tradition of Orthodoxy but rather with the sensual character of the liturgy, a combination of natural light and ecclesiastical architecture and a sudden insight into the religious significance of a Biblical story. His mother took him to church for the Monday liturgy during Holy Week. He remembers the incense rising from the censer, God's rays pouring down into the Church through a narrow window in the cupola and the incense rising in waves. For the first time, he consciously received the Word of God in his soul. For the first time, he understood something of what was being read in God's Church. It is the story of Job. What is great here is the mystery: how could God smite his servant just so that he could say how much he suffers for his sake? Earthly image and eternal truth touched each other here. The old grief, by a great mystery of human life, becomes quiet, tender joy. The young ebullient blood becomes a mild, serene, old age. Over all is God's truth, moving, reconciling and all-forgiving. Earthly life is already touching a new, infinite unknown. Minimal religious experience it may be, but it is channelled through the Orthodox tradition, as though in a kaleidoscope in which, just occasionally, fragments suddenly and unexpectedly come together to make a supremely wonderful and meaningful pattern that, as Bakhtin would put it, is inwardly persuasive.

As a child, Zosima had had a book called *One Hundred and Four Sacred Stories from the Old and New Testaments*, and learnt to read with it. Priests, he now says, should read to their simple flock from the Bible, especially to children: of Abraham and Sarah, of Isaac and Rebecca, of how Jacob went to Laban and wrestled with the Lord in his dream and said 'how fearsome is this place.' The Orthodox heart will understand everything. Read how Joseph's brothers sold him into slavery, how he seized his brother Benjamin in Egypt, the whole while loving them and tormenting them at the same time. Only a tiny seed is needed in the heart of a simple man. It will not die but live in his soul all his life, hiding there amidst the darkness, amid the stench of his sins, as a bright point, a great reminder. Read the story of the beautiful Esther and the arrogant Vashti or the parables of our Lord, chosen mainly from Luke, and Saul's speech from the Acts of the Apostles, and finally from the Lives of the Saints, at least the Life of Alexei the Man of God and our Mother Mary of Egypt. He who believes in the people of God will also see their holiness. Only the people with their spiritual power can convert our atheists. The people perish without the word of God, for their souls thirst for his Word and every experience of beauty. All things are good and beautiful because all is truth. He points to the mildness and trustfulness in the face of the horse or the ox. Everything except man is sinless and Christ is with them even before us. The Word is for all, every little leaf is striving towards the Word.

These recollections are followed by the story of Zosima's taciturn visitor, whose name is Mikhail. He admires Zosima, who concludes that he must be hiding some mysterious secret. He agrees that paradise is hidden within every one of us and that everyone is guilty before and for all. When everyone understands this, the Kingdom of Heaven will come to them. He says this is a matter of the soul, a psychological matter. A psychological change is necessary. In view of Dostoevsky's known reservations about contemporary psychology, it may be worth recalling the root of the word 'psychological'. Strictly speaking, the word psyche is Greek not for mind or spirit, but for soul and it is not unreasonable to assume that when Zosima's mysterious visitor uses the word here he, and probably Dostoevsky too, have in mind the faculty through which people intuit a spiritual realm rather than the subject matter of a science of the mind. Perhaps it would not be too far wide of the mark to suggest that what is at issue here is a choice of cognitive compasses. No science of self-interest, the mysterious visitor continues, will ever enable people to share their property and rights without resentment. The period of human isolation must end. The Russian word for isolation used here is *uedninenie*, which might equally well be translated as alienation or estrangement. Everyone tries to find fullness of life by separating himself off, but what follows is not fullness of life but total suicide. What is needed is not isolation but a general wholeness of humanity. When this happens, the Son of Man will appear in heaven. Zosima seems to say that the Kingdom of God will arrive only when the brotherhood of humanity has been achieved.

Suddenly the mysterious visitor blurts out his secret: he has killed a person. He tells how he murdered the woman he loved who had turned him down and arranged things so that the blame would fall on the servants. Nobody has ever suspected him. A servant was arrested but died unexpectedly before coming to trial. After that, the mysterious visitor's own punishment begins. At first, though he regrets killing the woman he loved, he suffers no remorse for the murder. Other circumstances ease his conscience. He throws himself into official and philanthropic work, but eventually starts brooding. Just then he meets and marries a wonderful and sensible girl, hoping to escape his old memories. He feels unworthy of her love and of his children, and begins to have horrible dreams. Finally, he dreams of confessing publicly. Zosima's duel makes up his mind. But he hates the thought of his wife dying of grief, his children being stripped of their rank and property, and the terrible memory that he will leave in their hearts. He has been in hell for 14 years. If he confesses, he will be in paradise. He continues to visit without confessing and begins to doubt the wisdom of it on many grounds. Zosima tells him to confess and again reads John 12: 24. Then he reads Hebrews 10: 31: 'It is a fearful thing to fall into the hands of the living God.' The mysterious visitor comes back and sits silently for two minutes. He tells Zosima to remember it. However, the next day is his birthday. At his party, he reads out a statement giving full details of his crime and produces forensic evidence. People don't believe him and decide that he has gone mad. Doctors confirm it. People blame Zosima for making him depressed. When Zosima gains access to him, the mysterious visitor whispers that he had intended to kill him on his last visit. He knew that he would not be able to face him if he did not give himself up, and he hated him for it. He soon dies himself. At first people turn against Zosima, then they begin to believe the mysterious visitor's testimony. As Caryl Emerson has remarked recently, the story plays the part in Zosima's testament that the legend of the Grand Inquisitor does in Ivan's confession. In both cases we are dealing with spiritual liminality or, more plainly, a threshold where a fateful spiritual choice has to be made. Emerson writes of 'his ecstatic words about hell instantly becoming paradise'.[231] That the choice of paradise may involve suffering both for oneself and for others is by no means excluded. But the price of continuing to suppress one's terrible secret is even greater. Zosima's quotation from Hebrews 'It is a fearful thing to fall into the hand of the living God' echoes his reference to Jacob's 'how fearful is this place.' To continue to live the lie, as the Grand Inquisitor does, is to cut oneself off from the divine. It seems to suggest that it may lead back to that terrifying abyss where the choice between faith and nothingness finds its origin. Both the Grand Inquisitor and the mysterious visitor have preserved long silences about terrible secrets. Both eventually break their silence. But whereas the Grand Inquisitor's confession is a long self-justification, Mikhail's is an expression of profound repentance. As well as serving as a counterpoint to the legend, the story of Mikhail problematizes Markel's dying epiphany and anchors it in the realm of hard moral choices: paradise comes at a cost; repentance and love, which Zosima connects, are here placed in dire conflict, for public confession will involve public disgrace and private misery for his loved ones. He hovers uncertainly a long time before the fateful choice is finally made and almost takes the opposite path.

VII

Zosima's Homilies

There follows a selection of Zosima's homilies, which take up and expand on themes that have already been introduced, but also give substance to the newly introduced ideas and experiences of Markel and the mysterious visitor. First of all Zosima talks about the Russian monk and his possible significance, and introduces a positive conception of solitude. He admits that there are sub-standard monks, but the ideal monk leads a life of solitude and fervent prayer in peace. (Solitude is once again *uedinenie*; peace is *tishina*.) They keep the image of Christ pure and undistorted, in the purity of God's truth. Although they are isolated from other people, therefore, they are close to Christ's image and God's truth. In a world that exalts itself above the people of God, the image of God and his truth are distorted. It has science, and science knows only what is subject to the senses. But the spiritual world, the higher half of man's being, is rejected altogether, banished with a sort of triumph. This world has proclaimed freedom, but knows only slavery and suicide. It tells people to satisfy their needs and to increase them. But what follows is isolation and spiritual suicide for the rich, and envy and murder for the poor. It generates many meaningless, pleasure-seeking and self-indulgent desires and people will even kill themselves if they are unable satisfy them. Instead of freedom they lapse into slavery; instead of serving brotherly love and human unity, they have fallen into disunity and isolation, as the mysterious visitor used to say. The way of the monk is very different: obedience, fasting and prayer are the way to real and true freedom. Who is more capable of upholding and serving a great idea — the isolated rich man or the one who is liberated from the tyranny of things and habits? The monk is reproached for his isolation and for forgetting his brotherly ministry to mankind, but we shall see who is more zealous in loving his brothers. The salvation of Russia will come from the people, and the Russian monastery has been with the people from time immemorial. The people will confront the atheist and overcome him, and there will be one Orthodox Russia. Watch over people and keep a watch on their hearts. Guide them in peace.

The next section in Alesha's notes is about masters and servants and whether it is possible for them to become brothers in spirit. Equality is only in man's spiritual dignity, says Zosima. Let us preserve the image of Christ, so that it may shine forth like a precious diamond to the whole world. He tells about meeting his former servant Afanasy again, now that he is a monk, and the communion between them. He talks about the future communion of mankind when each will seek to serve others. With Christ we shall bring this about. Scoffers dream of building a just order without Christ, but they will end by drenching the world with blood, for blood calls to blood, and he who draws the sword will perish by the sword.

There follows a vitally important section on prayer, love and contact with other worlds. Do not forget to pray, Zosima says, for prayer is education. Do not be afraid of men's sin. Love all of God's creation and you will perceive the mystery of God in things and you will come to love the whole world with a complete, universal love. Love the animals for they are sinless. Especially love children. A loving humility is a terrible power, the most powerful of all. Love is a teacher but it is difficult to acquire. All is like an ocean, all flows and connects. Touch it in one place and it echoes at the other end of the world. Ask gladness from God:

> On earth we seem in truth to be wandering and, if we did not have the precious image of Christ before us, we would perish and altogether lose ourselves, like the human race before the flood. Much on earth is concealed from us, but in place of it we have been granted a secret, mysterious sense of our living bond with another world, with a higher heavenly world, and the roots of our thoughts and our feelings are not here but in other worlds. That is why philosophers say it is impossible on earth to conceive the essence of things. God took seeds from other worlds and sowed them on this earth, and raised up his garden; and everything that could sprout sprouted, but lives and grows only through its sense of being in touch with other mysterious worlds; if this sense is weakened or destroyed in you, that which has grown up in you dies (XIV, 290–91).

The penultimate section asks whether one can be the judge of one's fellow creatures and speak of faith to the end. Do not judge anyone. No one should judge another without recognising that he is even guiltier than the accused for the crime in question. If you are surrounded by wicked and callous people, who do not want to listen to you, fall down before them and beg their forgiveness. If you desire revenge upon the wicked, fear that feeling most of all. You will understand that you too are guilty, for you might have shone forth before them, yet you did not. Throw yourself down on the earth and kiss it, love it tirelessly, insatiably, love all men, all things, seek this rapture and ecstasy. Water the earth with tears of joy and love those tears. Finally in a section on hell and hellfire, Zosima declares that hell is the suffering of being no longer able to love.

Zosima's testament is, of course, of vital importance for understanding the religious dimension of the novel. To a degree it fills out what he has said already, but without the ambiguity that inevitably occurs in interpersonal dialogue. It is, however, the product of interpersonal dialogue and relates back to it, a fact that is emphasized by the inclusion of the stories of Markel and Mikhail. The power of love and prayer are stressed again, as is the beauty of nature. The theses that we are all guilty for all and for everything, and that if only we realized that the world was paradise it would be, are repeated, and thus reinforced, not only by Zosima in his own right, but also by his dying brother Markel and by his mysterious visitor.

But it also juxtaposes a picture of humanity suffering a five-fold estrangement to a picture of humanity that is spiritually whole. The individual may be isolated from himself (inwardly divided), from other individuals and from human society as a whole, from 'God's creation' and from 'God's truth'. The consequences of such alienation (isolation, or estrangement) will be bloodshed and destruction. This picture is not very different from the Grand Inquisitor's picture of humanity unable to shoulder the burden of freedom and in need of the Catholic Church to bring happiness based on a lie. Only Zosima's creed offers reconciliation with and love of God's truth, his creation, other people and one's neighbour. It proclaims not a lie but the Truth. His testament points to various points of entry to this spiritual state: above all there is repentance and active love, or what the Slavophiles (and Dostoevsky in their wake) called *sobornost'*, the principle of unity of the Orthodox Church and the Russian people; where nature is concerned, there is the overwhelming sense of beauty; and, to guide us all, there is the precious image of Christ. Only a tiny seed is needed, says Zosima, in the heart of a simple person. It will not die, but live in his soul all his life, hiding there amidst the darkness.

But although Zosima speaks of 'God's creation', 'God's truth', and 'the Word of God', God is apparently still an elusive concept for him. Once again, his creed borders on that of Ivan. He concedes that philosophers say that it is impossible on earth to conceive the essence of things. By 'philosophers' he has no doubt in mind Kant and his successors, but, as we have remarked, this is also the case in the realm of apophatic theology. However, Zosima adds an important dimension, for he holds that here on earth, although much is concealed from us, we have been granted a secret, mysterious sense of our living bond with another world, with a higher heavenly world, and the roots of our thoughts and our feelings are not here but in these other worlds. That is why philosophers say it is impossible on earth to conceive the essence of things. God took seeds from other worlds and sowed them on this earth, and raised up his garden; and everything that could sprout sprouted, but lives and grows only through its sense of being in touch with other mysterious worlds; if this sense is weakened or destroyed in you, that which has grown up in you dies (XIV, 290–91).

Much of this is undoubtedly metaphorical, yet Zosima seems to want us to take literally his talk of an inner bond with other worlds. It is this that makes the difference between the individual who emerges with a shining faith from the silent darkness beyond human knowledge and the individual who is isolated and lost and knows only despair or rebellion. While he remains in this one, Zosima cannot, by definition, tell us anything further about these other worlds. Yet his faith is grounded in this conviction, and it is in this faith that, at the end of Part 2, he eventually dies. Nothing in his narrative, or in the texts he quotes, suggests that the pilgrimage is easy. From among the passages in the Old Testament that he recommends, one has only to think of the story of Job, who experiences to the full the sense of being abandoned by God, or of Jacob who went to Laban and wrestled with the Lord (Genesis 32: 24ff.) and said, 'how fearsome is this place' (Genesis 28: 17), to realize that his empathy with Ivan is born of a full understanding. Critics often present such passages as the key to Zosima's 'answer to Ivan'. Yet, of course, they are not answers to Ivan's questions. They are descriptions of the spiritual crossroads where, apparently, Zosima's and Ivan's paths have crossed and diverged.

VIII

More Patterns in the Religious Kaleidoscope

Having established the point of divergence and the alternative routes taken by Zosima and Ivan, what follows in the rest of the novel may well be described in terms of the Epstein model as 'minimal religion', both in its broader and its purer forms. Zosima's intimation that a life of repentance, love and belief in God and immortality can have its origin in the tiniest seed sown by someone else or, in mythological terms, by God, hints at such a state of affairs. So does his omission to give centrality, or indeed any place at all, to the Resurrection of Christ, a belief central to all branches of mainstream Christianity but given special emphasis in the Orthodox tradition. It is not simply that Zosima does not accord it primacy of place. Unlike St Paul, for whom it is of vital and central importance, he even omits it from his argument for the immortality of the individual soul. Dostoevsky himself, as we have seen, argues for immortality on the grounds that the human ideal is unrealisable in this life. Zosima, and we have to assume the narrator is content with this, sees belief in immortality as an inevitable consequence of living a life of active love, not as a consequence of belief in the resurrection of Jesus, as the early Church held and preached, and the doctrine of the Orthodox Church confirmed. Notwithstanding this omission, spiritual rebirth is central to the novel and to Zosima's teaching, though expressed through a strikingly different metaphor, that of the seed that falls to the ground and dies before springing again to life (John 12: 24). The metaphorical character of the image is underlined by the fact that seeds do not in fact behave in this way. Minimal religion (a religion liberated from an elaborate interpretative tradition) is therefore at the very centre of Zosima's creed. However, as we shall see, minimal does not necessarily mean superficial and certainly not trivial.

Part 3 begins with the observance of traditional monastic rites over the body of the dead Elder; with the malicious glee among some of the monks when the odour of corruption becomes noticeable, undermining Zosima's claims to saintliness in the eyes of those who subscribe to certain ancient traditions and whose faith depends on miracles; and with Alesha's dismay that his beloved elder's standing has thus been compromised. We are told, however, that it is not miracles but only 'a higher justice' that Alesha hungered for, once again echoing his brother Ivan's rebellion and the predicament of Job. He could not bear the thought that this most righteous of men should be the subject of such derision and spite, from a crowd that was so frivolous and so far beneath him. Why did Providence hide its finger, as if wanting to submit to the mute, blind, merciless laws of nature (XIV, 306–07)? Alesha's faith in God (unlike Ippolit's or Kirillov's in their respective novels) is not shaken, but something of yesterday's conversation with Ivan begins to trouble him. It is Rakitin who recognizes that he is in a state of rebellion, to which Alesha responds, echoing his brother, by saying that he does not rebel against God, but simply does not accept his world (XIV, 308).

In the remaining parts of the novel, the reader is often struck by echoes, situation rhymes and analogies with episodes from Ivan's confession to Alesha, and from Zosima's testament. Very often they strike a minimalist note in the purer sense, as when Grushenka tells Alesha the story of the peasant woman who dies and seeks forgiveness on account of a single onion (XIV, 319). Alesha responds to Grushenka's exaggerated gratitude by saying that he has just given her 'an onion'. The theme is taken up again in Alesha's dream at the side of Zosima's coffin, when Zosima assures him that there are many at the Wedding in Cana of Galilee who only gave one little onion (XIV, 327).[232]

Also clearly attributable to the category of minimal religion, or at least religiosity, are the many examples of conventional use of religious terminology, appeals to God or the devil, for example, whose status and significance for the speaker are more likely to derive from folk religion than from any subtle or profound religious faith.

But even the great spiritual experiences of Alesha and Dmitry may justifiably be said to be minimalist in that they are presented as direct expressions of religious experience only lightly touched by the forms of orthodox theology and dogma and often contaminated by decidedly unorthodox, if not heretical sources. Such is the case with Dmitry's 'hymn to joy' (deriving from Schiller)[233] or Alesha's belief in resurrection (deriving perhaps from Fedorov)[234] or the echoes in the characterization of Alesha and Zosima of writers with Catholic backgrounds such as George Sand[235] and Victor Hugo.[236] In the chapter 'Cana of Galilee', where Alesha returns to the hermitage and to Zosima's coffin with joy in his heart, he begins praying, though almost mechanically, and, we are told:

> Fragments of thoughts flashed in his soul, and caught fire like little stars, only to die out at once and be replaced by others, yet there reigned in his soul something whole, firm and soothing, and he was conscious of it himself (XIV, 235).

Father Paissy reads from John about the Wedding in Cana of Galilee. Alesha associates the first miracle with the joy brought by Christ. It is evident that he is falling asleep. He sees Zosima alive again. He is a guest at the wedding. Zosima asks if Alesha sees his sun, and Alesha says he is afraid to look. Zosima tells him not to be afraid. His greatness is awful but he is merciful. Tears of rapture fill Alesha's soul and he leaves. We have already referred to this passage more than once, but it is worth quoting it again in full in the light of Epstein's model, and we shall note, as we have before in a different context, that all but token reference to Orthodox ritual and traditional Christian doctrine has been suppressed; perhaps it would be more appropriate to say that, though channelled through it, Alesha's religious experience has been liberated from Orthodox ritual and traditional Christian doctrine, at the very moment when it might be expected to overwhelm him, at a moment when a performance of that ritual and a proclamation of that Gospel coincides with a profoundly emotional religious experience that seems to cry out for such an interpretation. So much so, indeed, that critics, especially those with Orthodox sympathies, have not been slow to provide it. But what is most significant is that the narrator does not do so. Indeed, we know from the evidence of his notebooks that, at least in one important respect, Dostoevsky suppressed his urge to provide it. Here is the passage again:

> [Alesha] did not stop on the veranda, but quickly went down the steps. Filled with ecstasy, his soul thirsted for freedom, room and space. Above him the heavenly vault stretched out, broad and measureless, full of silent, shining stars. From its zenith to the horizon, the still misty Milky Way ran its double course. The fresh night, silent to the point of motionlessness, lay upon the earth. The white towers and golden

domes of the church sparkled in a sapphire sky. The magnificent spring flowers in the flower beds near the house had fallen asleep until morning. The earthly silence seemed to merge with a heavenly silence; an earthly mystery touched a heavenly mystery... Alesha stood, looked and, as if suddenly felled, threw himself to the earth. He did not know why he was embracing it, he did not try to understand why he wanted so irresistibly to kiss it, to kiss it all, but he kissed it weeping, sobbing and watering it with his tears, and vowed ecstatically to love it, to love it forever. The words 'Water the earth with tears of joy and love those tears,' rang out in his soul. What was he weeping about? Oh, he wept in his ecstasy even about those stars that gleamed on him from the abyss and 'felt no shame for this rapture'. It was as if threads from all these numberless worlds of God came together at once in his soul, and it trembled all over, 'touching these other worlds'. He wanted to forgive everyone for everything and to ask forgiveness, oh, not for himself but for everyone, for everything, for 'others are asking forgiveness for me,' the words rang out again in his soul. But with every moment he felt clearly and almost palpably something as firm and unshakeable as this heavenly vault descend into his soul. Some sort of idea was beginning to reign in his mind, and to continue to do so for his whole life and to eternity. He had fallen to the ground a weak youth, and he rose to his feet a steadfast fighter for the rest of his life, and he felt this suddenly, in the very moment of his ecstasy. And Alesha would not ever forget that moment for the rest of his life. 'Someone visited my soul at that moment,' he would say afterwards with firm faith in his words (XIV, 328).

Not 'God visited my soul', but 'someone', note, although God's name has been invoked earlier in the same passage. There is at once a looseness and a precision about Alesha's formulations. The looseness derives from the novelty of the experience and his struggle to find his own inadequate words to describe it. The precision derives from his refusal to fall back on traditional, theological formulae, but to forge his own.

Although more elaborate and more intense, Alesha's experience seems not dissimilar to Ivan's after his third and final meeting with Smerdiakov and just before his encounter with his devil:

It was as if a sort of joy now descended into his soul. He felt an infinite firmness in himself: the end to his hesitations, which had tormented him so terribly all through those last days! The decision was taken, 'and now all will be changed,' he thought with happiness (XV, 68).

The same may be said of Dmitry's repeated references to the hand of God in his affairs. These may be moments of elation, and the name of God may be invoked, but there is no reason to assume that the Orthodox tradition in all its fullness lies behind them. Indeed, as we have seen, there is more in

Dmitry's words that remind us of Schiller than of Orthodoxy (XIV, 413; 425–26; 456–57; 458), even in his conviction that a new man has arisen inside him. His dream of the baby was a prophecy. God will bring joy to him as a prisoner: the men underground will start singing a tragic hymn to God, in whom there is joy. Dmitry says that he is tormented by God. How can man be virtuous without God? To whom will he be thankful? To whom will he sing a hymn? He can't understand how man can love mankind, as Rakitin avers, without God (XIV, 31). Even when Alesha tells Ivan that God has sent him to tell him that he did not kill his father, that it is God who has put it into his heart to do so, it is far from clear that he is echoing any particular religious tradition. Ivan says he cannot bear prophets and epileptics, and especially messengers from God, and suggests that they break off relations and go in opposite directions. Ivan goes off to talk to Smerdiakov (XV, 40–41).

Alesha is not liberated from his reservations about God's world as a consequence of his epiphany. We still find him intuitively siding with the rebels. And even his final speech at Iliusha's graveside is not an Orthodox homily, not even a paraphrase of his Elder, but something much more personal:

'Know that there is nothing higher, or stronger, or more healthy, or more useful afterwards in life, than some good memory, especially a memory from childhood, from the parental home. You hear a lot said about your education, yet some such beautiful, sacred memory, preserved from childhood, is perhaps the best education of all. If a person takes many such memories with him into life, then he is saved for his whole life. And even if only one good memory remains with us in our hearts, that alone may serve some day for our salvation' (XV, 195).

It is not Christ's death and resurrection that saves us, but a precious memory from childhood. Moreover, Alesha's 'just one memory' echoes Grushenka's and Zosima's (in Alesha's dream) 'one little onion'.

Kolia asks Alesha if it can really be true that, as religion says, we shall all rise from the dead, and come to life, and see one another again? 'Certainly we shall rise, certainly we shall see and gladly, joyfully tell one another all that has been,' says Alesha.

The echoes and situation rhymes that proliferate in the rest of the novel sometimes appear to be full of meaning, while other times they seem to be quite arbitrary. The existence of the former invites us to ask whether the latter are really arbitrary and may have a hidden meaning. The existence of the latter warns us not to interpret the former too generously.

For example, there are repeated allusions to folk religion, into which category must be put the mentions of icons (Khokhlakova's gift of an icon to Dmitry (XIV, 349); Kolia's swearing to his mother before the icon (XIV, 465); Iliusha's bed in the corner by the icons (XIV, 485)) and probably Iliusha's conviction that God is punishing him for his cruelty to the dog Zhuchka (XIV, 482). As with the case of the holy fool, motifs that sometimes seem to denote deep spirituality seem at others to be entirely devoid of it. Such is the case with all reflections of folk religion in the novel.

Allusions to religious movements or texts may extend the range of religious reference but in other respects may also seem almost arbitrary. For example, what are we to make of the fact that in exchange for the toy cannon Kolia has brought as a gift for Iliusha he had traded a copy of an ancient book entitled *A Relative of Mohammed or a healing folly* (XIV, 493)? What significance should we attach to the fact that the warden at Dmitry's prison has been reading the Apocryphal Gospels (XV, 26)? More tantalisingly, what, if anything, do we make of the fact that when Smerdiakov takes the bundle with 3,000 roubles in it from his sock and declares to Ivan that Dmitry is as innocent as can be, he puts his book, *The Homilies of Our Father among the Saints, Isaac the Syrian* over the money, to hide it. This is the kind of book that we should expect Zosima to have, not Smerdiakov. In fact a number of scholars have speculated on its influence on the characterization of Zosima and on Dostoevsky's preparations for the novel.[237] Has Smerdiakov even opened its pages? This is the sort of question on which one might expect a conference paper, though I have not yet come across one.[238] And how many readers notice that there is a reference to a second *Life of the Elder Zosima* (*Zhitie v boze pochivshego startsa otsa Zosimy*), this time published by the diocesan authorities? It is mentioned by the Counsel for the Defence (XV, 100) and attributed to Rakitin. That is all we hear of it and the narrator evidently prefers Alesha's notes. There is also the occasional reference to other Christian confessions, not simply to the Catholic Church, but even to the fact that Dr Herzenstube is, apparently, a Herrnhuter or Moravian (XV, 103).

Then, on the negative side there are the many echoes of Ivan's discourse and personal experience. In Lise's dream, for example, there are echoes of Ivan's hallucinatory encounter with his devil, and Father Ferapont's hunger-induced visions of little devils. Lise's little devils lurk in the corners waiting to pounce on her, she says. Then suddenly she wants to abuse God and they rush at her; she crosses herself and they draw back. Amazingly, Alesha says he has had the same dream himself (XV, 23).

More significantly, there are echoes, in caricatured or intellectually diminished form, of the sort of discourse on religious topics that we have already heard from Ivan or Rakitin. There is more from Rakitin, of course, and the greater part of Kolia's precocious views on the subject also belong to this category. He patronisingly tells Alesha that he has heard that he is a mystic, but a touch of reality will cure him. Obviously, as with much else, he has got this wrong, for the narrator has already told us otherwise as early as the novel's fourth chapter (XIV, 17). He says he has nothing against God, but that he is only a hypothesis, necessary for the sake of order. If there were no God he would have to be invented, he says, parroting Voltaire. To this Alesha replies that Voltaire believed in God and in mankind, but very little. Kolia says that he's a socialist, and much more in similar vein. Alesha says he does not despise him, but is sorry that his soul should already be perverted by all this crude nonsense, and the reader cannot help but agree. By this time we all are too familiar with his view (cf. Rakitin, Ivan) that it's possible to love mankind without believing in God, and do not require a caricature of it to press the point home (XIV, 499 ff). Kolia is also Ivan's unwitting disciple in his belief that he is innocent of an act, if he only has the idea and someone else carries it out. He tells Alesha how a peasant killed a goose at the market in accordance with 'basic principles' that he had expounded (XIV, 495–96).

It is Ivan's devil who bridges Ivan's relatively sophisticated viewpoint and its cruder expressions, combining in his conversation with Ivan accounts of earlier stages in his thinking (that, with the exception of the legend of the Grand Inquisitor, now embarrass Ivan) with satire on reasoning of the kind that we have encountered from Smerdiakov or even old Karamazov. He agrees with the narrator (or is it the other way round?) that proofs are no help to faith, especially material proofs. Thomas believed not because he saw the risen Christ, but because he wanted to believe even before that. (Compare the narrator's comments in XIV, 25 with Ivan's devil's in XV, 71.)

> 'Take spiritualists, for example … I like them so much … imagine, they think it supports faith when devils show their little horns to them from the other world. "This," they say, "is so to speak a material proof, that the other world exists." The other world and material proofs, hey presto! And, after all, who knows whether proof of the devil is also a proof of God? I want to join an idealist society and form an opposition within it: "I'm a realist," I'll say, "not a materialist,"'

Ivan recognizes his 'devil' as himself talking, an embodiment of himself, just one side of him, only the most loathsome and stupid of his thoughts and feelings. The devil's words contain more satire on vulgar religious philosophizing, for example,

> 'By some pre-temporal arrangement, which I have never been able to fathom, I am appointed to "negate" […] Without criticism, there would be only "Hosannah". But "Hosannah" alone is not enough for life, it is necessary that this "Hosannah" pass through the crucible of doubt, and so on, in the same vein' (XV,77).

Is this even satire on Dostoevsky himself? Ivan's devil too, just as is reported of Ivan, Zosima and Alesha, says he does not know whether he believes in God.

> 'Let's just say, if you like, that my philosophy is the same as yours, that would be correct. Je pense donc je suis, I'm quite sure of that, but all the

rest around me, all those worlds, God, even Satan himself — for me all that is unproven, whether it exists independently, or is only my emanation, a consistent development of my ego, which exists pre-temporarily and uniquely ...' (XV, 77).

The Devil says that he is intentionally leading Ivan alternately between belief and disbelief. He sows just a tiny seed of faith and from it an oak will grow. He says that even those who pray and eat locusts in the desert can contemplate such abysses of belief and unbelief at the same time that really it seems that only a hair's breadth separates them from falling in (XV, 80). And here Ivan's devil, or perhaps we should say Ivan himself, leads us back to that very abyss that, according to Epstein, lies at the very heart of the apophatic tradition, and to which, earlier in the novel, Zosima himself had drawn attention. Alesha decides that he is beginning to understand Ivan's illness: God, in whom Ivan did not believe, and God's truth were overcoming Ivan's heart:

'God will win!' he thought. 'He will either rise into the light of truth, or ... perish in hatred, taking revenge on himself and everyone for having served something he does not believe in' (XV, 89).

Even the Prosecutor at Dmitry's trial has more than a glimmering of the spiritual abyss over which humanity, and particularly the Karamazov brothers, hangs. He refers to the 'accursed questions (*prokliatye voprosy*)' that preoccupy the modern Russian (XV, 123). Having given an account of the travails of present-day Russia and of the 'Europeanism' of Ivan and the 'popular foundations' of Alesha's life-style, he says of Dmitry that he is capable of being sincerely noble at one moment and sincerely base the next (XV, 128).

'Why? Precisely because we are of a broad Karamazov nature — and this is what I am driving at — capable of containing all possible opposites and of contemplating both abysses at once, the abyss above us, an abyss of lofty ideals, and the abyss beneath us, an abyss of the lowest and foulest degradation' (XV, 129).

There is little doubt that 'the Karamazov nature' stands in Dostoevsky's mind for 'the Russian soul' and the Russian soul for the true condition of humanity as a whole.

So we come back full circle. According to this reading, the religious vision of Dostoevsky's most famous novel finds its origins in the abyss over which humanity hangs as it confronts the unknowable Godhead in silence and finds there either the divine presence or the spirit of nothingness. The institutions and the dogmas of the Church are there to guide us, but our own religious experience may be much more diverse and in essence much simpler. It is this picture of minimal religion (and indeed minimal atheism, for there is no institution yet to embody it) that Dostoevsky depicts, a picture in which the institutional Church plays a background part, for, as the narrator tells us on the occasion of little Iliusha's funeral:

> It was a very old church and rather poor, many of the icons were without settings, but somehow one prays better in such churches (XV, 192).

To put it another way, here is fertile soil for those seeds that have fallen to the ground and died, to rise again to new life. Sarah Hudspith, who considers John 12: 24 a suitable epigraph for the whole of Dostoevsky's oeuvre, puts the point very well when she says that a corn of wheat is a simple thing; it is also extremely small, but it has the potential to bring forth much fruit.[239] Does that mean that the tradition of Orthodoxy in its fullness is of no consequence in *The Brothers Karamazov*? Certainly not. The Orthodox tradition, though they may now sit lightly to it, is the channel through which both Zosima and Alesha have come to their religious visions. It is, to use a favourite Orthodox metaphor, the window through which they approach transcendent reality and whose theology has enabled them to formulate their own religious outlook on life. Without the presence of that tradition, Zosima's formulations would have been impossible and there would have been no possibility of Alesha's discipleship. However, the reader will have to look beyond Dostoevsky's text to find that tradition expressed in its fullness. The text repeatedly gestures in that direction without forcing the reader to go there.

X

Silence

In its quest for nothingness, the apophatic tradition gives special value to silence. Hesychasm, says C S Calian, is an internalized method of theologising through prayer. The ultimate aim is a mystical union with God within a context of silence. The word *hesychia* means tranquillity or peace in Greek. Ultimate tranquillity is a state of silence or quietude.[240] Or, in the words of Kallistos Ware, 'The hesychast, the person who has attained hesychia, inward stillness or silence, is par excellence the one who listens. He listens to the voice of prayer in his own heart, and understands that this voice is not his own but that of Another speaking within him.'[241]

Dostoevsky's novels do not, of course, immediately strike the reader as celebrations of silence. Neither his narrators nor his major characters, nor some of his minor ones, ever seem short of a word or two to say. Even Zosima jokes that he is so used to talking that it would be more difficult for him to be silent than to speak (XIV, 148). Like his critics, Dostoevsky himself was aware that he never conquered his tendency to overwrite. Yet even a superficial reader of *The Brothers Karamazov* will notice that moments of silence play a vital role in the novel's poetics. The great silences of Jesus and the Grand Inquisitor, which stand at the heart of the novel, together with the dramatic, even culpable, silences of characters at key moments in the development of the plot, will spring to every reader's mind. However, silence in this novel is more than a mere dramatic device. It emerges from close study as a major organising principle of the novel's narrative.

Silence is capable of many meanings, as a full list of the various adjectives used with the noun would show. Moreover, Russian is capable of more subtle shades of meaning than English, distinguishing between *molchanie* (absence or cessation of speech or conversation), *tishina* (tranquillity or absence of sound)[242] and *bezmolvie* (absence of speech or sound), words that evoke some of the most memorable lines in Zhukovsky or Pushkin, as well as the apophatic tradition in Russian Orthodoxy.

Reflection on great moments of silence in Russian literature, from Pushkin's 'the populace is silent'[243] to Tiutchev's *Silentium* or Jesus' silent kiss in 'The Grand Inquisitor', exposes two salient features. The first and third of these moments illustrate the ambiguity of silence. How much ink has been spilt over the meaning of the silence of the populace at the close of Boris Godunov, Jesus' silent kiss in Ivan's poem, the dumb show at the end of Gogol's *Revizor*, or the dots which close some of Pushkin's best-known lyrics...

Such ambiguity may have varying effects, depending on context. It may be used to open up dialogue or it may be used to close it down. There is no better example of Bakhtin's 'discourse with a loophole', for it is always possible to deny the other's interpretation of one's silence.[244] It can have a more devastating effect than any words. A short story by Leonid Andreev graphically makes the point. Making a distinction between *tishina* and *molchanie*, to which we shall return later, his narrator says, 'It was not a tranquil silence (*tishina*) because a tranquil silence is just the absence of sounds. This was the kind of silence (*molchanie*) 'which occurs when those who are silent might apparently have spoken, but have declined to do so'.[245] Father Ignatii, his protagonist, is driven out of his mind by the combined silences of his dead daughter and his wife, both of whom might have spoken but did not, and whose silences seem to converge on his guilt. This is also, of course, the strategy that the narrator of Dostoevsky's story 'The Gentle One' deploys on the story's heroine, with similarly fatal consequences.[246]

As Dostoevsky knew very well, the writer may intentionally exploit ambiguity. Someone has said: the greatest artists are those who know the limits of their own craft; the greatest writers are those who best understand the limits of language. However, Tiutchev's poem makes a different point. For Dostoevsky, it raises a fundamental question about the capacity of language ever to do justice to the complexity and profundity of reality, ever to convey the true meaning of life. At the very time when 'the crucial assemblages and transformations of material' for *The Brothers Karamazov* were taking place, Dostoevsky was seriously reflecting on the key line of Tiutchev's poem: 'a thought once uttered is a lie'.

In a variant to an article in *The Diary of a Writer* for October 1876 he wrote:

> The truth is that reality is profounder than any attempt by human fantasy or imagination to grasp it. In spite of the apparent simplicity of phenomena there is a terrible enigma in the fact that one seeks in vain in reality for beginnings and ends. Everything flows and has its being but you will never succeed in pinning anything down in concepts or words — it immediately becomes a falsehood. 'A thought once uttered is a lie' (XIII, i, 326).

Here Dostoevsky explicitly links what Bakhtin has called unfinalizability (*nezavershennost'*) with the ineffableness of truth, not just of God, but of all higher reality: there are no beginnings and no ends in the real world; reality is profounder than anything that human imagination can conceive; everything exists and is in a flux. But the moment you reduce it to words (or logarithms or reason, the Underground Man would have added) you enter the realm of lies. The Tiutchevan principle, as one might call it, affirms both that the deepest thoughts are incapable of being expressed in words and that in expressing a thought you inevitably distort it. But Dostoevsky goes further than this. His note firstly and most importantly affirms that there is a reality and there is a truth beyond the range of human language and human understanding. Only secondarily, but no less importantly, does he affirm that this truth or reality is ultimately inaccessible to the human imagination. These leitmotifs had come to prominence in Dostoevsky's fiction in *The Idiot* (VIII, 328). In 1877, shortly after the variant quoted, he was to publish in *The Diary of a Writer* his famous story 'The Dream of a Ridiculous Man' (XXV, 104–119), in which he re-mythologized the Fall as humanity's discovery of the lie.

The Brothers Karamazov harps on these themes too, sometimes to the point of caricature. There is no better illustration of the relationship between talkativeness and the lie than the speeches at Dmitrii's trial, in which stories (plausible, though patently false) are made up by the prosecuting and defending counsels about the events surrounding the murder. There was no murder. There was only a report of a violent death surrounded by reports of evidence.

The role of silence as an organising principle in the poetics of Dostoevsky's last novel is foreshadowed in the authorial preface itself, where the fictional author, having raised the question as to why he is writing two novels about his hero, reveals his strategy. When faced with problems which are difficult to solve, he says, he will leave them without solutions: 'Rather than waste time trying to solve such questions, I shall decide to leave them without any explanation' (XIV, 6).

When we turn to the characters and the unfolding drama of the novel, we notice that Ivan, Alesha, Kalganov and others are all reported at one stage or other in their lives, either by the narrator or by another character, to be taciturn (*molchaliv*). Characters in the novel often fall silent. We are told of silences that are restrained, impressive, resolute and earnest, mysterious, dignified. We are told of Ivan that he keeps silent and grins without saying a word, which is why people think he is so clever (XIV, 158); of Grushenka that she fell silent as though stifling something in her heart (XV, 189). Silence may betoken embarrassment, depression, suppression, resignation, anxiety, foreboding, cowardice, impotence, guilt, unsociability, piety, anger, cynicism, uncertainty, derision, the wish to imply something without actually saying it, and many more motives and states of mind. All these varieties of silence are exemplified in the novel and may be traced to individual moments in the narrative.

Very often, the moments of dramatic silence that occur between characters are almost surreal in their intensity, virtually impossible to reproduce in dramatisations of Dostoevsky's novel. The reader is familiar with them from his earlier works. Karamazov, we are told, was silent for about two minutes after his performance in the monastery (XIV, 85). This is perhaps more plausible because others continue talking. However, on receiving Dmitry's money from Alesha, Snegirev is silent for almost a whole minute and unable to utter a word (XIV, 190). And who will forget the scene of two minutes' total silence (XIV, 281) in which Zosima's mysterious visitor sits opposite him in his room, deciding whether or not to kill him? Katerina is likewise silent as she kneels before Dmitry. Ivan is silent at the trial. Some of these silences are not just dramatic occasions. They play an active, even a fateful role in the development of the plot.

For, example, Dmitry's reticence about the source of the money he spends at Mokroe (XIV, 440) complicates the investigation and acts against his interests. Ivan's silence, when faced with Smerdiakov's hints of what may happen to his father in his absence, is apparently taken by Smerdiakov as approval for his unvoiced plan to murder the old man (XIV, 244).

Though Alesha and Ivan are both characterized as taciturn, their silences are radically different. At first Fedor Karamazov does not distinguish the difference. He says of Alesha that he is much too silent and thinks too much. But Fedor Karamazov is mistaken. It is inner tranquillity (*tishina*) not the suppression of clamorous thoughts (*molchanie*) that underlies Alesha's silences.[247] Ivan's silence, on the other hand, is the result of psychological suppression. This turns out to be a vital difference, which not only distinguishes Alesha from Ivan, but also forms the axis of the thematic structure of the novel. For this reason we should pause a moment on Ivan.

Ivan has a secret. Dmitry says:

'Brother Ivan is a sphinx and is silent, whereas I am tormented by God [...] Ivan has no God. He has an idea beyond my comprehension. But he is silent. I think he must be a freemason. I have asked him about it, but he is silent. I wanted to slake my thirst at his spring, but he is silent. On only one occasion did he drop a hint.'

'What did he say?' asked Alesha hurriedly.

'I said to him, "If that's the case, then it must mean that everything is permitted?" He frowned. "Fedor Pavlovich," he said, "our dear daddy, was a swine all right, but he reasoned correctly"' (XV, 32)

The novel reveals what happens to Ivan when the secret is out, and when the economy of suppression ceases to be effective. The theme is paralleled in Katerina's outburst at the trial when she can no longer hold back her bitterness at her humiliation; or in the explosion of rage on the part of the older monks when Zosima's corpse exhales the odour of corruption; or in the Grand Inquisitor's tirade when confronted with the image of Jesus. And it is reinforced in some unexpected quarters. It is Snegirev who tells Alesha that silent and proud children may hold back their tears for a long time but are liable to break down suddenly under great pressure (XIV, 189). On the other hand, we learn of the relief of Zosima's mysterious visitor when he eventually breaks his long years of silence about the murder he has committed.

The many psychoanalytical studies of Ivan Karamazov are sufficient to remind us that he exemplifies Freudian repression.[248] Ivan has a secret. That is why he is silent. And Ivan's secret is one that in its complete form he cannot admit even to himself: that he lives on that perilous cliff edge between passionate belief and sheer unbelief, at least up to the point of composing his poem about the Grand Inquisitor, and arguably therefore at the time of his conversation with Alesha too.

Silence in Dostoevsky's novel is then a reflection of the inadequacy of language to express reality in its most important aspects, a narrative strategy to awaken and sustain interest, a source of dramatic intensity, a means of characterization, especially of neurotic characters, and a lever of plot development. That would be more than sufficient to attract our interest. But it is more than that. It is evident that silence plays a vital role in the view of reality and human values, which the text seeks to represent. And this is brilliantly dramatized in the novel's three key chapters, each focussing the personal drama of one of the brothers. These are 'The Grand Inquisitor' in the case of Ivan, 'Cana of Galilee' in the case of Alesha and 'In the darkness' in the case of Dmitry.

These are the three great moments of silence in the novel, each relating to one of the three brothers. Together they define the parameters of silence on the thematic level.

Ivan's legend is not just a fable of silence. It is also a fable of final outbursts. Ivan himself is breaking his silence to Alesha. He is telling him the secret (or that part of it of which he is conscious) that he withholds from Dmitry and from everybody else. But his mouthpiece, the Grand Inquisitor, has been silent on a superhuman scale. He has kept silence for ninety years. His secret — a secret that he cannot confess to a living soul — is that he does not believe in God. He does not believe in what stands before him. Yet he is still haunted by Christ's image. In this respect he is a model for all of Dostoevsky's atheists.

> 'The important thing was that the old man should speak out, that he should finally speak out after ninety years and say aloud what he has remained silent about for all those ninety years.'
>
> 'And the prisoner is silent too? He looks at him without uttering a word?'
>
> 'Yes, that is how it always has to be in such cases. The old man himself remarks to him that he has no right to add anything to what has already been said.'[...]
>
> 'When the Inquisitor had fallen silent, he waited for a moment to see what his prisoner would reply. His silence oppressed him. He saw that his captive was listening quietly and attentively the whole time, looking straight into his eyes, apparently wishing to raise no objection. The old man would have liked him to say something, however bitter, however terrible. But he suddenly approached the old man in silence and quietly kissed him on his bloodless ninety-year-old lips' (XIV, 228–29 and 239).

Here we have a juxtaposition of two silences, the one (Ivan's and the Grand Inquisitor's), the long obsessive guarding of a secret broken in a torrent of words in the form of a confession; the other, the silence of inner peace and tranquillity. It is the contrast between *molchanie* and *tishina*. But, if the Epstein model is right, it is more than this in the case of Ivan and the Grand Inquisitor, for what they are doing is not verbalising a long-hidden truth; they are verbalising a long-hidden half-truth. The other half, that Jesus in this interpretation perceives, is that they are still haunted by an underlying, unspoken and unacknowledged belief. They have mistaken its inexpressibleness for non-reality. They too, at the deepest level, live on the perilous cusp of belief and unbelief, and their confessions tell of what happens to the spiritually sensitive soul when that belief is denied.

Then there is Alesha. In his mystical experience, Alesha senses the thread of all God's innumerable worlds meeting in his soul; something as firm as the heavenly vault itself entering it; the sensation of someone visiting it; an idea gaining ascendancy over his mind that would last for the rest of his life. Just before this, the narrator records the autumn flowers falling asleep till morning and then earthly silence (*tishina*) seems to merge with heavenly silence (*tishina*), earthly mystery with heavenly mystery (XIV, 328). It is reminiscent of Zosima's recollection of the birds falling silent against a background of tranquillity and universal prayer: 'The little birds fell silent; everything was praying to God silently (*tikho*) and magnificently' (XIV, 267). Alesha has experienced the silence not simply of the soul but of Creation itself.

Finally, there is Dmitry's moment, the moment when his father is killed, though he does not know it at the time. He is there in the garden at the fateful hour.

> But everywhere there was a deathly silence (*molchanie*) and, as if by design, complete calm (*zatish'e*), not a breath of wind. 'And only the silence (*tishina*) whispers': for some reason this line of verse flashed through his mind (XIV, 353).

As usual, when Dmitry quotes verse, he misquotes, this time from Pushkin's *Ruslan and Liudmila*. But in this scene there is an extraordinary mixture of sensations: a deathly silence (*mertvoe molchanie*), complete calm (*polnoe zatish'e*) and the whisper of silence (*shepchet tishina*). A dark, menacing, brooding silence is juxtaposed to, perhaps even merges with, complete tranquillity. And indeed, in subjective terms, this is an accurate reflection of the reality of the moment. While Fedor Pavlovich is actually being murdered, an act with fateful consequences for Dmitry too, the hand of God seems to have held Dmitry back. Afterwards Dmitry would say, 'God [...] protected me at that time' (XIV, 355).

The idea of silence overcomes Dmitry again at other moments of stress. Later, under investigation, he misquotes Tiutchev: '"Be patient, be humble and be silent," he completed his thought with a line of poetry, and gathered his strength again in order to continue' (XIV, 423).

If there are two kinds of silence, and the narrator seems to be pointing us towards the silence of tranquillity, Dostoevsky as author does not grant an easy victory. As always, he puts his fondest ideas to the severest test, in this case the test of parody. For the most devoted adherents of the life of silence are, as we have seen, Zosima's fanatical opponents in the monastery, led by father Ferapont. Father Ferapont and Father Jonah are great observers of fasts and silence. Among Zosima's opponents were some of the oldest monks, strictest in their devotions, committed adherents of a life of fasting and silence, who have kept silent during the life of the great Elder, but whose lips are suddenly unsealed after his death, greatly influencing the young monks with still immature ideas.

Ferapont parodies the life of silence not only in his person, but also in the imagery he chooses. As he makes his protest against the dead Elder, he turns towards the setting sun and falls to the ground with a mighty cry. Exclaiming 'Christ has conquered the setting sun' (XIV, 304), he falls face downwards on the ground and bursts into sobs, crying like a little child.

At first we may be struck by the repetition of sacred motifs associated with Alesha and Zosima (the setting sun, falling down on the ground and sobbing, childlikeness). But not only is the language different: there is far too much noise and anguish, even physical violence, about Ferapont's performance. It is evident that his silence has not been the silence of tranquillity; it is the silence of a suppressed anger now bursting forth. It is *molchanie*, not *tishina* that he has discovered in his long devotion to the monastic life, a *molchanie* in which he is tormented by visions of cosmic chaos embodied in his little devils. In reality, Ferapont is not much of an adversary for Zosima. He exemplifies the very principles that Zosima opposes, dressed up in the clothes of sanctity. The silence (*molchanie*) associated with Ferapont, Ivan, the Grand Inquisitor, are signs of illness, of psychological dysfunction. But the tranquillity (*tishina*) of Zosima, or Alesha, and, in a fleeting but significant moment, of Dmitry, finds its roots in the ancient Orthodox tradition. Zosima advocates the life of the Russian monk, particularly those who long for solitude and fervent, silent prayer (*tishina molitvy*, XIV, 284).

It is evident that silence and discourse coexist in Dostoevsky's text in opposition to each other, if not in a dialectical relationship. Elsewhere I have argued that for Dostoevsky human language is 'fallen discourse'.[249] The underlying thought is expressed in the famous line from Tiutchev which Dostoevsky pondered as he laid the foundations for his final novel. But it only put succinctly what he already knew very well and what his narrators and characters had long protested, namely that human beings are fated to use a discourse which is inadequate to their higher nature, the deepest spiritual realities and the fullness of God. When they try to talk of God, as Myshkin observes, they somehow miss the main point (VIII, 182), and this always seems to be the outcome when people try to express their deepest thoughts.

However, it is also arguable that there is a dialectic of silences at work in the deep structure of Dostoevsky's novels, in which the silence of closure is in opposition to the silence of openness and that, notwithstanding a certain lack of consistency in Dostoevsky's use of the words, a dialectic between *molchanie* and *tishina*. The first silence is a silence of boundaries, a silence of prohibitions and taboos; ultimately it is the silence of chaos and non-existence. It is the silence which demarcates, distinguishes, selects and measures and which therefore underlies scientific classification and rational thought. Like theological dogma, it has its place. But access to the divine source of life is to be accomplished only through spiritual tranquillity, *hesychia*, which relates to the unsayable.

Silences — different varieties of silence — lead us on the one hand into the duality of inwardly divided characters and on the other into the spiritual unity of those characters who are relatively whole. The former is the silence of the person trying to impose his or her own pattern on the raw material of experience by censoring out the unclassifiable, the Elihu whose 'ignorant words cloud my [God's] design in darkness' (Job, 38: 2), who has tried to understand the ineffable with what Ivan Karamazov would call his Euclidian mind, and who has been forced into inevitable distortions. The latter is the silence of Job, who hearkens to the ultimate tranquillity of Nature beyond the tumult and clamour of immediate experience, the person who attends to the words of the Lord addressing him from out of the whirlwind. We may know a character by the nature of his or her silence or, in the case those denied, or spared, such intense experiences, by the nature of their talkativeness.

ESSAY VI

Conclusion

In this concluding essay I make no claim to originality. As I did in essay two, I shall selectively revisit earlier work by other scholars, but this time not to raise questions so much as to show how these scattered findings may be integrated into the model that I have suggested.

The chapter on *The Brothers Karamazov* shows that it is perfectly possible to read Dostoevsky convincingly through the prism of the Epstein model, once this model has been translated into synchronic terms and modified to take account of the fact that the Soviet experience had not yet occurred. In fact, this rather significant modification is less damaging than it might seem at first sight, since it explains why Dostoevsky is often said to have anticipated, or even prophesied, Soviet Russia and other atheistic totalitarian states of the twentieth century. The novel gives clear hints of that originary silence of darkness that may lead to the fullness and tranquillity of faith on the one hand or the desolation of the abyss of nothingness on the other; it puts the conflict between these two outcomes at centre stage in the persons and philosophies of life of Ivan and Zosima, and to varying degrees in those of their acolytes. It also presents us with evidence that the two responses are not necessarily polar opposites, but may interact and overlap, and that any individual may flip uneasily between the two. It also presents us with many examples of what Epstein calls minimal religion — what earlier I called the shoots of a new Christianity — in a variety of different forms, especially those forms of religious experience which are no longer underpinned by institutions, ritual and dogma. In fact minimal religion, in Dostoevsky as in actual historical experience, may combine Christian elements with pagan elements and with motifs from other religious traditions altogether. Such minimal religion emerges from the energy sapping and ultimately unresolved battle between theism and atheism that characterizes Dostoevsky's mature novels.

However, there are some forms of religious experience in Dostoevsky that deserve further elaboration. In earlier chapters, I have tended to relegate the folk traditions of the Orthodox Church, Russian sectarianism and Old Belief to the margins, and to suggest simply that they furnish us with examples of minimal religion. But there is another, and possibly more fruitful, way of interpreting the place of folk religion (as we may call it all for brevity's sake) in his scheme of things for, as we have seen, Dostoevsky ultimately placed his faith in the capacity of the Russian peasant to see to the heart of things and to conserve in his soul the essence of the Christian faith, in spite of his lack of education and his tragic historical experience. Although Dostoevsky sometimes took this attitude to the point of self-caricature, he drew heavily on Russian folk religion as a source of positive spiritual insight. He was also aware that some of these folk traditions — that of the Holy Fool, for example — were ambiguous in their spiritual worth. And there were others that fed on a fascination with spiritual darkness.

Some of these traditions were received in written form and have, it has been persuasively argued, fed into the depiction and even the discourse of Zosima in *The Brothers Karamazov*. Sergei Hackel[250] has discussed a number of these. For example, there was the Elder Amvrosy of the monastery at Optina Pustyn, who, as was his custom, probably gave Dostoevsky various books on the occasion of his brief visit to the monastery with Vladimir Solovev in the summer of 1877. Hackel argues that the monk Parfeny's travel tales may have influenced Zosima's style of presentation, and that Dostoevsky was also able to draw on Parfeny's earlier account of a visit to the Elder Leonid. The newly canonized Tikhon of Zadonsk, whom Dostoevsky declared he had long ago welcomed into his heart, was richly represented in his library, and he openly acknowledged the influence on Zosima of certain of Tikhon's homilies. Most important of these religious sources, Hackel suggests, may have been Isaac of Syria's *Ascetic Discourses*, translated into Russian from the Greek; these are mentioned in the notebooks for the novel and several times in the novel itself: as we have seen, Grigory had a manuscript copy of *The Discourses*, though he understood very little of it; Smerdiakov had a printed copy which he used to hide the money; Ivan spotted it when he visited Smerdiakov. None of this seems to be of positive spiritual significance, but Hackel speculates that Isaac of Syria's view of the value of tears as the fruit of penitence and spiritual perception, and a stage on the way to divinisation, may lie at the root of Zosima's advocacy of tears. Similarly there are parallels, but not exact equivalences, between Isaac's and Zosima's description of an exalted spiritual state; while Isaac's insistence that 'paradise is the love of God' finds an echo, though not an exact equivalent, in Zosima's doctrine on human and divine love. These and other sources in Orthodox hagiography have been well attested in the work of Hackel, Vetlovskaia, Linnér, Stanton and others, and the reader fascinated by the richness of this subtext may turn to their pages. For our purposes it is sufficient to note firstly that in each case it is the spiritual ethos rather than the precise doctrine or practice that interests Dostoevsky, and which he imports into his own text. This is particularly noteworthy in the case of Kliment Zedergolm's *Life of the Elder Leonid* that, Leonard Stanton argues, was used by Dostoevsky as a source for *The Brothers Karamazov*.[251] Stanton draws particular attention to those elements of Zedergolm's presentation of Leonid's life that foreground aspects of Orthodox theology deriving from the apophatic tradition: the possibility of divinisation of the individual believer; the belief that spiritual truth is inaccessible by means of reason, but acquired in silence; the authority that derives from spiritual knowledge rather than from reason. In addition, Stanton finds passages in the *Life of Leonid* that, he shows, Dostoevsky probably imported directly (if in disguised form) into the text of his novel. Once again, this is of less importance to our theme than the fact that Dostoevsky's understanding and depiction of the Eldership and its theological roots in the hesychast tradition, and on the margins of the life of the Orthodox Church, itself exercised a strong influence on his conception of the true character and sources of spiritual knowledge.

This point is reinforced by Michel Niqueux[252] who, in a recent survey of the importance for Dostoevsky of the Russian sects and Old Believers, concludes that although he certainly read widely about dissenting religious groups, including those with European sources, such as the shtundists and spiritualists, and although he occasionally wrote about them, and even had some personal familiarity with their adherents in Siberia and in St Petersburg, he was not in the end interested so much in their ethnographical features as in the character of their spiritual life.

While it is hardly surprising that the lives of the Orthodox saints had some bearing on Dostoevsky's depiction of Zosima, it is quite easy to overlook the fundamental importance of sectarians and Old Believers for the dynamics of religious experience in his work. Though he was not drawn to sectarianism as a solution to his religious questing, there is no doubt that he was deeply fascinated by it in his attempt to diagnose Russia's religious predicament. This fascination long pre-dates his exile to Siberia and finds its earliest expression in the short story 'The Landlady' whose hero is reportedly writing a history of the Russian Church. The antecedents of the sinister Murin have been much discussed, and there can be little doubt that there are several vaguely identifiable sources outside Dostoevsky's own fertile imagination, including West European literature, notably the stories of E T A Hoffmann. Yet the dark and sinister side of the Russian religious tradition was already haunting Dostoevsky's mind. Murin has been seen by some as exhibiting features (physical as well as spiritual) of the Old Believers, as well as of the castrates and the flagellants. Mikolka in *Crime and Punishment* (who falsely confesses to Raskolnikov's crime) is presented as a schismatic. We have already seen how the theme of Old Belief and sectarianism resurfaces in *The Idiot*, principally through Rogozhin. Niqueux reaches the interesting conclusion that if the flagellants (*khysty*) are linked in Dostoevsky's mind with irrational and religious immanentism, the castrates are connected in his work with murder and revolution, for example in Petr Vekhovensky's ambitions for Stavrogin as a false tsar, and that their significance therefore far exceeds the purely contextual, and has far-reaching metaphorical significance for him. That this is the case seems to be confirmed by the links between Smerdiakov and the sectarians in *The Brothers Karamazov*, and by Smerdiakov's links with Ivan. In other words, although it is impossible to pin down exactly how Dostoevsky saw these connections, two very important facts emerge. The first is that he saw a progression from true Christianity to socialistic atheism not only in the development of Western civilisation (which he emphasizes in his anti-Western polemics and most commentators emphasize as a consequence) but also in the development of Russia's home-grown traditions via the link between sectarianism and revolution. The second is that the dynamic religious processes that we have been examining in Dostoevsky's work, and which are thrown into relief by the juxtaposition with Epstein's model, are to be seen not only in the philosophising of his intellectual heroes, but even more clearly within the traditions of Russian sectarianism itself. Here, in the soul of the Russian peasant in whom Dostoevsky put so much faith, and not only in the mind of the enlightened intellectual who has lost his roots in the soil, is the ultimate meeting-place of spiritual enlightenment with spiritual darkness. Here is the place where Christianity and gnosticism merge, where religious spirituality and nationalism lie down together, where religious fanaticism and political revolution join forces. And should one doubt that Dostoevsky actually made these connections, one has only to look at his plans for his unwritten *Life of a Great Sinner*, which fed into all his later novels. Of the projected hero, he wrote:

> The loss of faith in God has a colossal effect on him. [...] He darts about among the younger generations, among atheists, Slavs and Europeans, Russian heretics and dwellers in the wilderness, among priests. He falls under the influence of a proselytising Polish Jesuit, and descends from him into the depths of *khlystovshchina* [the sect of the flagellants], and finally finds Christ and the Russian land, the Russian Christ and the Russian God (XXVIII, i, 329).

Then, in a letter to Apollon Maikov from Dresden, dated 25 March/ 6 April 1870, he wrote, somewhat differently:

> (The general title of the novel is *The Life of a Great Sinner*, but every story will have a separate name.) The main question, which is dealt with in all the parts, is the one that has tormented me consciously and unconsciously all my life — the existence of God. The hero, in the course of his life, is now an atheist, now a believer, now a fanatic, now a sectarian, then an atheist again (XXIX, 117).

Nor was he immune to the infection himself, as his own identification of Russian nationality with a profession of the Russian Orthodox faith confirms. It is in these regions, surely, that Dostoevsky intuited, beyond the torments of his own mind, the existence in Russia's historical experience of that mix of light and darkness that was capable of deeply sinister developments as well as of pointing towards a spiritual rebirth.

Dostoevsky's world is not then bathed in the warm glow of Orthodoxy; nor does he depict a world in which peace and turmoil are equally balanced. Most of his characters, most of the time, live on the troubled surface of a reality that is characterized by turbulence, conflict and instability. Like

Ivan Karamazov in theory, and Dmitry Karamazov in practice, they may find temporary solace in the sensuous pleasures of life. But there are also small oases of spiritual tranquillity for the privileged few. In *Crime and Punishment*, *The Idiot* and *The Devils*, such moments are indeed hard to find and their ability radically to transform lives may seem doubtful. Yet in *The Brothers Karamazov*, the reader is given more hope. So long as the individual retains his sense of being in touch with other mysterious worlds, through the seeds that God sowed in this world, there is hope, whereas, if this sense is weakened or destroyed in the individual, that which has grown up in him or her dies (XIV, 290–91). Of course, the image of Christ preserved in the monastery plays its essential part in this process, but the richness of the Orthodox tradition as a whole has faded into the background.

We noted a number of examples of folk religion in the essay on *The Brothers Karamazov*, in some cases identified as such by the narrator, places where Christian traditions merge with and pick up deep-rooted pagan superstitions. The appearance of little devils to Ferapont (not to mention Alesha, Lise and Ivan Karamazov) is a prominent example, the more significant in that it occurs within the heart of a Christian community and is accompanied by eccentric, not to say unorthodox, theological speculation. Such chaos monsters, representing the threat of an originary chaos to an established cosmos, are common to most if not all ancient religions and are embodied, in the Christian tradition, in the person of Satan. However we interpret Ivan's devil — psychological interpretations seem the most convincing to many readers — Satan steps onto the stage in person in Ivan's legend of the Grand Inquisitor. One of his temptations, it will be remembered, is to yield to the demand for the miraculous. That temptation is also foregrounded in the events following Zosima's death, when many of the monks expect his sanctity to be confirmed by miracles. When this does not happen, the views of his detractors seem to receive confirmation. The sub-text reminds us that Jesus (according to Mark, 8: 12, for example) despaired of a generation that demanded signs and said that no sign would be given them.[253] While it may be doubtful that Dostoevsky had this explicitly in mind, the implied rejection of the demand for the miraculous, both in the story of Zosima and in 'The Grand Inquisitor', could be read as a response to the visions of Ippolit or Kirillov, or to Holbein's picture of Christ taken down from the Cross, in which Christ's divinity turns out to be illusory. Put more succinctly, the response would be that the requirement that Christians believe in the historical veracity of the Resurrection accounts is totally unnecessary in the light of Jesus's own dismissive attitude to signs and wonders. The important thing is what Bakhtin would have called the inwardly persuasive nature of the underlying myth of spiritual resurrection in each individual life and at the end of time. Such an interpretation would also be in keeping with the preference of the narrator for psychological interpretations of religious phenomena. If this is a permissible reading, then the novel points to one more alternative form of minimal religion, one that anticipates developments in twentieth century Western theology and perhaps points in the direction of a Jungian analysis.

Finally, there is the question, raised in Epstein's model, of the development of non-Christian faiths. There are of course references, especially to Islam, in *The Brothers Karamazov*, but they are entirely of a negative kind. There is no suggestion that they would find fertile soil in Russia. However, a growing number of critics have found interesting parallels between the spirituality of Dostoevsky's novels and that of non-Christian faiths. Since this lies outside the remit of this book, they will receive no more than a mention here, but they are worth noting because they seem to draw on a common pool of spirituality that underlies not only the Judeo-Christian and Muslim traditions but also Buddhism and even, it has been argued, Shamanism. Tatiana Kasatkina refers to a number of recent studies in which Myshkin has been likened to an arctic shaman or a Sufi mystic 'gifted with a profound apophatic intuition' which has as much in common with Buddhism as with Islam and draws on a common spiritual source.[254]

Hence the importance of minimal religion, the small seeds mentioned by Myshkin and Ippolit, Grushenka's parable of the onion, the passing reference to the traditions, rituals and dogma of the Church, the importance of good, though fragmentary, memories from childhood. Hence, also, the strategic placing of the passage from John, 12: 24, which forms the epigraph to *The Brothers Karamazov*. In this light, the rationale of *Notes from Underground*, *Crime and Punishment*, *The Idiot* and *The Devils* becomes clearer too. While they are not permeated with the spirit of Orthodoxy, they do all, in their different ways, show the presence of new shoots of faith appearing in the atheistic gloom: The Underground Man's intuition that there is a better way; Sonia's simple faith; Raskolnikov's future renewal and rebirth; the hints at the close of *The Idiot* that Myshkin's passage through their lives has had some positive effect on at least Vera, Kolia and Radomsky; Verkovensky senior's death-bed conversion; all point the way towards the more spacious panorama of *The Brothers Karamazov*. Why are his novels not depressing? Possibly because in conceding the darkness that hangs over the face of the earth, they also depict a light that repeatedly breaks through and remind the reader of the promise that the light has vanquished the darkness.

If Dostoevsky chiefly depicts 'minimal religion' in his novels, one is entitled to ask, why have critics consistently got it wrong? One type of answer perhaps lies in the religious or antireligious predispositions of critics themselves and an implicit commitment to showing the coherence of literary texts and to providing a key to their interpretation. This book is, of course, not immune to such an accusation; the important thing in reading Dostoevsky is to find a key to coherence, which makes full allowance for the fact that his text so often nearly collapses into incoherence; for the fact that, drawing on a tradition of writing that Derrida has characterized as logocentric, it is nevertheless so vulnerable to deconstruction. Another type of answer lies in Dostoevsky's own pious words about his intentions and his known commitment to Orthodoxy, particularly towards the end of his life. But how could any truly attentive reader of his novels be misled into believing that the lure of unbelief had gone away? How, for that matter, could any attentive reader be misled into thinking the opposite, that his belief was simply a matter of self-delusion? That these are rhetorical questions will be plain to any reader who has not started reading this book at the end.

Ultimately, we have proposed, Dostoevsky's is not a binary world, though it, like the individual personality, has a seemingly irresistible tendency to express itself in such terms. The contending principles have a common origin which lies outside the text (like the vanishing point in a picture): everything depends on which route the individual takes from the silence of darkness or how individuals navigate their way between. The choice determines not only an abstract philosophy of life, but also one's relationship to the universe, the natural world, to society, to oneself, to other people and to the world to come, even to the business of thinking and philosophising itself, in other words to how one regards human discourse, in particular religious discourse, whether one sees it as an expression of one's sense of wholeness or as an analytic tool in the service of one's own will and the creation of one's own system of values.

The model that we have proposed has certain advantages from the point of view of the critic, for it accommodates both Dostoevsky's wish to make us choose between the Orthodox tradition and atheism and the countervailing impression that to make such a choice is arbitrary. In other words, it saves us from having to choose between a 'Christian' reading and a 'non-Christian' reading, a religious reading and a post-modernist reading. On the contrary it obliges us to accommodate the two, for in Dostoevsky's world the reality of their coexistence is unavoidable. Moreover, the religious dynamic of Dostoevsky's novels clearly corresponds to a process that continues recognisably in our own day. Dostoevsky undoubtedly hoped that these shoots of a new faith would lead back to a renewed form of Russian Orthodoxy. This may be so, though today it is looking somewhat doubtful. That does not, however, necessarily mean that they do not possess their own validity. As Myshkin says, when atheists talk about religion, they always seem to miss the whole point and to be talking about something quite different (VIII, 182).

There is no real doubt about Dostoevsky's personal faith in his experience of God as a supernatural power; nor is there any doubt about his persistent private reservations about whether such a belief is ultimately based on an illusion. There is also no doubt of his belief in the supreme value of such experiences in human affairs even if they are indeed ultimately based on an illusion. In other words, Dostoevsky personally placed his faith in the empowering value of the image of Christ, whether there was a supreme transcendent reality or not. The alternatives would seem to be that nihilistic darkness that haunts his intellectual heroes or a life devoted to limited sensual and materialistic pursuits. All three positions, and his oscillation between them, are amply documented in his non-fictional writing, and his fictional world depicts a reality in which all three conclusions are possible.

It does not insist on the rightness of any one of them. There is no way of determining whether the religious experiences of his characters are merely projections of their own ideals, expressed in culturally available images, or whether they reflect a reality which ultimately escapes definition but which human beings try constantly to capture and transmit through such images. The surprising thing is that the images that he enlists are so varied and so loosely connected to the Orthodox Tradition. It is possible to read them in one way or the other. There is no way of determining the issue, and this is precisely the point.

In addition to dramatising such basic questions, Dostoevsky loses no opportunity to show his reader that religious experiences come in a wide variety of forms, some of them of much greater value for the purpose of human fulfilment than others. Not only atheistic nihilism, but also some forms of religion are destructive of human fulfilment, and such experiences seem to come to individuals who are themselves psychologically maimed or inadequate, or unable to grasp the difference between literalism and the poetic interpretation of religious imagery and narrative. In *The Brothers Karamazov*, Dostoevsky actually locates many such individuals within the confines of the monastery, the very institution whose historical destiny, according to his own beliefs, was to preserve the precious image of Christ. Other inadequate characters seem to be provoked into making their views explicit by visiting the monastery. So even the most sacred institutions of the Church are not immune, indeed they seem to harbour, even provoke, some of the most negative aspects of spirituality. This is one of the most remarkable features of Dostoevsky's depiction of religious experience and practice, namely that he not only juxtaposes it with powerful expressions of antireligious thought and practice, but also exposes its own weaknesses; moreover, he does this not only in relation to those forms of Christianity to which he was in principle opposed, because he considered them degenerate, but also in relation to Orthodoxy itself.

I have used what I have called the Epstein model as an explanatory tool to account for the interrelationship of these varieties of religious experience within Dostoevsky's text. Some readers may still be uneasy at the thought that Epstein's model is itself incapable of verification and may be a distortion of actual historical processes. Indeed it may. We can only judge it by its efficacy in clarifying such processes. That is why, in spite of a temptation to jettison it for fear of arousing such objections, I have nevertheless persevered with it. At the end of the day, it does not matter for my purposes whether its tracing of the dramatic oppositions of non-rational religious faith and forms of nihilistic atheism in Russia to the peculiarities of apophatic theology is correct or not. What matters is whether it casts light on the dynamic structure of religious experience in Dostoevsky's fiction. I believe, and have argued, that it does.

Endnotes

1 My allusion here is to the distinction that Brian McHale makes between modernism and postmodernism in terms of their alleged epistemological and ontological dominants. See McHale (1987), pp. 3–4.
2 See Frank 1976, pp. 42–53; Kjetsaa 1987, pp. 1–18.
3 Dolinin 1964, i, p. 61.
4 Grossman 1922, p. 68.
5 Hudspith 2004, p. 167.
6 On the importance of memory in Dostoevsky, see Thompson 1991.
7 Dolinin 1964, i, p. 97.
8 Frank 1976, p. 78.
9 In addition to the sources quoted above (note 3), a detailed account of Dostoevsky's reading may be found in Catteau 1989, pp. 33–62.
10 Dolinin 1964, i, p. 169.
11 Frank 1976, pp. 195, 201, 210.
12 Belinsky 1948, iii, pp. 707–17, 709.
13 Gibson 1973, p. 10.
14 There was as yet no translation of the whole Old Testament into modern Russian.
15 Frank 1983, p. 23.
16 L'vov 1956, pp. 165–90, 188: 'We shall be with Christ'.
17 Kjetsaa 1984.
18 It is striking, for example, how little space Nicholl (1998) devotes to the major novels.
19 Dolinin 1964, i, p. 254.
20 Dolinin 1964, i, p. 250.
21 Dolinin 1964, i, pp. 346–47. There is an excellent discussion of these issues in Frank 1983, pp. 194–98.
22 Dolinin 1964, i, p. 281. Although they varied in frequency and intensity, Dostoevsky's epileptic fits continued until the end of his life. See Catteau 1989, pp. 90–134.
23 For a detailed account of the content of *Time* and *The Epoch*, see Chances 1974.
24 Kjetsaa 1987, p. 285.
25 Liza Knapp makes these notes her point of departure in her fascinating new book, Knapp 1996.
26 For a recent discussion of the image of the Russian Christ as Dostoevsky saw it see Schoultz 1998.
27 Knapp 1996.
28 Kjetsaa 1984, p. 39.
29 Sutherland 1977, pp. 85–98.
30 *Neizdannyi Dostoevskii* 1971, p. 675.
31 See Murav 1992, pp. 66ff.
32 Zakharov 1997.
33 Zakharov 1994a; Esaulov, in Zakharov (ed.) 1998.
34 See Cox 1969, pp. 140ff.

35 Kjetsaa 1987, p. 222.
36 Esaulov, in Zakharov (ed.) 1994.
37 Gibson 1973, pp. 92–93.
38 For an account of the psychological strategies underlying this interaction, see Jones 1990, pp. 77–95.
39 See Miller 1997.
40 Miuller, in Zakharov (ed.) 1998.
41 Morson 1997.
42 See Leatherbarrow 1982; also Leatherbarrow, The Devil's Vaudeville, in Pamela Davidson (ed.), *Russian Literature and the Demonic*, Oxford, Berghahn (forthcoming).
43 See Egeberg 1997.
44 Fridlender 1959, pp. 191ff.; Gibson 1973, pp. 112–13.
45 Gibson 1973, pp. 112–13.
46 Gibson 1973, p. 38.
47 See Thompson 2001.
48 Dostoevskaia 1971, p. 201.
49 Compare, for example, Timofeeva's account of Dostoevsky's ranting in 1873–1874 about the coming of the Antichrist (Dolinin 1964, ii, p. 170) or Leskov's account of his sullen, ill-tempered, stubborn defence of Orthodoxy against Protestantism (Leskov 1958).
50 Zernov 1961, p. 232.
51 Gibson 1973, p. 142.
52 Gibson 1973, p. 153.
53 Gibson 1973, pp. 154–68.
54 See Linnér 1975; Hackel 1983; Stanton 1995.
55 An English translation of extracts from this letter can conveniently be found in Leatherbarrow and Offord (trans. and ed.) 1987, pp. 125–26.
56 Cox 1969, p. 210.
57 Gibson 1973, p. 14.
58 L'vov 1956, p. 188: We shall be with Christ; 'A speck of dust'.
59 See Nicholl 1997, pp. 119–76.
60 See the excellent new book by Hudspith 2004.
61 See Futrell 1981. It is worth noting in this connection that one of the books in Dostoevsky's personal library was A. Gusev, *Nravstvennyi ideal buddizma v ego otnoshenii k khristianstvu*, (*The ethical ideal of Buddhism in its relationship with Christianity*) St Petersburg, 1874 (Grossman 1922, p. 43).
62 Pattison and Thompson 2001.
63 Pattison and Thompson 2001, p. 4.
64 Pattison and Thompson 2001, p. 11.
65 Guardini 1933, 1963.
66 Barth 1933.
67 Thurneysen 1921.
68 Pattison and Thompson 2001, p. 16.
69 Gibson 1973.
70 Sutherland 1977.
71 Pattison and Thompson 2001, pp. 1–2.
72 Camus 1951, p. 52 (footnote).
73 James 1960.
74 I have not forgotten that George Pattison's own contribution, the final essay in the book, is on Dostoevsky and Kierkegaard ('Freedom's dangerous dialogue: Reading Dostoevsky and Kierkegaard together', pp. 237–56), but although Kierkegaard's influence in the twentieth century has been considerable, he can scarcely be regarded as a twentieth-century philosopher in his own right, and Pattison does not treat him as one.
75 Pattison and Thompson 2001, p. 69.
76 Pattison and Thompson 2001, pp. 103ff.

77 Pattison and Thompson 2001, p. 135.
78 Pattison and Thompson 2001, p. 70.
79 Pattison and Thompson 2001, p. 94.
80 Pattison and Thompson 2001, p. 76.
81 Pattison and Thompson 2001, p. 75.
82 Pattison and Thompson 2001, p. 87.
83 Perlina 1985.
84 Pattison and Thompson 2001, p. 95.
85 Pattison and Thompson 2001, p. 107.
86 Pattison and Thompson 2001, p. 103.
87 Heller 1961, p. 181.
88 Pattison and Thompson 2001, p. 104.
89 Sutherland 1984, pp. 1, 26.
90 Pattison and Thompson 2001, p. 106.
91 See, for example, Smart 1989, pp. 10–21.
92 Figes 2002, pp. 297–301.
93 Pattison and Thompson 2001, pp. 31–40.
94 Pattison and Thompson 2001, pp. 226–36.
95 Pattison and Thompson 2001, pp. 134–55.
96 Pattison and Thompson 2001, pp. 226–36.
97 Pattison and Thompson 2001, pp. 31–40.
98 Sarah Hudspith has remarked that the only character to mention the resurrection of Christ in *The Brothers Karamazov* is Ivan's devil. But, strictly speaking, the reference is to Christ's ascension, not to his resurrection (Hudspith 2004, p. 122; XV, 82).
99 Pattison and Thompson 2001, pp. 41–50.
100 Pattison and Thompson 2001, pp. 116–33.
101 Notably, Linnér 1975; Hackel 1983; Stanton 1995.
102 Pattison and Thompson 2001, pp. 31–40.
103 Smart 1989, p. 20.
104 Pattison and Thompson 2001, pp. 173–88.
105 Stanton 1995.
106 Pattison and Thompson 2001, p. 113; Florovskii 1981, p. 300.
107 See Golosovker 1963.
108 For a thorough discussion of this tradition in relation to Russian fiction and intellectual history, see Stanton 1995.
109 Jones 1997a.
110 Hudspith 2004, p. 129.
111 See Clark 1981, pp. 178–82.
112 Letter to Dostoevsky, from St Petersburg, 22 December 1849.
113 See his famous letter to Fonvizina, from Omsk, 20 February 1854, XXVIII, i, 176.
114 Rozanov 1972, pp. 75–76.
115 Camus 1962, p. 1891.
116 Shestov 1903, 1969.
117 See Kasatkina 2004, pp. 399–405.
118 See Sutherland 1977.
119 Camus 1962, p. 1891.
120 Weil 1952, p. 239.
121 Onasch 1993a, p. 148.
122 Shestov 1903, 1969.
123 Zakharov 1994, p. 49.
124 See Børtnes 1983, pp. 407–10.
125 For example, Antonii 1921.
126 Berdiaev 1923.
127 For further references see Terras 1981.

128 For a brief account of the richness of Dostoevsky's reading of Biblical and religious texts, see Belknap 1990, especially pp. 19–21.
129 I have in mind Iuliia Denisovna Zasetskaia. See Jones 1994. See also Leskov 1956–1958, vol. xi, p. 148.
130 Pattison and Thompson 2001, p. 42.
131 Kjetsaa 1984, p. 37. I have throughout used this book as my source for markings in Dostoevsky's copy of the New Testament. I have not taken into account finger nail markings made in Siberia since it is reasonable to assume that passages so marked would have been marked additionally with a writing implement, when one became available, if they had had an overriding significance for Dostoevsky.
132 Pattison and Thompson 2001, p. 73.
133 Kjetsaa 1984, p. 36.
134 Kjetsaa 1984, p. 18.
135 Kjetsaa 1984, pp. 55–56.
136 Vermes 2004, p. 284.
137 Young 2003. It is controversial, among others reasons, because of its failure to mention the central Christian doctrine of the Resurrection of Jesus.
138 Kjetsaa 1984, p. 73.
139 Kjetsaa 1984, p. 23.
140 Those who wish to follow up these references in further detail without having to count them themselves are referred to the notes to the Academy Edition of *The Brothers Karamazov* (XV, pp. 523ff.) or alternatively to the end-notes to Richard Pevear and Larissa Volokhonsky's English translation of the novel (1992), pp. 779ff.
141 For an accessible and scholarly discussion of these and related issues, see Vermes 2000.
142 Coates 1998.
143 See the discussion in Børtnes 1983, p. 404: 'Bakhtin's christotelic definition of Dostoevskii's art demonstrates the absurdity of those who have accused him of being a relativist.'
144 Kermode 1979, pp. 3–4.
145 Hackel 1983, pp. 164–65.
146 Note Leont'ev's famous critique (1886). Orlando Figes has recently argued that the ambition to create a heaven or earth, although heretical, was particularly prevalent among the uneducated Russian peasantry and thus facilitated the development of socialism and revolutionary sympathies (Figes 2002, p. 308).
147 If it is argued that it would be theologically improper for Alesha to look directly at the transfigured Christ, it should be borne in mind that it is Zosima, in the dream, who is urging him to do so. So if Alesha is behaving properly, Zosima is not.
148 Hackel 1983, p. 152. There is no doubt that Dostoevsky understood this doctrine. See Børtnes 1983, p. 402.
149 Bakhtin 1975, pp. 154ff.
150 Lossky 1974, pp. 150–51.
151 Jones 1990, pp. 170ff.
152 Kjetsaa 1984, p. 25.
153 Pattison and Thompson 2001, pp. 116–133.
154 Lossky 1974, pp. 66–7. Sven Linnér refers to St Serafim of Sarov (1759–1833) as an example of an elder in his book 1975, p. 103. But there appears to be no hard evidence that Dostoevsky knew of his work.
155 Epstein 1982, 1999a.
156 Epstein 1999b.
157 Lossky 1957, p. 25.
158 With the exception of Frank, who noted this convergence of theology and atheism many years ago. See Frank 1956, pp. 179–80.
159 Epstein 1999b, p. 355.
160 Goodchild 2002, p. 10.

161 For a recent essay on this theme, see Christa 2002.
162 Figes 2002, p. 339.
163 Pattison and Thompson 2001, p. 227.
164 Pattison and Thompson 2001, p. 75.
165 On another approach to Dostoevsky and Heidegger, see Gerigk 2002.
166 Leatherbarrow 1982.
167 Bethea 1989, especially pp. 62–104.
168 Peace 1971.
169 Futrell 1981.
170 Murav 1992.
171 Epstein 1999b, p. 355.
172 Lossky 1957. See pp. 25–28 for the source of this paraphrase.
173 Lossky 1957, pp. 38ff.
174 Lossky 1957, p. 26.
175 Pattison and Thompson 2001, p. 227.
176 Peace 1971, p. 91.
177 Pattison and Thompson 2001, p. 38.
178 Hackel 1983, p. 142.
179 Figes 2002, pp. 294–95. Figes acknowledges Stanton 1995, p. 46.
180 Dolinin, i, p. 281. Although they varied in frequency and intensity, Dostoevsky's epileptic fits continued until the end of his life. See Catteau 1989, pp. 90–134.
181 I say, 'it appears', because the reader does not know what happens in Myshkin's mind following the 'complete breakdown of his mental organs' at the close of the novel (VIII, 508).
182 Epstein 1999b, p. 353.
183 Pattison and Thompson 2001, pp. 103–115.
184 'Dear Lord and Father of mankind' by Whittier (1807–92).
185 For an interesting discussion of the influence of the structure of Job (and the Old Testament more generally) on the dialogic structure of Dostoevsky's novels, see Liakhu 1998.
186 Pattison and Thompson 2001, pp. 69–99.
187 Sarraute 1956, p. 10 (my translation).
188 Tunimanov 2002.
189 Not acknowledged as a masterpiece by everyone, of course. John Jones could not bring himself to include a chapter on *The Idiot* in his *Dostoevsky* 1985.
190 Morson 1997.
191 Miller 1981.
192 Jackson 1966.
193 Barthes 1964.
194 Egeberg 1997.
195 Wasiolek 1967, pp. 10–12. Whereas references to the Russian original are given in the text, further references to Strelsky's English translation of the notebooks (Wasiolek, 1967) are given in the endnotes. It should, however, be noted that this translation is based upon the Russian edition of 1931 in which the sequence of the notes, together with the dates ascribed to them, sometimes differs significantly from the revised version of Dostoevsky's text (published in 1974), which I have used.
196 Wasiolek 1967, p. 204.
197 Wasiolek 1967, pp. 12–13.
198 Wasiolek 1967, pp. 173–74.
199 Lord 1970, in which Chapter VI, 'An epileptic mode of being', argues that Myshkin is actually a schemer and manipulator and that his 'redeeming characteristics' are 'comparatively unimportant' (p. 82).
200 Morson 1997, p. 114.
201 Egeberg 1997, p. 168.

202 See also 'A Weak Heart', II, 47–48, published in 1848.
203 Proctor 1969, pp. 9–10.
204 See Schmid 1973.
205 See Jones 1999.
206 Poole 2002, pp. 398 ff.
207 Poole 2002, p. 413.
208 I have given a detailed analysis of *The Double* and the problems it raises for the reader in Jones 1990, pp. 35–58.
209 Todd 2002.
210 Jakobson 1987, p. 87.
211 Todd 2002, p. 161.
212 Miller 1981.
213 Jones 1999.
214 Solzhenitsyn 1968, p. 426.
215 Seeley 1999, pp. 86–87. The essay in which this view is developed was first published in 1961.
216 Rahv 1962, p. 21. The article was first published in 1960.
217 Laing 1971.
218 Jones 1990, pp. 75–145.
219 From Pushkin's poem 'A Hero' (1830), which Dostoevsky, as usual, quotes not quite accurately. The original reads 'is dearer to us': *'T'my nizkikh istin nam dorozhe/ Nas vozvyshaiushchii obman'*.
220 Seeley 1983, p. 120.
221 Johnson 2004.
222 Vetlovskaia 1977, gives a subtle and much quoted analysis of the rhetorical devices used by Dostoevsky to incline his readers towards his positive characters (Zosima and Alesha) and against his negative ones (particularly Ivan).
223 Exactly what Dmitry (and Dostoevsky) meant by Sodom is not entirely clear, but it apparently stands for the realm of sensuality.
224 Sutherland 1977.
225 Dostoevsky 1992, p. 169. The distinction is of course unknown to Christian theology.
226 Ward 2004, p. 90.
227 This is an allusion to the thought of the eccentric Russian philosopher Nikolai Fedorov, whom Dostoevsky met towards the end of his life. For a post-Soviet Russian appraisal, see Semenova 1990. For a selection of his works in English see Fedorov 1990. For an appraisal of his significance for Dostoevsky, see Lord 1970, pp. 175–200.
228 By the time that Dostoevsky wrote this, he was familiar with the Radstockist movement (an English conservative evangelical movement led by Lord Radstock) in Russia. However, the novel is set in the 1860s before Radstock's first visit and so the allusion to 'Lutheranizing philanthropists' is correct. One of these was Iuliia Zasetskaia. See Jones 1994. Later, in Book 6, in the course of Zosima's testament, there is a reference to Lutherans stealing away the Orthodox flock because Orthodox priests claim they are too poorly paid (XIV, 265).
229 An important extra-textual reason for Jesus' silence, of course, is that if Dostoevsky had put new words into Jesus' mouth, or even recontextualised old words, he would have laid himself open to accusations of heresy and blasphemy.
230 Jones 1990.
231 Emerson 2004, p. 163.
232 See Morson 2004.
233 See, for example, Lyngstad 1975.
234 See Lord 1970, pp. 175–85.
235 See Pouzyna 1939.
236 See, for example, Hackel 1983, pp. 162–64.
237 Cf. Terras 1981, pp. 22–23; Hackel 1983, pp. 142–47, 153–54, 159–60.

238 Since writing this, I have found one, already mentioned above (Johnson 2004, p. 84).

239 Hudspith 2004, p. 129.

240 Calian 1978, p. 128.

241 Ware 1965, p. 262; quoted by Calian.

242 Anticipating this stage of my argument I have invariably translated '*tishina*', '*tikhi'i*, etc. by 'silence' or 'silent' in the quotations above, rather than by 'tranquility', 'calm', etc., which might sometimes seem more felicitous.

243 Pushkin, *Boris Godunov*: the final stage direction: *narod bezmolvstvuet* (the populace is silent).

244 Bakhtin 1972, pp. 400 ff.

245 Andreev 1900.

246 I have discussed the use of 'discourse with a loophole' as a psychological strategy in my article '*The Eternal Husband*: discourse with a noose', Jones 1995.

247 See Miller 1992, p. 107.

248 Among others, see Seeley 1983.

249 Jones 1990, pp. 181–84.

250 Hackel 1983.

251 Stanton 1995, pp. 151ff.

252 Niqueux 2002.

253 It is true that Matthew and Luke say that Jesus made an exception for the 'sign of the prophet Jonah', who dwelt in the whale's belly for three days, seen in retrospect by the Gospel-writers as an anticipation of the Resurrection, and that the later and more theologically sophisticated Gospel of John highlights the many signs and wonders that Jesus performed to manifest his supernatural character, but in the synoptic Gospels Jesus as a rule refuses to comply with the demand for a sign from heaven, commenting that those that demanded it belonged to 'an evil and adulterous generation' (Matthew, 12: 39, 16: 4; Luke, 11: 29).

254 Kasatkina 2004, pp. 457–58.

Select Bibliography

This bibliography includes all sources mentioned in this book together with others that formed essential background reading. Where reference to the original text is critical (as, for example, with Dostoevsky himself), or where there is no translation, sources in the original language are listed. Where this is not the case, translations into English or, failing these, into other West European languages have been preferred. The non-specialist reader should not imagine that this is a complete list of scholarly work on the subject, which would have extended this bibliography far beyond the limits of what is reasonable in a book of this kind. Apart from the standard bibliographies, additional titles may conveniently be found in the 'current bibliographies' published in *Dostoevsky Studies*, the Journal of the International Dostoevsky Society. Where authors whose names are normally written in the Latin script (for example, Young) have published in the Cyrillic script, they are placed alphabetically where the original spelling would require it (that is, under Y) and the re-transliterated Latin form (in this case, Iang) is placed in brackets alongside.

Allain, Louis, 1981, *Dostoïevski et Dieu: la morsure du divin*, Lille, Presses universitaires de Lille.

Amelin, G G and Pilshchikov, I A, 1992, *Novyi Zavet v Prestuplenii i nakazanii* F M. Dostoevskogo, *Logos*, 3, pp. 269–79.

Andreev, Leonid, 1900, Molchanie, *Zhurnal dlia vsekh*, 12 December, pp. 1427–1438.

Antonii, 1921, Metropolitan of Kiev and Halych, *Slovar' k tvoreniiam Dostoevskogo*, Sofia, Russkobolgarskoe knigoizdatel'stvo.

Bakhtin, M M, 1972, *Problemy poetiki Dostoevskogo*, Moscow, Khudozhestvennaia literatura.

Bakhtin, M M, 1981, Discourse in the Novel, in Michael Holquist (ed.), Caryl Emerson and Michael Holquist (trans.), *The Dialogic Imagination*, Austin, University of Texas Press, pp. 259–422.

Bakhtin, M M, 1984, *Problems of Dostoevsky's Poetics*,. Emerson, Caryl (ed. and trans.), Booth, Wayne C (introd.), Manchester, Manchester University Press.

Barth, Karl, 1933, *The Epistle to the Romans*, Hoskyns, E C (trans.), Oxford, Oxford University Press.

Barthes, Roland, 1964, *La Tour Eiffel*, Paris, Delpire.

Belinskii, V G, 1948, *Sobranie sochinenii v trekh tomakh*, 3 vols., Moscow, OGIZ.

Belknap, R, 1990, *The Genesis of 'The Brothers Karamazov'*, Evanston, Northwestern University Press.

Berdiaev, N, 1934, *Dostoievsky: an Interpretation*. D Attwater (trans.), London, Sheed and Ward.

Berman, Marshall, 1982, *All that is Solid Melts into Air: the Experience of Modernity*, New York, Verso.

Bethea, David M, 1989, *The Shape of the Apocalypse in Modern Russian Fiction*, Princeton, Princeton University Press.

Bodin, Per-Arne, 2001, Byzantine Hesychasm and the theme of Sophia in Russian Thought, in Kjetsaa, Geir, Lönngren, Lennart and Opeide Gunnar (eds), *Translating Culture, Essays in Honour of Erik Egeberg*, Oslo, Solum Vorlag, pp. 39–53.

Borisova, V V, 1991, *Sintetizm religiozno-mifologicheskogo podteksta v tvorchestve F. M. Dostoevskogo (Bibliia i Koran)*, in *Tvorchestvo F. M. Dostoevskogo: iskusstvo sinteza: monografiia*, Ekaterinburg, Izd. Ulral'skogo Universiteta, pp. 63–89.

Børtnes, J, 1978, The Function of Hagiography in Dostoevskij's Novels, *Scando-Slavica*, 24, pp. 27–33.

Børtnes, J, 1983, Polyphony in *The Brothers Karamazov*: variations on a theme, *Canadian-American Slavic Studies*, 17, 3, pp. 402–11.

Børtnes, J [Biortnes, Iu], 1994a, *Russkii kenotizm: k pereotsenke odnogo poniatiia*, in Zakharov V N (ed.), *Evangel'skii tekst v russkoi literature XVIII-XX vekov*, 1, Petrozavodsk, Izd. Petrozavodskogo Universiteta, pp. 61–65.

Børtnes, J, 1994b, Dostoevskij's *Idiot* or the Poetics of Emptiness, *Scandoslavica*, 40, pp. 5–14.

Børtnes, J, 1995, Dostoevskian Fools – Holy and Unholy, in Lunde, Ingunn (ed.), *The Holy Fool in Byzantium and Russia*, Bergen, Russisk institutt, Skrifter, 8, pp. 18–35.

Børtnes, J [Biortnes Iu], 1998, *"Khristos-otets": k probleme protivopostavleniia ottsa krovnogo i ottsa zakonnogo v Podrostke Dostoevskogo*, in Zakharov V N (ed.) *Evangel'skii tekst v russkoi literature XVIII-XX vekov*, 2, Petrozavodsk, Izd. Petrozavodskogo Universiteta, pp. 409–15.

Børtnes, J, 1998, Religion, in Jones, Malcolm V and Miller, Robin Feuer (eds), *The Cambridge Companion to the Classic Russian Novel*, Cambridge, Cambridge University Press, pp. 104–29.

Brincken, Alexandra v. d., 1933, George Sand et Dostoievsky, *Revue de littérature comparée*, 13, pp. 623–29.

Bulanov, A M, 1994 Stat'ia Ivana Karamazova o tserkovno-obshchestvennom sude v ideino-khudozhestvennoi strukture poslednego romana Dostoevskogo, in *F. M. Dostoevskii: materialy i issledovaniia*, Leningrad, Nauka, 12, pp. 125–36.

Calian, C S, 1978, Hesychasm and Transcendental Meditation: Sources for Contemporary Theology?, *Eastern Churches Review*, 10, 1-1, pp. 126–40.

Camus, Albert, 1951, *The Rebel*, Bower, Anthony (trans.), Harmondsworth, Penguin.

Camus, Albert, 1962, Questionnaire pour Spectacles, *Théâtre, récits, nouvelles*, Paris, Gallimard, pp. 1891–92.

Cassedy, Steven, 1982, The Formal Problem of the Epilogue in *Crime and Punishment*: the Logic of Tragic and Christian structures, *Dostoevsky Studies*, 3, pp. 171–90.

Catteau, Jacques, 1989, *Dostoevsky and the Process of Literary Creation*, Littlewood, Audrey (trans.), Cambridge, Cambridge University Press.

Catteau, Jacques, 1984, The paradox of the legend of the Grand Inquisitor in *The Brothers Karamazov*, in Jackson R L (ed.), *Dostoevsky: new perspectives*, Englewood Cliffs, Prentice Hall, pp. 243–54.

Chances, Ellen, 1974, *Pochvennichestvo*: Ideology in Dostoevsky's Periodicals, *Mosaic*, 7, ii , pp. 71–88.

Christa, Boris, 2002, Dostoevskii and money, in Leatherbarrow W J (ed.), *The Cambridge Companion to Dostoevskii*, Cambridge, Cambridge University Press, pp. 93–110.

Clark, Katerina, 1981, *The Soviet Novel, History as Ritual*, Chicago, University of Chicago Press.

Coates, Ruth, 1998, *Christianity in Bakhtin, God and the Exiled Author*, Cambridge, Cambridge University Press.

Cox, R L, 1969, *Between Heaven and Earth: Shakespeare, Dostoevsky and the Meaning of Christian Tragedy*, New York, Holt, Rinehart & Winston.

Cunningham, David S, 2001, *The Brothers Karamazov* as trinitarian theology, in Pattison, George and Thompson, Diane O (eds), *Dostoevsky and the Christian Tradition*, Cambridge, Cambridge University Press, pp. 134–55.

Dilaktorskaia, O D, 1995, Skoptsy i skopchestvo v izobrazhenii Dostoevskogo: k istolkovaniiu povesti "Khoziaika", *Philologica*, 2, 3/4, pp. 59–86.

Dolinin, A S, (ed.), 1964, *F. M. Dostoevskii v vospominaniakh sovremennikov*, 2 vols., Moscow, Khodozhestvennaia literatura.

Dostoevskaia, A G, 1971, *Vospominaniia*, Moscow, Khudozhestvennaia literatura.

Dostoevsky, F M, 1972–1990, *Polnoe sobranie sochinenii v tridtsati tomakh*, 33 vols., Leningrad, Izd. Nauka.

Dostoevsky, Fyodor, 1992, *The Brothers Karamazov*, Pevear, Richard and Volokhonsky, Larissa (trans.), New York, Alfred A. Knopf.

Dudkin, V V, 1998, *Dostoevskii i Evangelie ot Ioanna*, in Zakharov, V N (ed.) *Evangel'skii tekst v russkoi literature XVIII-XX vekov*, 2, Petrozavodsk, Izd. Petrozavodskogo Universiteta, pp. 337–48.

Durylin, 1928, Ob odnom simvole u Dostoevskogo, in *Dostoevskii. sbornik statei*, Moscow, Gosudarstvennaia akademiia khudozhestvennykh nauk, 3, pp. 163–99.

Efimova, N, Motiv bibleiskogo Iova v *Brat'iakh Karamazovykh*, in *Dostoevskii: materialy i issledovaniia*, Moscow, Nauka, 11, pp. 122–31.

Egeberg, E, 1997, How should we then read *The Idiot?*, in Knut Andreas Grimstad and Ingunn Lunde (eds), *Celebrating Creativity, Essays in Honour of Jostein Børtnes*, Bergen, University of Bergen, pp. 163–69.

Egeberg, E, 1998, F. M. Dostoevskii v poiskakh polozhitel'no prekrasnogo cheloveka. *Selo Stepanchikovo i Idiot*, in Zakharov, V N (ed.), *Evangeli'skii tekst v russkoi literature XVIII-XX vekov*, 2, Petrozavodsk, Izd. Petrozavodskogo Universiteta, pp. 385–90.

Eikeland, K, 1997, Functions of hagiographic discourse in the Life of Father Zosima, in Knut Andreas Grimstad and Ingunn Lunde (eds), *Celebrating Creativity, Essays in Honour of Jostein Børtnes*, Bergen, University of Bergen Press, pp. 151–62.

Emerson, Caryl, 2004, Zosima's "Mysterious Visitor": Again Bakhtin on Dostoevsky, and Dostoevsky on Heaven and Hell, in Robert Louis Jackson (ed.), *A New Word on 'The Brothers Karamazov'*, Evanston, Northwestern University Press, pp. 155–79.

Epstein, Mikhail, 1999a, Minimal Religion (1982), in Epstein, Mikhail N, Genis, Alexander A and Vladiv-Glover, Slobodanka M (eds), *Russian Postmodernism: New Perspectives on Post-Soviet Culture*, New York, Berghahn Books, pp. 163–71.

Epstein, Mikhail, 1999b, Post-atheism: From Apophatic Theology to "Minimal Religion", in Epstein, Mikhail N, Genis, Alexander A and Vladiv-Glover, Slobodanka M (eds), *Russian Postmodernism: New Perspectives on Post-Soviet Culture*, New York, Berghahn Books, pp. 345–93.

Ermilova, G, 1999, Khristologiia Dostoevskogo, *Dostoevskii i mirovaia kul'tura*, 13, pp. 37–44.

Esaulov, I A, 1994, Kategoriia sobornosti v russkoi literature, in Zakharov V N (ed.), *Evangel'skii tekst v russkoi literature XVIII-XX vekov*, 1, Petrozavodsk, Izd. Petrozavodskogo Universiteta, pp. 32–60.

Esaulov, I A, 1995, *Kategoriia sobornosti v russkoi literature*, Petrozavodsk, Izd. Petrozavodskogo Universiteta.

Esaulov, I A, 1997, *Sobornost'* in Nineteenth-Century Russian Literature, in Børtnes, Jostein and Lunde, Ingunn (eds), *Cultural Discontinuity and Reconstruction; the Byzanto-Slav Heritage and the Creation of a Russian National Literature in the Nineteenth Century*, Oslo, Solum Forlag, pp. 29–45.

Esaulov, I A, 1998a, Paskhal'nyi arkhetip v poetike Dostoevskogo in Zakharov, V N (ed.), *Evangel'skii tekst v russkoi literature XVIII-XX vekov*, 2, Petrozavodsk, Izd. Petrozavodskogo Universiteta, pp. 349–62.

Esaulov, Ivan, 1998b, Iurodstvo i shutovstvo v russkoi literature: nekotorye nabliudeniia, *Literaturnoe obozrenie*, 3, pp. 108–12.

Esaulov, I A, 2001, The categories of Law and Grace in Dostoevsky's poetics, in Pattison, George and Thompson, Diane O (eds), *Dostoevsky and the Christian Tradition*, Cambridge, Cambridge University Press, pp. 116–33.

Evnin, F, 1997, Dostoevskii i voinstvuiushchii katolitsizm 1860–1870-kh godov, *Russkaia literatura*, 1, pp. 29–41.

Fedorov, Nikolai Fedorovich, 1990, *What was Man created for? The Philosophy of the Common Task*, Kutaissoff, Elisabeth and Minto, Marilyn (Selected works trans. and abridged), Honeyglen Publishing.

Figes, Orlando, 2002, *Natasha's Dance, A Cultural History of Russia*, London, The Penguin Press.

Florovskii, G, 1981, *Puti russkogo bogosloviia*, Paris.

Frank, Joseph, 1976, *Dostoevsky, The Seeds of Revolt, 1821–1849*, Princeton, Princeton University Press.

Frank, Joseph, 1983, *Dostoevsky, The Years of Ordeal, 1850–1859*, London, Robson Books.

Frank, Joseph, 1987, *Dostoevsky, The Stir of Liberation*, London, Robson Books.

Frank, Joseph, 1995, *Dostoevsky, The Miraculous Years, 1865–1871*, London, Robson Books.

Frank, S L, 1956, *Real'nost' i chelovek: metafizika chelovecheskogo bytiia*, Paris, YMCA Press.

Fridlender, G M, 1959, Roman *Idiot*, in Stepanov, N L *et al.*, *Tvorchestvo F. M. Dostoevskogo*, Moscow, Izd. ANSSSR, pp. 173–214.

Futrell, Michael, 1981, Buddhism and *The Brothers Karamazov*, *Dostoevsky Studies*, 2, pp. 155–62.

Gacheva, A and Tikhomirov, B, 1999, Novye materialy k istorii znakomstva Dostoevskogo s ideiami N. F. Fedorova, *Dostoevskii i mirovaia kul'tura*, 13, pp. 205–58.

Gaustad, Randi, 1997, Rebuilding Gothic on Russian Soil: the Roles of Religion and Intertwining of Minds in Dostoevskii's *The Landlady*, in Grimstad, Knut Andreas and Lunde, Ingunn (eds), *Celebrating Creativity, Essays in Honour of Jostein Børtnes*, Bergen, University of Bergen Press, pp. 205–15.

Gerigk, Horst-Jürgen, 2002, Dostoevskij und Heidegger: eschatologischer Dichter und eschatologischer Denker, in Stepanian, Karen (ed.), *XXI vek glazami Dostoevskogo: perspektivy chelovechestva*, Moscow, ID Graal, pp. 81–98.

Gibson, A Boyce, 1973, *The Religion of Dostoevsky*, London, SCM Press.

Golosovker, Ia E, 1963, *Dostoevskii i Kant*, Moscow, ANSSSR.

Golubov, Alexander, 1976, Religious Imagery in the Structure of *The Brothers Karamazov*, in Freeborn, Richard, Milner-Gulland, Robin and Ward, Charles A (eds), *Russian and Slavic Literature: 1700–1917*, Slavica, Bloomington, p. 113–36.

Goodchild, Philip, 2002, *Capitalism and Religion, the Price of Piety*, London, Routledge.

Gornostaev, A K, 1929, *Rai na zemle: k ideologii tvorchestva F. M. Dostoevskogo*, Seine, Harbin.

Gorodetzky, Nadejda, 1951, *Saint Tikhon Zadonsky: Inspirer of Dostoevsky*, London, SPCK.

Gourg, Marianne, 2002, Le discours d'Ordynov: quelques remarques sur la poétique de *La Logeuse*, in Albert, Marie-Aude (ed.), *Diagonales dostoïevskiennes, mélanges en l'honneur de Jacques Catteau*, Paris, Presses de l'Université de Paris-Sorbonne, pp. 113–20.

Grossman, L P, 1922, *Seminarii po Dostoevskomu*, Moscow-Petrograd, GIZ.

Guardini, Romano, 1933, *Der Mensch und der Glaube: Versuche über die religiöse Existenz in Dostojewskijs grossen Romanen*, Leipzig, Hegner.

Guardini, Romano, 1963, *L'Univers religieux de Dostoïevski*, Engelmann, Henri and Givord, Robert (trans), Paris, Editions du Seuil.

Gusev, 1874, *Nravstvennyi ideal buddizma v ego otnoshenii k khristianstvu*, St Petersburg.

Hackel, S, 1983, The Religious Dimension: Vision or Evasion? Zosima's discourse in *The Brothers Karamazov*, in Jones, Malcolm V and Terry, Garth M (eds), *New Essays on Dostoyevsky*, Cambridge, Cambridge University Press, pp. 139–68.

Halacińska-Wertelak, H [Khalatsin'ska-Verteliak, Kh.], 2000, Evangelie ot Sviatogo Ioanna i epizod romana *Brat'ia Karamazovy*, *Dostoevskii i mirovaia kul'tura*, 15, pp. 112–19.

Hamilton, W, 1968, Banished from the land of unity: Dostoevsky's religious vision through the eyes of Dmitry, Ivan and Alyosha Karamazov, in Altizer, T J J and Hamilton W (eds), *Radical theology and the Death of God*, Harmondsworth, Penguin, pp. 65–94.

Heller, Erich, 1961, *The Disinherited Mind*, Harmondsworth, Penguin,.

Hollander, R, 1974, The apocalyptic framework of Dostoevsky's *The Idiot*, *Mosaic*, 7, pp. 123–39.

Hudspith, Sarah, 2004, *Dostoevsky and the Idea of Russianness, A New Perspective on Unity and Brotherhood*, London, RoutledgeCurzon.

Ivanov, V V, 1994, Iurodivyi geroi v dialoge ierarkhii Dostoevskogo, in Zakharov, V N (ed.), *Evangel'skii tekst v russkoi literature XVIII-XX vekov*, 1, Petrozavodsk, Izd. Petrozavodskogo Universiteta, pp. 201–09.

Ivanov, V V, 1998, Isikhazm i poetika kosnoiazychiia u Dostoevskogo, in Zakharov, V N (ed.), *Evangel'skii tekst v russkoi literature XVIII-XX vekov*, 2, Petrozavodsk, Izd. Petrozavodskogo Universiteta, , pp. 321–27.

Ivanov, V V, 2001, O evangel'skom smysle metafory sna v ode A. S. Pushkina "Prorok" i romanakh F. M. Dostoevskogo *Prestuplenie i nakazanie* i *Idiot*, in Zakharov, V N (ed.), *Evangel'skii tekst v russkoi literature XVIII-XX vekov*, 3, Petrozavodsk, Izd. Petrozavodskogo Universiteta, pp. 346–59.

Jackson, Robert Louis, 1966, *Dostoevsky's Quest for Form, A Study of his Philosophy of Art*, New Haven, Yale University Press.

Jackson, Robert Louis, 1993, *Dialogues with Dostoevsky. The Overwhelming Questions*, Stanford, Stanford University Press.

Jackson, Robert Louis (ed.), 2004a, *A New Word on 'The Brothers Karamazov'*, Evanston, Northwestern University Press.

Jackson, Robert Louis, 2004b, Alyosha's Speech at the Stone: "The Whole Picture" in Jackson, Robert Louis (ed.), *A New Word on 'The Brothers Karamazov'*, Evanston, Northwestern University Press, pp. 234–53.

James, William, 1960, *The Varieties of Religious Experience, a Study in Human Nature*, London, Fontana.

Johae, Antony, 1981, Idealism and the dialectic in *The Brothers Karamazov*, in Leon Burnett, (ed.), *F. M. Dostoevsky 1821–1881: A Centenary Collection*, Oxford, Holdan Books, pp. 109–17.

Johae, Antony, 1992–1993, Dostoevsky's Walls and Holbein's Paintings, *Germano-Slavica*, pp. 102–5.

Johae, Antony, 2001, Towards an iconography of *Crime and Punishment*, in Pattison, George and Thompson, Diane O (eds), *Dostoevsky and the Christian Tradition*, Cambridge, Cambridge University Press, pp. 173–88.

Johnson, Lee D, 2004, Struggle for Theosis: Smerdyakov as Would-Be Saint, in Robert Louis Jackson (ed.), *A New Word on 'The Brothers Karamazov'*, Evanston, Northwestern University Press, pp. 74–89.

Jones, John, 1985, *Dostoevsky*, Oxford, Oxford University Press.

Jones, Malcolm V, 1990, *Dostoevsky after Bakhtin*, Cambridge, Cambridge University Press.

Jones, Malcolm V, 1994, Dostoevsky, Zasetskaya and Radstockism, *Oxford Slavonic Papers*, N.S., 27, pp. 106–120.

Jones, Malcolm V, (1995), *The Eternal Husband*: discourse with a Noose, *Essays in Poetics*, Autumn, 20, pp. 46–59.

Jones, Malcolm V, 1997a, The Death and Resurrection of Orthodoxy in the Works of Dostoevskii, in Børtnes, Jostein and Lunde, Ingunn (eds), *Cultural Discontinuity and Reconstruction, the Byzanto-Slav Heritage and the Creation of a Russian National Literature in the Nineteenth Century*, Oslo, Solum Forlag, pp. 143–67.

Jones, Malcolm V, 1997b, Silence in *The Brothers Karamazov*, in Gerigk Horst-Jürgen (ed.), *'Die Brüder Karamasow', Dostojewskijs letzter Roman in heutiger Sicht*, Dresden, Dresden University Press, pp. 29–45.

Jones, Malcolm V, 1999, The Narrator and Narrative Technique in Dostoevsky's *The Devils*, in Leatherbarrow, W J (ed.), *Dostoevsky's 'The Devils': a Critical Companion*, Evanston, Northwestern University Press, pp. 100–118.

Jones, Malcolm V, 2001, *Roman-nevaliashka*: Further Thoughts on the Structure of Dostoevsky's *Idiot*, in Kjetsaa, Geir, Lönngren, Lennart and Opeide, Gunnar (eds), *Translating Culture, Essays in Honour of Erik Egeberg*, Oslo, Solum Forlag, pp. 129–39.

Jones, Malcolm V, 2002, Dostoevskii and Religion, in Leatherbarrow, W J (ed.), *The Cambridge Companion to Dostoevskii*, Cambridge, Cambridge University Press, pp. 148–74.

Jones, Malcolm V, 2003, Modelling the religious dimension of Dostoevsky's fiction, in Zohrab, Irene (ed.), *Slavonic Journeys across two Hemispheres. Festschrift in Honour of Arnold McMillin, New Zealand Slavonic Journal*, 37, pp. 41–53.

Kantor, Vladimir, 2001, Pavel Smerdiakov and Ivan Karamazov: The problem of temptation, in Pattison, George and Thompson, Diane O (eds), *Dostoevsky and the Christian Tradition*, Cambridge, Cambridge University Press, pp. 189–25.

Kasatkina, T, 1998, "Khristos vne istiny" v tvorchestve Dostoevskogo, *Dostoevskii i mirovaia kul'tura*, 11, pp. 113–20.

Kasatkina, T, 2004, *O tvoriashchei prirode slova: ontologichnost' slova v tvorchestve F. M. Dostoevskogo kak osnova 'realizma v vysshem smysle'*, Moscow, IMLI RAN.

Kaye, Peter, 1999, *Dostoevsky and English Modernism 1900–1930*, Cambridge, Cambridge University Press.

Kermode, Frank, 1979, *The Genesis of Secrecy*, Cambridge, Harvard University Press.

Kiiko, E I, 1976, Iz istorii sozdaniia Brat'ev Karamazovykh: Ivan i Smerdiakov, *Dostoevsky: materialy i issledovaniia*, 2, Leningrad, Nauka, pp. 125–29.

Kiiko, E I, 1980, Dostoevsky i Renan, *Dostoevsky: materialy i issledovaniia*, 4, Leningrad, Nauka, pp. 106–22.

Kirillova, I A, 1992, K probleme sozdaniia khristopodobnogo obraza: (Kniaz' Myshkin i Avdii Kallistratov), in *Dostoevskii: materialy i issledovaniia*, 10, Moscow, Nauka, pp. 172–76.

Kirillova, Irina, 2001, Dostoevsky's markings in the Gospel according to St John, in Pattison, George and Thompson, Diane O (eds), *Dostoevsky and the Christian Tradition*, Cambridge, Cambridge University Press, pp. 41–50.

Kjetsaa, Geir, 1987, *Fyodor Dostoyevsky, A Writer's Life*, London, Macmillan.

Kjetsaa, Geir, 1984, *Dostoevsky and His New Testament*, Oslo, Solum Forlag A.S.

Knapp, Liza, 1996, *The Annihilation of Inertia, Dostoevsky and Metaphysics*, Evanston, Northwestern University Press.

Kotel'nikov, V, 1998, Khristoditseia Dostoevskogo, *Dostoevskii i mirovaia kul'tura*, 11, pp. 20–28.

Kozulin, Alex, 1990, *Vygotsky's Psychology, a Biography of Ideas*, New York, Harvester-Wheatsheaf.

Krieger, M, 1962, Dostoevsky's *Idiot*: the Curse of Saintliness, in Wellek, René (ed.), *Dostoevsky*, Englewood Cliffs, Prentice Hall, pp. 39–52.

Kristeva, J, 1987, *Soleil noir, dépression et mélancholie* Paris, Editions Gallimard.

Kunil'skii, A E, 1994, Problema "smekh i khristianstvo" v romane Dostoevskogo *Brat'ia Karamazovy*, in Zakharov, V N (ed.), *Evangel'skii tekst v russkoi literature XVIII-XX vekov*, 1, Petrozavodsk, Izd. Petrozavodskogo Universiteta, pp. 192–200.

Kunil'skii, A E, 1998, O khristianskom kontekste v romane F. M. Dostoevskogo *Idiot*, in Zakharov, V N (ed.), *Evangel'skii tekst v russkoi literature XVIII-XX vekov*, 2, Petrozavodsk, Izd. Petrozavodskogo Universiteta, pp. 391–408.

Kunil'skii, A E, 2001, F. M. Dostoevskii v vospriiatii nekotorykh tserkovnykh avtorov, in Zakharov, V N (ed.), *Evangel'skii tekst v russkoi literature XVIII-XX vekov*, 3, Petrozavodsk, Izd. Petrozavodskogo Universiteta, pp. 420–29.

Laing, R D, 1971, *Self and Others*, Harmondsworth and New York, Penguin.

Leatherbarrow, W J, 1982, Apocalyptic Imagery in *The Idiot* and *The Devils*, *Dostoevsky Studies*, 3, pp. 43–52.

Leatherbarrow, W J and Offord, D S (trans. and eds), 1987, *A Documentary History of Russian Thought from the Enlightenment to Marxism*, Ann Arbor, Ardis .

Leatherbarrow, W J, 2000, The Devil's Vaudeville, in Davidson, Pamela (ed.), *Russian Literature and the Demonic*, Oxford, Berghahn pp. 279–306.

Leatherbarrow, W J (ed.), 2002, *The Cambridge Companion to Dostoevskii*, Cambridge, Cambridge University Press.

Leont'ev, K, 1886, O vsemirnoi liubvi, rech' F. M. Dostoevskogo na Pushkinskom prazdnike, *Vostok, Rossiia i slavianstvo, sbornik statei*, Moscow, 2, pp. 280–309.

Leskov, N S, 1958, O kufel'nom muzhike i proch, in *Sobranie sochinenii*, 11 vols, Moscow (1956–58), Gos. izd. khudozhestvennoi literatury, 11, pp. 134–56.

Liakhu, L, July–August, 1998, O vlianii poetiki Biblii na poetiku F. M. Dostoevskogo, *Voprosy literatury*, pp. 129–43.

Linnér, Sven, 1975, *Starets Zosima in 'The Brothers Karamazov', A Study in the Mimesis of Virtue*, Stockholm, Almqvist and Wiksell International.

Lord, Robert, 1970, *Dostoevsky, Essays and Perspectives*, London, Chatto and Windus.

Losskii, N O, 1953, *Dostoevskii i ego khristianskoe miroponimanie*, New York, Izd. imeni Chekhova.

Lossky, Vladimir, 1957, *The Mystical Theology of the Eastern Church*, James Clarke, London.

Lossky, Vladimir, 1974, *In the Image and Likeness of God*, New York.

Lotman, L M, 1972, Romany Dostoevskogo i russkaia legenda, *Russkaia literatura*, 15, 2, pp. 129–41.

Lunde, I, 1998, Ot idei k idealu – ob odnom simvole v romane Dostoevskogo *Podrostok*, in Zakharov, V N (ed.), *Evangel'skii tekst v russkoi literature XVIII-XX vekov*, 2, Petrozavodsk, Izd. Petrozavodskogo Universiteta, pp. 416–23.

L'vov, 1956, Zapiska o dele petrashevtsev, *Literaturnoe nasledstvo*, Moscow, ANSSSR, 63, pp. 165–90.

Lyngstad, Alexandra, 1975, *Dostoevskij and Schiller*, The Hague, Mouton.

McHale, B, 1987, *Postmodernist Fiction*, New York and London, Methuen.

Mead, G H, 1974, *Mind, Self and Society from the Standpoint of a Social Behaviorist*, Chicago, Chicago University Press.

Meerson, Olga, 1995, Ivolgin and Holbein: Non-Christ risen vs. Christ non-risen, *Slavic and East European Journal*, 39, pp. 100–13.

Miller, Robin Feuer, 1981, *Dostoevsky and 'The Idiot', Author, Narrator and Reader*, Cambridge, Harvard University Press.

Miller, Robin Feuer, 1992, The Brothers Karamazov, *Worlds of the Novel*, New York, Twayne .

Miller, Robin Feuer, 1997, Dostoevskii's Parables: Paradox and Plot, in Børtnes, Jostein and Lunde, Ingunn (eds), *Cultural Discontinuity and Reconstruction, the Byzanto-Slav Heritage and the Creation of a Russian National Literature in the Nineteenth Century*, Oslo, Solum Forlag, pp. 168–84.

Milosz, Czeslaw, 1977, *Dostoevsky and Swedenborg, Emperor of the Earth*, Berkeley, University of California Press.

Morson, Gary Saul, 1997, Tempics and *The Idiot*, in Grimstad, Knut Andreas and Lunde, Ingunn (eds), *Celebrating Creativity, Essays in Honour of Jostein Børtnes*, Bergen, University of Bergen, pp. 108–34.

Morson, Gary Saul, 2004, The God of Onions: *The Brothers Karamazov* and the Mythic Prosaic in Jackson, Robert Louis (ed.), *A New Word on 'The Brothers Karamazov'*, Evanston, Northwestern University Press, pp. 107–24.

Müller, Ludolf, 1982, *Dostojewskij, sein Leben, sein Werk, sein Vermächtnis*, Munich, Erich Wewel Verlag.

Müller, L [Miuller, L], 1998, Obraz Khrista v romane Dostoevskogo *Idiot*, in Zakharov V N (ed.), *Evangel'skii tekst v russkoi literature XVIII-XX vekov*, 2, Petrozavodsk, Izd. Petrozavodskogo Universiteta, pp. 374–84.

Murav, Harriet, 1992, *Holy Foolishness, Dostoevsky's Novels and the Poetics of Cultural Critique*, Stanford, Stanford University Press.

Neizdannyi Dostoevskii, 1971, *Literaturnoe nasledstvo*, Moscow, ANSSSR, 83.

Neuhäuser, Rudolf, 1986, *The Brothers Karamazov*: A Contemporary Reading of Book VI, "A Russian Monk", *Dostoevsky Studies*, 7, pp. 135–51.

Nicholl, Donald, 1997, *Triumphs of the Spirit in Russia*, London, Darton, Longman and Todd.

Niqueux, Michel, 2002, Dostoïevski, les sectes russes et les vieux-croyants, in Albert, Marie-Aude (ed.), *Diagonales dostoïevskiennes, Mélanges en l'honneur de Jacques Catteau*, Paris, Presses de l'Université de Paris-Sorbonne, pp. 149–59.

Ollivier, S [Olliv'e, S], 1994, Polemika mezhdu Polem Klodelem i Andre Zhidom po povodu obraza Iisusa Khrista v tvorchestve Dostoevskogo, in Zakharov, V N (ed.), *Evangel'skii tekst v russkoi literature XVIII-XX vekov*, 1, Petrozavodsk, Izd. Petrozavodskogo Universiteta, pp. 210–21.

Ollivier, S, 1997, Dostoevskii's *The Landlady* and The Icon of the Mother of God, in Jostein Børtnes and Ingunn Lunde (eds), *Cultural Discontinuity and Reconstruction, the Byzanto-Slav Heritage and the Creation of a Russian National Literature in the Nineteenth Century*, Oslo, Solum Forlag, pp. 202–16.

Ollivier, S [Olliv'e, S], 1998, Dostoevskii i Shatobrian, in Zakharov V N (ed.), *Evangel'skii tekst v russkoi literature XVIII-XXX vekov*, 2, Petrozavodsk, Izd. Petrozavodskogo Universiteta, pp. 328–36.

Ollivier, Sophie, 2001, Icons in Dostoevsky's works, in Pattison, George and Thompson, Diane O (eds.), *Dostoevsky and the Christian Tradition*, Cambridge, Cambridge University Press, pp. 51–68.

Onasch, K, 1961, *Dostoevskij als Verführer*, Zurich, EVZ-Verlag.

Onasch, K, 1976, *Der Verschweigene Christus: Versuch über die Poetisierung des Christentums in der Dichtung F. M. Dostojewskijs*, Berlin, Union Verlag.

Onasch, K, 1980, Der hagiographische Typus des "Jurodivyj" im Werk Dostoevskijs, *Dostoevsky Studies*, 1, pp. 111–22.

Onasch, K, 1985, F. M. Dostoevskij: Biographie und religiöse Identität. Versuch einer Synopse, *International Journal of Slavic Linguistics and Poetics*, 31-32, pp. 295–308.

Onasch, K, 1993a, Dostoevskij und die Lehrtradition der Orthodoxen Kirche, in Jones, Malcolm V (ed.), *Dostoevsky and the Twentieth Century, the Ljubljana Papers*, Nottingham, Astra Press, pp. 137–48.

Onasch, K, 1993b, Dostoewskijs alternative Orthodoxie, *Sinn und Form*, 45, 5, pp. 725–33.

Orwin, Donna, 2004, Did Dostoevsky or Tolstoy believe in Miracles?, in Jackson, Robert Louis (ed.), *A New Word on 'The Brothers Karamazov'*, Evanston, Northwestern University Press, pp. 125–41.

Panichas, G, 1985, *The Burden of Vision: Dostoevsky's Spiritual Art*, Gateway Editions, Chicago.

Pascal, Pierre, 1970, *Dostoïevski, l'homme et l'oeuvre*, Lausanne, Slavica.

Pattison, George and Thompson, Diane O, 2001, Introduction: Reading Dostoevsky religiously, in Pattison, George and Thompson, Diane O (eds), *Dostoevsky and the Christian Tradition*, Cambridge, Cambridge University Press, pp. 1–28.

Pattison, George, 2001, Freedom's dangerous dialogue: reading Dostoevsky and Kierkegaard together, in Pattison, George and Thompson, Diane O (eds), *Dostoevsky and the Christian Tradition*, Cambridge, Cambridge University Press, pp. 237–56.

Peace, Richard, 1971, *Dostoyevsky: an Examination of the Major Novels*, Cambridge, Cambridge University Press.

Peace, Richard, 2001, *Khoziaika*, Structure and Confusion, in Kjetsaa, Geir, Lönngren, Lennart and Opeide, Gunnar (eds), *Translating Culture, Essays in Honour of Erik Egeberg*, Oslo, Solum Vorlag, pp. 236–45.

Peace, Richard, 2001, Starets Zosima: pravoslavie i "miry inye", *Filologicheskie zapiski*, 16, pp. 24–42.

Perlina, Nina, 1985, *Varieties of Poetic Utterance, Quotation in 'The Brothers Karamazov'*, Lanham, University Press of America.

Pike, C, 1984, Dostoevsky's "Dream of a Ridiculous Man": seeing is believing, in Andrew, J (ed.), *The Structural Analysis of Russian Narrative Fiction*, Keele, Essays in Poetics, pp. 26–63.

Piksanov, N K, 1991, Khristos v soznanii Dostoevskogo, in *Siuzhet i vremia: sbornik nauchnykh trudov*, Kolomna, Kolomenskii Pedagogicheskii Institut, pp. 183–87.

Pletnev, R, 1982, Ob iskushenii Khrista v pustyne i Dostoevskom, *Russian Language Journal*, 36, 1323–24, pp. 66–74.

Pletnev, R V, 1994, Dostoevskii i Evangelie, in *Russkie emigranty o Dostoevskom*, Sankt-Peterburg, Andreev i synov'ia, pp. 160–90.

Pomomareva, G B, 2001, *Dostoevskii: ia zanimaius' etoi tainoi*, Moscow, Akademkniga.

Poole, Roger, 2002, Towards a Theory of Responsible Reading: How to Read and Why, in Cappelhørn, Niels Jørgen, Deuser, Hermann and Stewart, Jon (eds), *Kierkegaard Studies, Yearbook 2002*, Berlin, Walter de Gruyter, pp. 395–442.

Pouzyna, Ivan, 1939, George Sandet Dostoïevski, la parenté littéraire des *Frères Karamazov* et du *Spiridion*, in *Etudes*, Paris, 1, pp. 345–60.

Prestel, D K, 1998, Father Zosima and the Eastern Orthodox Hesychast Tradition, *Dostoevsky Studies*, New Series, 2, 1, pp. 41–59.

Proctor, Thelwall, 1969, *Dostoevskij and the Belinskij School of Literary Criticism*, The Hague-Paris, Mouton.

Pyman, Avril, 1983, Dostoevskii's influence on religious thought in the Russian Silver Age, *Canadian-American Slavic Studies*, Fall, 17, 3, pp. 287–324.

Pyman, Avril, 2001, Dostoevsky in the prism of the orthodox semiosphere, in Pattison, George and Thompson, Diane O (eds), *Dostoevsky and the Christian Tradition*, Cambridge, Cambridge University Press, pp. 103–15.

Rahv, Philip, 1962, Dostoevsky in *Crime and Punishment*, in Wellek, René (ed.), *Dostoevsky*, Englewood Cliffs, Prentice Hall, pp. 16–38.

Rosen, Nathan, 1971, Style and Structure in *The Brothers Karamazov*: the Grand Inquisitor and the Russian Monk, *Russian Literature Triquarterly*, 1, pp. 352–65.

Rothe, Hans, 1997, Dostojewskijs Weg zu seinem "Grossinquisitor", in Gerigk, Horst-Jürgen (ed.), *'Die Brüder Karamasow', Dostojewskijs letzter Roman in heutiger Sicht*, Dresden, Dresden University Press, pp. 159–204.

Rozanov, V, 1972, *Dostoevsky and the Legend of the Grand Inquisitor*, Roberts, Spencer E (trans.), Ithaca, Cornell University Press.

Russell, Henry M W, 2001, Beyond the will: Humiliation as Christian necessity in *Crime and Punishment*, in Pattison, George and Thompson, Diane O (eds), *Dostoevsky and the Christian Tradition*, Cambridge, Cambridge University Press, pp. 226–36.

Sandoz, Ellis, 2000, *Political Apocalypse, A Study of Dostoevsky's Grand Inquisitor*, Second Edition Revised, Wilington, ISI Books.

Sarraute, Natalie, 1956, *L'ère du soupçon*, Paris, Editions Gallimard.

Schmid, Wolf, 1973, *Der Textaufbau in den Erzählungen Dostoievskijs*, Munich, Wilhelm Fink Verlag.

Schoultz, Oscar von [Shul'ts, O fon], 1998, Russkii Khristos, in Zakharov, V N (ed.), *Evangel'skii tekst v russkoi literature XVIII-XX vekov*, 2, Petrozavodsk, Izd. Petrozavodskogo Universiteta, pp. 31–41.

Schoultz, Oscar von [Shul'ts, O fon], 1999, Khristos Dostoevskogo, in Zakharov, V N (ed.), *Oskar von Shul'ts, svetlyi, zhizneradostnyi Dostoevskii*, Petrozavodsk, Izd. Petrozavodskogo Universiteta, pp. 301–339.

Seeley, Frank, 1983, Ivan Karamazov, in Malcolm V Jones and Garth M Terry (eds), *New Essays on Dostoevsky*, Cambridge, Cambridge University Press, pp. 115–36.

Seeley, Frank, 1999, *Saviour or Superman, Essays Old and New on Tolstoy and Dostoevsky*, Nottingham, Astra Press.

Semenova, Svetlana, 1990, *Nikolai Fedorov, tvorchestvo zhizni*, Moscow, Sovetskii pisatel'.

Sepsiakova, I P, 1998, Khristianskii ideal i postmodernizm, in Zakharov, V N (ed.), *Evangel'skii tekst v russkoi literature XVIII-XX vekov*, 2, Petrozavodsk, Izd. Petrozavodskogo Universiteta, pp. 537–48.

Sharakov, S L, 2001, Ideia spaseniia v romane F. M. Dostoevskogo *Brat'ia Karamazovy*, in Zakharov, V N (ed.), *Evangel'skii tekst v russkoi literature XVIII-XX vekov*, 3, Petrozavodsk, Izd. Petrozavodskogo Universiteta, pp. 391–98.

Shestov, Lev, 1903, *Dostoevskii i Nitshe – filosofiia tragedii*, St Petersburg.

Shestov, Lev, 1969, Dostoevsky and Nietzsche: the Philosophy of Tragedy, in *Dostoevsky, Tolstoy and Nietzsche*, Bernard Martin (introd. and trans.), Ohio, Ohio University Press, pp. 141–322.

Smart, Ninian, 1989, *The World's Religions*, Cambridge, Cambridge University Press.

Solzhenitsyn, 1968, *V pervom krugu*, London, Flegon Press.

Stanton, Leonard J, 1995, *The Optina Pustyn Monastery in the Russian Literary Imagination, Iconic Vision in Works by Dostoevsky, Gogol, Tolstoy and Others*, New York, Peter Lang.

Sutherland, Stewart, R, 1977, *Atheism and the Rejection of God: Contemporary Philosophy and 'The Brothers Karamazov'*, Oxford, Blackwell.

Sutherland, Stewart, 1984a, *Faith and Ambiguity*, London, SCM Press.

Sutherland, Stewart, 1984b, *God, Jesus and Belief*, Oxford, Blackwell.

Terras, V, 1981, *A Karamazov Companion*, Madison, University of Wisconsin Press.

Thompson, Diane O, 1991, *'The Brothers Karamazov' and The Poetics of Memory*, Cambridge, Cambridge University Press.

Thompson, Diane O, 1997a, Motifs of Compassion in Dostoevsky's Novels, in Børtnes, Jostein and Lunde, Ingunn (eds), *Cultural Discontinuity and Reconstruction, the Byzanto-Slav Heritage and the Creation of a Russian National Literature in the Nineteenth Century*, Oslo, Solum Forlag, pp. 185–201.

Thompson, Diane O, 1997b, The problem of conscience in *Crime and Punishment*, in Grimstad, Knut Andreas and Lunde, Ingunn (eds), *Celebrating Creativity, Essays in Honour of Jostein Børtnes*, Bergen, University of Bergen, pp. 190–204.

Thompson, D O [Tompson, D O], 1998, Problemy sovesti v *Prestuplenii i nakazanii*, in Zakharov, V N (ed.), *Evangel'skii tekst v russkoi literature XVIII-XX vekov*, 2, Petrozavodsk, Izd. Petrozavodskogo Universiteta, pp. 363–73.

Thompson, Diane O, 2001, Problems of the biblical word in Dostoevsky's poetics, in Pattison, George and Thompson, Diane O, (eds), *Dostoevsky and the Christian Tradition*, Cambridge, Cambridge University Press, pp. 69–99.

Thurneysen, Eduard, 1921, *Dostojewski*, Munich, Raiser.

Tikhomirov, B N, 1994, O "khristologii" Dostoevskogo, in *Dostoevskii: materialy i issledovaniia*, 11, Moscow, Nauka, pp. 102–21.

Tikhomirov, B, 1999, Khristos i istina v poeme Ivana Karamazova "Velikii Inkvizitor", *Dostoevskii i mirovaia kul'tura*, 13, pp. 147–77.

Tikhomirov, B, 2000, Dostoevskii i gnosticheskaia traditsiia (k postanovke problemy), *Dostoevskii i mirovaia kul'tura*, 15, pp. 174–81.

Todd, William Mills, III, 1997, On the Uses and Abuses of Narrative in *The Brothers Karamazov'*, in Gerigk, Horst-Jürgen (ed.), *'Die Brüder Karamasow', Dostojewskijs letzter Roman in heutiger Sicht*, Dresden, Dresden University Press, pp. 75–87.

Toichkina, A, 1998, Problema ideala v tvorchestve Dostoevskogo 1860s- kh godov (roman *Idiot*), *Dostoevskii i mirovaia kul'tura*, 11, pp. 29–34.

Troyka, C M, 1993, Faith and Rebellion: the Tragic Poles of Dostoevsky's Theodicy, in Jones, Malcolm V (ed.), *Dostoevsky in the Twentieth Century: the Ljubljana Papers*, Nottingham, Astra Press pp. 119–36.

Tucker, J, 1997, Dostoevsky's *Idiot*: defining Myshkin, *New Zealand Slavonic Journal*, pp. 23–40.

Tunimanov, V, 1998, Bog ili absurd? (etiko-religioznyi aspekt temy 'Al'ber Kamiu i Fedor Dostoevskii'), *Dostoevskii i mirovaia kul'tura*, 11, pp. 95–109.

Tunimanov, V, 2002, Podpol'e i zhivaia zhizn', in Stepanian, K (ed.), *XXI vek glazami Dostoevskogo: perspektivy chelovechstva* Moscow, ID 'Graal'', pp. 11–22.

Vermes, G, 2000, *The Changing Faces of Jesus*, London, The Penguin Press.

Vermes, G, 2004, *The Authentic Gospel of Jesus*, London, Penguin Books.

Vetlovskaia, V E, 1971, Literaturnye i fol'klornye istochniki *Brat'ev Karmazovykh*: Zhitie Alekseia cheloveka bozhiia i dukhovnye stikhi o nem, in Kirpotin, V Ia (ed.), *Dostoevskii i russkie pisateli: Traditsii, novatorstvo, masterstvo: sbornik statei*, Moscow, Sovetskii pisatel'.

Vetlovskaia, V E, 1977, *Poetika romana 'Brat'ia Karamzazovy'*, Leningrad, Nauka.

Vetlovskaia, V E, 1981, Od odnom iz istochnikov *Brat'ev Karamazovykh*, *Izvestiia Akademii nauk SSSR. Seriia literatury i iazyka*, 40, pp. 436–45.

Vetlovskaia, V E, 1983, Pater Seraphicus, in Fridlender, G M (ed.), *Dostoevskii: materialy i issledovaniia*, 5, pp. 163–78.

Vetlovskaia, V E, 1984, Alyosha Karamazov and the hagiographic hero, in Jackson, R L (ed.), *Dostoevsky: New Perspectives*, Englewood Cliffs, Prentice Hall pp. 206–26.

Vetlovskaia, V E, 1998, Apokrif *Khozhdenie Bogoroditsy po mukam v Brat'iakh Karamazovykh* Dostoevskogo, *Dostoevskii i mirovaia kul'tura*, 11, pp. 35–47.

Vetlovskaia, V E, 1986, Rhetoric and poetics: the Affirmation and Refutation of Opinions in Dostoevsky's *The Brothers Karamazov*, in Miller, Robin Feuer (ed.), *Critical Essays on Dostoevsky*, Boston, G. K. Hall, pp. 223–33.

Viktorovich, V, 1996, Slavianofil'stvo Dostoevskogo: tri obrashcheniia, *Volga*, 8-9, pp. 113–31.

Vladimirtsev, V P, 2001, "Sibirskaia tetrad'" F. M. Dostoevskogo: khristianskii – kul'turnyi i rechevoi – sloi, in Zakharov, V N (ed.), *Evangel'skii tekst v russkoi literature XVIII-XX vekov*, 3, Petrozavodsk, Izd. Petrozavodskogo Universiteta, pp. 337–45.

Ward, Bruce, K, 1986, *Dostoevsky's Critique of the West: the Quest for Earthly Paradise*, Waterloo, Ontario, Wilfrid Laurier University Press.

Ware, Timothy, 1963, *The Orthodox Church*, Harmondsworth Penguin.

Ware, Kallistos, October 1965, The Power of the Name: the Function of the Jesus Prayer, *Theology Today*.

Wasiolek, Edward (ed.), 1967, *Dostoevsky, the Notebooks for 'the Idiot'*, Strelsky, Katharine (trans.), Chicago and London, University of Chicago Press.

Weil, Simone, 1952, *The Need for Roots*, London, Routledge and Kegan Paul.

Whitcomb, C, 1992, The Temptation of Miracle in *Brat'ja Karamazovy*, *Slavic and East European Journal*, 36, 2, pp. 189–201.

White, H, 1993, Dostoevsky's Christian Despot, *Russian Language Journal*, 47, 156–58, pp. 65–79.

Young, Sarah [Iang, S.], 2001, Bibleiskie arkhetipy v romane F. M. Dostoevskogo *Idiot*, in Zakharov, V N (ed.), *Evangel'skii tekst v russkoi literature XVIII-XX vekov*, 3, Petrozavodsk, Izd. Petrozavodskogo Universiteta, pp. 382–90.

Young, Sarah, 2003, Dostoevsky's *Idiot* and the Epistle of James, *The Slavonic and East European Review*, 3 July, 81, pp. 401–20.

Zakharov, V N, 1994a, Simvolika khristianskogo kalendaria v proizvedeniiakh Dostoevskogo, in Zakharov, V N (ed.), *Novye aspekty v izuchenii Dostoevskogo*, Petrozavodsk, Izd. Petrozavodskogo Universiteta, pp. 37–49.

Zakharov, V N (ed.), 1994b, *Evangel'skii tekst v russkoi literature XVIII-XX vekov*, 1, Petrozavodsk, Izd. Petrozavodskogo Universiteta.

Zakharov, V N, 1997, Umilenie kak kategoriia poetiki Dostoevskogo, in Grimstad, Knut Andreas and Lunde, Ingunn (eds), *Celebrating Creativity, Essays in Honour of Jostein Børtnes*, Bergen, University of Bergen, pp. 237–55.

Zakharov, V N (ed.), 1998, *Evangel'skii tekst v russkoi literature XVIII-XX vekov*, 2, Petrozavodsk, Izd. Petrozavodskogo Universiteta.

Zakharov, V N (ed.), 2001, *Evangel'skii tekst v russkoi literature XVIII-XX vekov*, 3, Petrozavodsk, Izd. Petrozavodskogo Universiteta.

Zander, L A, 1948, *Dostoevsky*, London, SCM Press.

Zenkovsky, V V, 1962, Dostoevsky's Religious and Philosophical Views, in Wellek, René (ed.), *Dostoevsky: A Collection of Critical Essays*, Englewood Cliffs, Prentice Hall, pp. 130–45.

Zernov, N, 1944, *Three Russian Prophets, Khomiakov, Dostoevsky, Soloviev*, London, SCM Press.

Zernov, N, 1961, *Eastern Christendom: a Study of the Origin and Development of the Eastern Orthodox Church*, London, Weidenfeld And Nicolson.

Ziolkowski, Eric J, 2001, Reading and incarnation in Dostoevsky, in Pattison, George and Thompson, Diane O (eds), *Dostoevsky and the Christian Tradition*, Cambridge, Cambridge University Press, pp. 156–70.

Ziolkowski, Margaret, 2001, Dostoevsky and the kenotic tradition, in Pattison, George and Thompson, Diane O (eds), *Dostoevsky and the Christian Tradition*, Cambridge, Cambridge University Press, pp. 31–40.

Zohrab, Irene, [Zograb, I.], 1998, Ob odnom intertekste v *Brat'iakh Karamazovykh*, in Zakharov, V N (ed.), *Evangel'skii tekst v russkoi literature XVIII-XX vekov*, 2, Petrozavodsk, Izd. Petrozavodskogo Universiteta, pp. 424–41.

Zvoznikov, A A, 1994, Dostoevskii i pravoslavie: predvaritel'nye zametki, in Zakharov, V N (ed.), *Evangel'skii tekst v russkoi literature XVIII-XX vekov*, 1, Petrozavodsk, Izd. Petrozavodskogo Universiteta, pp. 179–91.

Index

References to Dostoevsky himself, which occur on every page, are naturally omitted, as are the many references to individual works, both by Dostoevsky and other writers. In addition to individual entries, listed in alphabetical order, some are grouped in clusters under a general heading. Such are the entries for The Bible, Dostoevsky, and Russian Orthodoxy, where subsidiary entries may be sought where appropriate.

Printed in the United Kingdom
by Lightning Source UK Ltd.
107400UKS00001BA/304-330